TREE of HATE

TREE of HATE

Propaganda and Prejudices Affecting United States Relations with the Hispanic World

by *Philip Wayne Powell*

Basic Books, Inc., *Publishers*

New York / *London*

© 1971   by Basic Books, Inc.
Library of Congress Catalog Card Number: 79–158442
SBN 465–08750–7
Manufactured in the United States of America
DESIGNED BY THE INKWELL STUDIO

FOR

DIANA LINDA

A young lady of exemplary courage

I nere could tell from what roote this huge

Large spreading Tree of hate from Spayne to us,

From us agayne to Spayne, took the first growth.

No? Then Ile tell you: let us season our sorrow

With this discourse.

OLD ENGLISH PLAY,

Dick of Devonshire, 1625

Preface

Spain was the first summit power of modern times, preeminent in Europe and presiding over an empire that dwarfed those of Rome and Genghis Khan. Spain was also the first global power to assume what came to be called "the white man's burden" and, simultaneously, to defend Christendom against the powerful thrusts of a Eurasian infidel.

With tasks and goals of such magnitude, Spain inevitably depleted herself in blood and treasure and went into decline in Europe, where her long sway finally receded before France and England, successors at the summit. But the centuries of Spanish imperial power created a host of enemies who, mixing fear, envy, and the intense hatreds of religious conflict, made Spain and Spaniards the first to feel the impact of the printing press as a propaganda weapon. Spanish power was the target of devastating attacks, which launched a Western fashion of denigrating Spain, Spaniards, and most of their works—propagandas which became entrenched as History.

The story of this Black Legend, which purports a unique Spanish depravity, should be of singular interest to the citizens of a summit power now burdened with similar twin responsibilities of defense of the West and aid to backward nations while also suffering the blows of global propagandas designed to destroy us. And knowledge of the growth and perennial fruiting of that "large spreading tree of hate" is essential to an understanding of the vast Hispanic world that is so vital to the survival and well-being of Western civilization.

PHILIP WAYNE POWELL

Santa Barbara, California

Contents

Contents

Part iii
Echoes of the Legend

Portfolio of Engravings by Theodore De Bry, 1598, pages 81–90

Part i

Dimensions of the Black Legend

Chapter 1

INTRODUCING THE HISPANOPHOBIC FALLACY

*"Let him who will portray me," said
Don Quijote, "but let him not malign
me; for patience is very often lost
when insults are heaped upon it."*
Don Quijote, part II, chapter 59

We of the United States, presently championing the values of Western civilization, have never achieved a truly sympathetic understanding of a vast part of that civilization—that which speaks in Spanish and Portuguese. Yet the Iberian peoples served as a shield and spear of Christian West against the infidel East for a thousand years; and the Spanish language, today, is second to English in Western usage. Since World War II the government and people of the United States have participated in attempts to ostracize Spain not only from the Western but also from the global community of nations. We have also dangerously neglected and incompetently managed our relationships with Latin America, the largest portion of the Hispanic world and a cornerstone of our foreign policy. Also in recent years we have given insultingly short shrift to Portuguese claims upon our understanding of them as fellow allies in Western unity against Eurasian communism.[1]

Some of our citizenry have long been aware that there is something tragically wrong in all this; that the chasms between us and Hispanic countries seem more often to widen than to contract, and that this is a mutual peril and a powerful weapon for those who seek to damage or destroy us. The basic causes of our faulty comprehension of the Hispanic world and our dangerous depreciation and neglect of this great cultural community are mainly, without our realizing it, deeply rooted in the past.

All too many among our political and intellectual leaders view Latin America in such terms as dictators versus democrats; or as a small, white, rich aristocracy lording it over faceless millions of Indian underdogs; or as an exercise in vast salvation through our own good works and financial largess. Such abstractions are absurdly simplistic because they lack historical perspective. This kind of distortion—a composite formed from our defective education, irrepressible missionary urges, and Marxian class struggle, and wrapped sometimes in the panicky feeling that Communists are ten feet tall in Latin America—is simply the latest chapter in a long story of our refusal to recognize, respect, and sympathetically appreciate the complexities of a vast Hispano-Catholic-mestizo-Indian-Negro-mulatto society that is not only vital to our well-being but also a gigantic section of that Western tradition that we seek to defend.

Our national habit of condescension and oversimplification of virtually all phenomena of the Hispanic world is a habit that stretches from our elementary schools to universities to the White House, and it grows out of ancestral antagonisms that have come to constitute a perennial prejudice as unjustifiable as it can be dangerous. The very depth of this prejudice renders it difficult to discern, especially when camouflaged by relatively superficial immediacies—such as, for example, an Argentine political crisis, a Guatemalan revolution, a Bay of Pigs episode, and the kidnapping of an ambassador. It is a prejudice that defies correction, for it is pervasive among so many of the teachers, writers, and politicians who guide our attitudes concerning Hispanic countries and their relationships to us.

The fact that this is basically an anti-Spanish complex that has its roots in the distant past is little known and even less considered. (The Spanishness in Latin America is far less congenial to us than is sympathy for Indian America.) The depth of the roots hides them from the view of a people normally unwilling to look farther back than yesterday's headlines to find the cause of anything. But the branches and fruit of this attitude can often be seen: disparagement and neglect of Hispanic cultures, governmental arrogance or touristic condescension, a notoriously insulting American colony exclusivism (a special brand of apartheid), or that utterly naïve faith that we can produce Latin American experts overnight.

It is the greatest misfortune that the myths of hispanophobia, in the West generally and in our country particularly, bear the stamp of intellectual respectability. Thus, by comparison with such prejudices as "white supremacy" or so-called antisemitism, which do not bear such a stamp (quite the contrary), it is difficult indeed to gain a hearing for the injustices of the hispanophobic fallacies. Our intelligentsia quite generally approve and practice disparagement of Hispanic culture and accompany it with a continuing belief in a unique Spanish backwardness. Precisely because this prejudice has been so long pervasive in our intellectual circles and political leadership, it demands even more attention than is now given to biases that are already clearly recognized.

The anti-Spanish views that have been particularly influential in shaping Western thought originated among Frenchmen, Italians, Germans, and Jews. They were spread widely in the sixteenth and seventeenth centuries by energetic use of the printing press. Along with this, the passions of the Protestant Revolt blended with the anti-Spanish aims of Holland and England to form the "large spreading Tree of hate," which flowered into a Western world fashion during the Age of Enlightenment, when so many of today's dogmas took classic form.

Heroes of anti-Spain run the gamut from Francis Drake to Theodore Roosevelt, from William the Silent to Harry Truman, from Bartolomé de las Casas to the Mexican Lázaro Cárdenas, or from Oliver Cromwell's Puritans to the Communists in an Abraham Lincoln Brigade—from romantic to prosaic and from near sublime to thoroughly ridiculous. There is far less distance in concept than there is in time between Anglo-Dutch hatred of Philip II and its echoes in today's university classrooms; between the "anti-Spain" of the Enlightenment and the "anti-Spain" of the West's latter-day intellectual circles.

Propagandistic distortion of Spain and Spanish America, their people and most of their works, long ago merged into the patterns of dogmatic anti-Catholicism. This twisted mixture lives on in popular literature and prejudices and continues to bolster our Nordic [or WASPish?] superiority complex and to distort Latin American and United States historical perspectives. If only for this reason, professoriates and other intellectual leadership should favor whatever can be done to eliminate from our national life erroneous views of the Hispanic world.

Successful propaganda is usually guided by intellectuals and educated men who become passionately committed to a cause (or are paid, in some form, to do so)—men who are acquainted with the tools needed to shape men's minds. So it was, very often, in the case of anti-Spanish propagandas, both in the past and more recently. Unfortunately, the lending of intellectual heroes to propagandistic advocacy, whether in the sixteenth, eighteenth, or twentieth century, too often speeds the sanctification of error. In the case of the anti-Spanish Legend, the errors have also been exposed and opposed by men of high intellectual stature from the sixteenth century to the present, but such corrections have never kept pace with the spread of "big lies" purposely designed for appeal to or manufacture of, wide popular prejudice. Scholarly contradiction of popular misconceptions concerning Hispanic historical phenomena is known only in limited circles, and the number of the informed is kept limited by the failure to make large contrary efforts.

Of Nordic Heroes and Spanish Villains

Nordic myth has been due in no small part to the fact that the maps are hung with the North up and the South down.

SALVADOR DE MADARIAGA [2]

The stereotyped Spaniard as portrayed in our schoolbooks, popular literature, movies and television, is usually a swarthy fellow with black, pointed beard, morion, and wicked Toledo blade. He is, of course, treacherous, lecherous, cruel, greedy, and thoroughly bigoted. Sometimes he takes the form of a cowled, grim-visaged Inquisitor. In more recent times, and with somewhat better humor, he has appeared as a kind of slippery, mildly sinister, donjuanesque gigolo. But whatever the guise, he is most likely to be cast as foil for the Nordic ego.

Historic and literary conflict between Nordic hero and Spanish villain, so popular in the English-speaking world since the days of Francis Drake and the Spanish Armada, has built in us, as it did in our forebears, a firm faith in Nordic superiority. The Spanish "heavy" continues to personify, far beyond historic realities, the evils of Roman Catholic State-Church, the barbarities of New World conquest, and a generalized moral-physical-intellectual inferiority by comparison with Nordic virtues.[3]

From schoolbooks to cape-and-sword novels and back again, the villainous Spaniard seldom has a chance against Nordic heroes. Perhaps this is just as well, for, contrary to our popular beliefs, the authentic Spaniard, especially in his imperial heyday, was a first-rate soldier and diplomat, with many victories to his credit. It might be rather disillusioning for our school children and our public to learn how often he thwarted the aims of our Nordic ancestors. A few examples out of many include: the defeat of John Hawkins and Francis Drake at Vera Cruz, Mexico, in 1568; successful defense of Cartagena against the fleet of Lord Vernon in 1740; Spanish-Argentine defeat of two successive English invasions in 1806 and 1807; the relative failure of Cromwell's "western design" against the Spanish Indies, in comparison to its grand objectives; overall Spanish success in maintaining and even expanding American territorial holdings against English and other threats and attacks.

For history's stereotyped Spaniard, the Nordic literary dice are invariably loaded. Who, for example, ever heard of humane, well-educated Spanish conquistadores who had virtues and vices like people such as Henry VIII's and Elizabeth I's Englishmen? [Walter Raleigh was really a sort of Renaissance Spaniard in English dress.] Or was there a generous, very human, and quite trustworthy Spanish hero behind that swishing Toledo blade? [For a couple of rather perverted exceptions see my Bibliography, pp. 190–191.] Or was there an enlightened, just, and humane Spanish Inquisitor? Or a Spanish sea captain honestly and gallantly victorious over, say, an Englishman?

The stock Spanish villain has company in stereotype. For example, the sentimentalized "good" missionary friar who is so effective in revealing how "bad" other Spaniards have been. Such padres are a kind of continuing echo of the famous champion of the Indians, Bartolomé de las Casas, and they may reflect the fact that much history of Spain in America was written by churchmen who pulled no punches when criticizing soldiers, captains, or other secular officials with whom they disagreed.

There is also the implacably tyrannical, hardhearted *hacendado* and the slinky, treacherous Mexican "greaser"; these gringo versions of Spanish depravity have had considerable popularity with Hollywood scenarists and the writers of horse operas. The following description is typical: "She sent for the Mexican at once, and the man came in a few moments, a venomous looking specimen of his race, slinking, yellow-eyed, with nicotine ingrained to his very soul" (Max Brand, *Destry Rides Again*, p. 69).

There is also the bandit-type guerrilla fighter, ruthlessly tough and a constant reminder that Spaniards can fight only as guerrillas and that Spain has been a unique breeding ground for bandits. Ernest Hemingway's *For Whom the Bell Tolls* and its movie echo helped bring the Spanish guerrilla up-to-date, though softened by political sympathies and Ingrid Bergman.

The historical and fictional Spanish villain is often outdone by the grotesquerie of travel literature dealing with Spain and its people. This brand of distortion began in the late fifteenth and early sixteenth centuries, when the political and cultural jaundice of Italian and some other travelers began creating the racially inferior, gloomy, treacherous, and excessively haughty Spaniard.

The compatriots of Machiavelli penned the earliest widely publicized accounts of travel in Spain, and they began the habit in the West of exaggerating and distorting Spanish customs on the basis of superficial knowledge, in terms such as: "They are very miserly, and . . . very accomplished in robbery. . . . They have no aptitude for literature. . . . They appear to be religious but, in reality, are not. . . . The Spaniards are so careless in land cultivation and so stupid in the mechanical arts that what would be done in other places in a month is done by them in four." [4]

The famous Italian ambassadors who made such comments at a time when Spaniards were entering a golden imperial and cultural age, established a tradition of shallow and unfavorable comment that continues to the present. "These accounts, translated into French and English, contributed heavily to the creation of a fantastic image of Spain and Spaniards, for, although they were accurate in many things, they also contained a multitude of exaggerations." [5]

The distortions in foreign accounts of Spain reached such a point in the later part of the nineteenth century that the famous Spanish novelist, Juan Valera, was stirred to bitter sarcasm against those who absorbed the ridiculous stereotypes of Spain and Spaniards.

Any Spaniard who has been for a time outside Spain can tell what foreigners ask him or tell him about his country. They have asked me if, in Spain, we hunt lions; they have explained to me what tea is, supposing that I had never seen or tasted it. And highly educated persons have lamented to me that our national costume (which they believe to be the *traje de majo*) is not worn for all court functions and other solemn occasions; and it is a pity we do not all dance the bolero, the fandango, and the cachucha. It is difficult to persuade half the inhabitants of Europe that practically all our women do not smoke, or that they do not wear daggers in their garters. The compliments which they accord us are usually so rare and so grotesque that they are really insults or ridicule.[6]

A turn-of-the-century writer lamented that most travelers to Spain never took the trouble to learn about the country before going there, nor did they even bother to learn the language, so indispensable for any understanding of Spain and Spaniards.[7] Both observations are still accurate; I would add, with *caveat,* that in these later days we have the elbow-bending American bullfight aficionado to enlighten us on *cosas de España,* dogging the footsteps of Hemingway and Barnaby Conrad. The "bull bums" have been infesting the Peninsula for some years; if you see one coming, run for cover and pray that he never writes a book on Spain!

Other peoples and nations, of course, are made to suffer from national or racial stereotypes and caricatures. But purposefully tortured history, along with an overabundnace of insulting travel literature, has afflicted Spain and Spaniards with more than their fair share of such burdens. It would not be too bad if this prejudicial potpourri consisted only of the lazily romantic, guitar-*cum*-balcony Andalusian lover, or a bullfighting Tyrone Power, treading Hollywood's blood and sand; or the passionately sinister Carmen, with stiletto in stocking. Some Spaniards, to be sure, were a bit nonplussed when they saw *Carmen Jones,* but they had become rather affectionately resigned to the foreign Carmen of Bizet. Some thought that a flamboyant chocolate-colored version was carrying it a bit too far, but they gamely made the best of it. "No longer does Carmen belong to us, not even as adopted sister. Although, on second thought, Who is this Carmen Jones, beautiful Negress, if not an example and one more proof of Spanish expansive power and universality? Authentic or imported, the Spanish flavor is very contagious among other races and environments" (*ABC,* Madrid, May 6, 1955).

If stereotypes like the penny-squeezing Scot, the skirt-chasing Frenchman, the Shylock Jew, Colonel Blimp, the "nigger mammy," or the loudmouthed Yankee tourist were all, we might call it good clean fun and let it go at that. But some distortions are so loaded with poison and insult that the damage is too great for good humor or repair. Thus, the *Pravda* and *Izvestia* versions of us and our history, such snappy stuff as photos of Negro lynchings, germs from the Korean War, the latest rehash of the "martyrdom" of the Rosenbergs, or the strained verses of a Yevtushenko exploiting the Kent State killings, are already an accepted picture of the United States over much of the globe. The insidious Latin American literature of "Yankeephobia," with more than half a century of cumulative effect in embittering inter-American relations, has been steadily building a massive and highly insulting caricature of us as a nation. Like the centuries-old defamation of Spain, this now classic view of us from our southern exposure is a witch's brew of truth, half-truth, propaganda, prejudice, and political expediency, easily intensified and exploited by our sworn enemies. It will cost us far more in applied intelligence than in applied dollars to counteract this "black legend." A legend, by the way, that originated among Latin American intellectuals and is largely perpetuated by them.

The Jew who is interested in historical justice and who can, perhaps, still taste the poison of the famed "Protocols of the Elders of Zion" or more recent anti-Jewish propagandas, should have little trouble understanding the long-suffering Spaniard, even though Jews themselves have contributed to past and continuing denigration of Spain.[8] Sober reflection upon the kind of damage done our national psychology by Hollywood stereotypes of the arrogantly evil German officer (in both World

Wars I and II), who is always outwitted by those fine clean fellows of British or American intelligence, would provide examples for any thoughtful essay upon the propagandistic defamation of Philip II and his subjects.

Definitions of the *Leyenda Negra*

The main pillars upon which the anti-Spanish Black Legend rests are: (1) the fear, envy, and hatred of those—mainly Italians, Germans, French, English, Dutch, Jews, and Portuguese—who clashed with Spanish political, military, economic, or religious power in Europe during some four centuries after the fourteenth; (2) similar antagonisms of those peoples and nations—especially Dutch, English, French, and Portuguese—who challenged Spanish sway in the New World; (3) purposeful defamation of certain individual Spaniards [e.g., Torquemada, Philip II] and Spanish policies, actions, and institutions [e.g., Inquisition, New World conquest and exclusivism, sack of Rome]—mainly by writers from rival nations; (4) the merging of the residues of 1, 2, and 3 into a broader, more intellectualized denigration of Spain as the "horrible example" of all that the Enlightenment was supposed to flog [Church-State evils, intolerance, traditionalism, obscurantism], rationalized and dogmatized in the eighteenth and nineteenth centuries; (5) uncritical popular and, more significantly, intellectual acceptance of anti-Spanish distortions, especially in those nations and peoples shaping Western ways of thought after Spain lost hegemony in Europe.

The Black Legend is sometimes described as the cumulative denigration of Spain's actions in the Americas. But this definition is not complete; it derives mainly from the tendency of Americanists to truncate their view of the Hispanic world by venturing east of the old Line of Demarcation only reluctantly. It further stems from wide Dutch and English propagandas against Spain's seaborne empire. This limitation often exaggerates, relatively speaking, the importance of the Spanish bishop, Bartolomé de las Casas, and his harsh indictment of Spanish New World conquest (see Chapter 2, pp. 30–36). As we shall see, there were other important aspects of Black Legend origin and growth.

Spain's Julián Juderías, who first gave wide publicity to the Black Legend label, early in this century, can still be credited with the following generally satisfactory definition:

The Black Legend is an atmosphere created by the fantastic accounts of Spain which have been published in almost all countries; the grotesque descriptions which are forever being made of the character of Spaniards as individuals and collectively; the negation, or, at least, the systematic ignorance of whatever is favorable and worthy of honor in the various manifestations of culture and art; the accusations which are always being launched against Spain, based upon happenings which are exaggerated, badly interpreted, or false in entirety; and, finally, the affirmation, contained in seemingly respectable and authentic books, and many times reproduced, commented on, and amplified in the foreign press, that our country constitutes, from the point of view of tolerance, of culture, and of political progress, a lamentable exception among European nations. In short, we understand as the Black Legend the legend of inquisitorial Spain—ignorant, fanatical, incapable, now as in the past, of being considered among the civilized nations, since we always prefer violent repression and we are the enemy of progress and of innovations. Or, in other terms, the legend which began to spread in the sixteenth century, on the heels of the Protestant Reformation, and which, since then, is unfailingly used against us, especially in critical moments of our national life.[9]

The basic premise of the Black Legend is that Spaniards have shown themselves, historically, to be *uniquely* cruel, bigoted, tyrannical, obscurantist, lazy, fanatical, greedy, and treacherous; that is, that they differ so much from other peoples in these traits that Spaniards and Spanish history must be viewed and understood in terms not ordinarily used in describing and interpreting other peoples. Thus, Spaniards who came to the New World seeking opportunities beyond the prospects of their European environment, are contemptuously called cruel and greedy "goldseekers," or other opprobrious epithets virtually synonymous with "Devils"; but Englishmen who sought New World opportunities are more respectfully called "colonists," or "homebuilders," or "seekers after liberty." [10] The following example shows how this operates even at university levels, where a distinguished professor of history wrote in two of his works widely disseminated for teaching purposes: "[The U.S.] were settled by homemakers and state builders alive with English ideas of self-government: Mexico was conquered by Spanish adventurers who wanted to go home with their plunder." "The conquistadores came from Spain to seek their fortune in the shape of gold and silver and to return home with it as soon as possible." [11] The truth is, of course, that the oldest homes in America are those built by the Spanish conquerors; they lived in them, too—sort of like colonists.

When Spaniards expelled or punished religious dissidents, this came to be known as "bigotry," "intolerance," "fanaticism," and a cause of their decline. When Englishmen, Dutchmen, or Frenchmen did the same thing, it is known as "unifying the nation," or safeguarding it against treason or foreign conspiracy. The killing of Indians by Spaniards became "atrocities," or "ruthless extermination"; but when Englishmen ran Irishmen to death by the thousands in their own bogs, or slaughtered them after surrender, this was called "the Irish problem."

A sordid tinge is always given to the Spanish interest in and profit from the New World's mineral wealth; but when this same wealth was piratically stolen from them by Elizabethan Sea Dogs it was regarded as an heroic step in building England, nation and empire. Likewise, when Anglo-Americans stumbled over each other in the rush for California gold, it was described as the "cornerstone" of a "great commonwealth." [12] To give this kind of comparative injustice a more modern twist, when Francisco Franco warned the West of the dangers of Russian Communism, in 1944, and offered to mediate between Axis and Allied Nations to fend off a Russian advance into the foreseeable vacuum of an unconditionally surrendered Germany, this was rejected because of its "Fascist" source; when we got the Churchillian "iron curtain" message in 1947 and began to take defensive steps *vis-à-vis* our erstwhile Red ally, this was usually called something like "leadership of the Western world." [13] In essence, if one wishes to understand typical Western world comments on Spain and her history, a special vocabulary must be mastered. And there is abundant irony in the recent realization, and exhortations, that we must similarly learn a distinctive terminology in order to understand the voice of Russian Communism.

It is a common belief that for several centuries now, Spain has been rather out of step with the Western world. Is there, perhaps, something to be said for the other side of this coin? The distinguished Spanish scholar, Américo Castro, surely had this possibility in mind when he wrote: "We . . . have to search for the meaning of Spanish civilization and its high values independently of the idea of material happiness. . . . Today, more than in any other moment in the history of the world, we can contemplate with serenity such a state of things, because today it is pertinent to ask whether this so-called 'progress', which has for its base a pure intellectualism and a craving for epicurean joys—whether this 'progress' may not be, after all, more productive of horrors than of benefits" (Inaugural Lecture, Princeton University, 1940). These words are even more pertinent, of course, some three decades later.

That other-side-of-the-coin question can be, if seriously and fairly examined, a nagging one, like: Did Spain reach the great heights of her intellectual "Golden Age" *in spite of* the Inquisition, or *because of* it? Such questions always seem easily answered, at first glance—and such quick answers fit so comfortably into our preconceived notions about Spain that they are surely the safest. In later pages, however, let us live a bit more dangerously.

Propaganda and misconceptions relating to Spanish conquest, rule, and cultural action in the Americas are not chronologically first in the story of the Black Legend. However, since Latin America is today so vital to us, so often misunderstood in its history, and so closely related to the Legend's most pervasive clichés and stereotypes, let us look first at Spain's phenomenal New World action. By contrasting common myths and harmful half-truths with scholarly views, we shall be better able to understand the fallacious nature of the Legend's distortions, which echo so offensively even unto our own times.

Chapter 2

SPAIN IN AMERICA: THE REAL AND THE UNREAL

*La atroz codicia, la inclemente saña,
Crimen fueron del tiempo y no de
España.*[1]

*That error is most dangerous which
has a great deal of truth mixed with
it.*

SIDNEY SMITH

Spanish rule in the Americas, spanning more than three centuries—four, if we include Cuba and Puerto Rico—was one of the greatest imperial achievements in all history. In opening such vast territories to European view, and then in managing them, Spaniards expanded mankind's material and intellectual horizons enormously. The most suitable parallel to Spain's activities beyond the confines of the known world, would be twentieth-century entry into space. If one restricts comparison to global limits, this tremendous Spanish achievement must be classed with the creation and durability of Roman and English empires, for nothing less will do.

The size and complexity of this Spanish imperial process stagger the imagination and confound the scholars. Written records of it exist by the ton, for it is probably the best documented period of all history prior to the nineteenth century.[2] The immensity of Spanish Empire bureaucracy, with characteristically Hispanic emphasis upon law and legions of lawyers, plus royal concern for preservation of records, assured that tremendous amounts of official paper—hallmark, seemingly, of high civilization—would record Spanish action overseas.

Those imperial centuries were rich in human diversity; in addition to the many-faceted Spaniard himself, other Europeans, Africans of sundry shades and levels of culture, and native Indians also of varied hue and achievement, formed a kaleidoscope of mankind's worst, best, and indifferent. They spread over the New World with its tremendous geographic size and variety, and caused appalling problems in social, political, and economic development that still exist.

Faulty generalizations about this large area and its several centuries of recorded history are all too frequent, even among those more than a little acquainted with the subject. The documentation is still largely unexploited; the geographic variations are so many; and the racial and cultural mixture of European, Indian, and African is so confusing that it is, even for experts, hard to make final judgments or definitive statements. The overwhelming complexity of it all—too often ignored by teachers and writers—is the reality; simplistic generalizations are the unreality.

By comparison with commonly held views on Spain in America, certain facts and interpretations—based upon scholarly investigations, a certain amount of logic, and some knowledge of human behavior—can be advanced toward revising popular misconceptions. Then, with more clarity, causes of these misconceptions, largely rooted in themes of the Black Legend, can be indicated.

The Spanish Conquest

The common belief that Spain's conquest in America was thoroughly and systematically characterized by unique cruelty, rapaciousness, greed, and general depravity is simply not borne out by the evidence. Let us put it more bluntly: *there is nothing in all Spanish history to prove that Spaniards, then or now, are characteristically more cruel, more greedy, or more depraved than other peoples.* I do not believe that any reputable scholar, free of racial and religious prejudices, would contradict that statement.

Conquests of this kind, with an advanced culture establishing dominance over lesser ones, have been all too often attended by cruelties—on both sides; by looting—on both sides; and by atrocities which most contestants and spectators would normally consider criminal. The mere fact that human beings are involved, whether civilized or savage, assures this. There is abundant evidence of such atrocities, Indian as well as Spanish, in the conquest period. There is also ample proof that such atrocities were viewed and punished as crimes committed against prevailing law. Such criminality was punishable—and, when possible, usually punished—in the ways of most civilized societies. When one understands that the Spain of the conquest period was a deeply civilized nation by all discernible European standards of that day, this becomes quite comprehensible. In jurisprudence, diplomacy, monarchical religious and imperial concepts, and total culture, Spain was a European leader throughout the sixteenth century and in much of the next.

A belief common among Englishmen, and one which we inherit, is that the English would have treated American Indians in more humane fashion than did the Spaniards. There is not a shred of evidence to uphold this comparative view, and, on the contrary, much to disprove it. In anything like similar circumstances, our English forebears treated Indians with a callousness and cruelty every bit the equal of Spanish behavior or worse. English government and people, and their New World progeny, exhibited for the most part, a supreme unconcern for the protection and welfare of the American Indian. This unconcern is particularly glaring by contrast with the enormous Spanish effort, governmental and individual, to behave in contrary fashion.

The English theme "we would have treated the Indians better than did the Spaniards" goes back to Elizabethan times. It is well illustrated in English popular literature, in a 1942 biography of Francis Drake, insisting that he demonstrated that "the English way of making friends of the less forward races is better than the [Spanish] way of converting them by massacre and cruelty into slaves." The Spaniards "learned nothing ever. They were among gentle, kindly natives, but they killed and went short of service. They tortured and made bitter enemies. They never condescended to make a friend. They were the lords of the world. For their captives there were the iron rule and the booted heel." [3] This, of course, does not even begin to approximate an accurate picture of Spain's Indian policies or of England's by contrast. More than one volume could be written on the subject of Spanish diplomacy among the native races, including gifts, honors and titles, protection and privileges, education, and other actions, which today would be automatically labeled as both practical and humanitarian.

For those who may still believe the myth that English humanitarianism was superior by contrast with that of the Spaniards, there is much corrective literature. For example, there are the following statements:

Elizabeth's reign was one of the most barbarous cruelty, in comparison with which the repressive measures of Mary pale to insignificance. And this reign was succeeded by one of equal cruelty under James I. . . . The people [by the time of Charles I] had been disciplined in the cruel methods of their erstwhile masters, and they had become as ferocious as Henry or Elizabeth or James.[4]

The study of contemporary Europe [that is, especially the sixteenth century] reveals plainly the universal pattern of cruelty, intolerance, and inhumanity which characterized the social, religious, and economic life of the continent. Humanitarianism was as yet a merely latent and undeveloped concept of human relations, and the disregard of the inherent rights of every individual was universal. For a conqueror to act with compassion toward the vanquished was still generally conceived as a sign of weakness.[5]

Habits of "frightfulness," acquired by the English in their prolonged aggression against the remnants of the Celtic Fringe in the highlands of Scotland and the bogs of Ireland, were carried across the Atlantic and practiced at the expense of the North American Indians.[6]

Some of our own and English bedevilment in this matter comes from using nineteenth- and twentieth-century attitudes as launching pads for moralistic missiles aimed at sixteenth-century Spaniards. But some of it is also based on the general Nordic superiority complex, on our latter-day sympathy for the Indian underdog, and, more importantly, simple ignorance of Spanish and Spanish American history. While nearly every English-speaking person is aware of, say, Cortés' victory and attendant killing of Indians, which is normal in warfare, not one in 10,000 ever heard of his and Spanish officialdom's sincere attempts to avoid such Indian depletion, during and after the Conquest.

Decrease in Indian population, which was from multiple causes, was a serious concern of Spain's royal officials and monarchy throughout the sixteenth century and later; it was repeatedly treated in royal cédulas, viceregal correspondence, etc. That is why our distinguished authority on Latin America, Professor Lewis Hanke, can make such statements as this: "No European nation . . ., with the possible exception of Portugal, took her Christian duty toward native peoples so seriously as did Spain." [7]

It is commonly believed, and too often taught and written, that practically all Spaniards came to the New World as seekers after gold, with a snide implication that there was something reprehensible in this. The Spanish goldseeker became a stereotype centuries ago and remains so to this day. That Spaniards were not by any means unique in their interest in gold, and that many other things of the New World attracted them, is illustrated by these words of Professor Irving Leonard:

The Conquistador . . . had a powerful reason for seeking so relentlessly the gold that was indispensable in the new economy [of Europe]. If he was too beguiled by a symbol of wealth and eventually paid dearly for his mistake in his own and his country's ruin, he was not unique in the history of mankind and there are indications in more modern times that others have not learned his lesson. . . . After 1500 particularly [the Conquistador's] imagination was kindled to an almost mystical exaltation of adventure and romance by the many books which began to pour from the presses. These [novels of chivalry] brought to his fevered mind seemingly authentic accounts of fantastic places, riches, monsters, and enchantment, and he burned to discover and possess for himself the realities that they described. To the Conquest itself, as a result, was imparted a spirit of romance and chivalry which gave these expeditions, as Irving has aptly remarked, "a character wholly distinct from similar enterprises undertaken by other nations."

Again, commenting on Bartolomé de las Casas' simplistic abstraction of his countrymen as "goldseekers," Leonard remarks:

Inherent in this concept is the implication that the Spaniard, more than any other European, was animated by a lust for metallic wealth. Yet the inhabitants of the Spanish Peninsula are not today, and have never been, characteristically more acquisitive than their continental neighbors. On the contrary, the Spanish and the Portuguese are among the least materialistic peoples of western Europe.[8]

Usually, little thought is given to the possibility that Spaniards were simply seeking to better their lot, were often guided to America by genuine religious zeal, or were simply colonizing homeseekers, or were engaged in trade, in ranching, in government service, and in all other branches of human activity. Logic and the evidence point to the fact that most Spaniards coming to the New World, even during the conquest period (until about 1560), were guided by the varieties of motive that usually influence other men and women in such migrations. Here is a random sample.

Though not generally known, the Spanish conquistadores came to the New World in quest of drugs as well as gold. "The caduceus (medical symbol) is as much a symbol of Spanish conquest as the sword and cross," says Dr. Francisco Guerra, visiting Professor of Pharmacology at the [University of California] Medical School in Los Angeles and Professor of Pharmacology at the University of Mexico. Spain brought to the New World a knowledge of medicine at least the equal of any in the world at the time, he says.[9]

Incidentally, several outstanding characteristics of the Spanish conquest, especially in contrast with the English, should be noted. The Spanish government made every effort to keep criminals and other socially undesirable elements from migrating to America; British policies included the dumping of criminals in Australia and the Americas. Spaniards, unlike so many of their English counterparts, felt no need to go to America to escape religious or other persecutions in the home country. One of our historians, writing in a college textbook, implies that Spaniards should not be considered true colonists (like the English) because they were not migrating to escape oppressive conditions in Europe.[10]

Closely paralleling the goldseeker distortion is the common misconception that only Englishmen came to the New World to build homes; that Spaniards came merely to loot and then return to the mother country with their ill-gotten gains. The oldest homes in America are those built by Spaniards, conquistadores who were also colonists. The second voyage of Columbus, in 1493, carried some 1,500 colonists, along with all the paraphernalia (seeds, plantings, livestock, etc.) normally needed in such enterprises. And the Spanish governor, Nicolás de Ovando, coming to the New World in 1502, had aboard his fleet some 2,000 colonists, officials, clergy, etc. After 1500, ships and fleets going from Spain to the New World regularly carried Spanish women, children, servants, officials; in short, nearly every imaginable type of human cargo.[11] On the farthest frontiers, even when Spaniards first arrived, Spanish women and families commonly accompanied their men, facing all the dangers and hardships that our ancestors encountered in frontier expansion. In our misconceptions about such Spanish home-building and colonizing in the New World, we usually underrate the fortitude and adventurous spirit of Spanish women and their loyalty to their men; a number of fascinating volumes could and should be written about Spanish women in the conquest and colonization of the Americas.[12]

In our simplistic habit of fastening upon Spaniards all opprobrium as "Indian killers" and "goldseekers," plus several other stigmas, we overlook some of the inevitabilities in such a conquest-colonization process.

The Spanish Conquest in America was far more characteristically an achievement of diplomacy than of war. This had to be, for Spanish exploratory and invading forces were so small that they could not otherwise have survived and conquered. In comparison with Spanish astuteness in diplomacy, the more famous firearms, horses, and steel sword were often less significant. As one scholar puts it, "the Spanish conquerors could have taught lessons to many of the chancelleries of Europe." [13] One has to go no further than the easily available story of Cortés in Mexico, classical example of a diplomatic process which occurred over and over again. Spaniards were constantly in need of Indian allies—and they sought them by diplomatic means; sometimes with exemplary show of strength and astuteness, often by gifts, "honeyed words," and agreement to help certain Indian tribes and nations against traditional enemies.[14] Spanish leaders of conquest, in the spirit of their European times, were often quite Machiavellian in all this; but Indian leaders were similarly proficient. [In any case, when did devious diplomacy become a crime? After World War II?] The more spectacular clash of arms too frequently eclipses the fascinating and very significant interplay of diplomatic forces in Spanish-Indian impact.

It is also quite accurate to characterize Spanish success in America as a process of Indians conquering Indians, under white supervision. The American Indian was often more the conqueror of his own race than were the Spaniards. This could occur because there was generally no underlying Indian loyalty to a concept of being Indian. Thus, Tlaxcalans took great delight in helping Spaniards defeat such a hated, perennial enemy as the Aztecs; and Aztecs, in turn, helped Spaniards fight and colonize on later frontiers. Anything resembling a broad, effective confederacy of Indian peoples brought together by the common purpose of defeating or exterminating the white man is hard to discern in most of this conquest story. And anyone puzzled by this point need only recall how Iroquois, Algonquins, Hurons, and others fought each other at European behest and under European aegis in our own colonial history. If one also recalls how Europeans of that day fought each other so often and so mercilessly, even with common bonds of Christianity, race, and culture, it is not difficult to appreciate that Spanish invaders were able to exploit Indian rivalries and hatreds to win an upper hand, often with relatively little bloodshed.

In some other ways, too, the authentic version of Spanish conquest differs much from our usual heroes-and-villains portrayals. It was, for example, a vast middle-class process—not a Grandee in sight!—rather than invasion by a haughty Spanish aristocracy. Seldom in the ranks of the conquistadores was there anyone more aristocratic than the bottom rungs of the lesser nobility and even those, in our modern terminology, would certainly be called middle class. Most of the ranks in exploratory and conquering forces were less than this. Thus, Spanish Conquest and occupation of America were carried out by levels of society approximately the equivalent of those who left England to build log cabins in the New World. Also, as various scholars have pointed out, this conquest was usually quite democratic, strongly characterized by private initiative, by the rise, sometimes through popular election, of leaders from the ranks, and by a kind of group sharing of costs, dangers, and rewards, akin to small business corporations.[15]

In light of this, the constant bickering, disunity, feuds, and even miniature civil wars, that occurred among the conquistadores are quite understandable. These were not professional soldiers operating under tight discipline and firm line of command from Crown down to general to private; they were a highly variegated representation of almost every type (except high nobility, of course) to be found in the Spain of that day. And seeking opportunity, risking their lives at nearly every turn, they quite naturally expected rewards in loot, or in Indian labor and tributes, or in lands, or government posts, or whatnot. When all is considered, these men should be judged, as Salvador de Madariaga has pointed out, not so much by how barbarous they were, but rather by how well they behaved in the midst of incredible dangers and almost unlimited temptations. The fact that they were deeply civilized—that is, every bit as sophisticated as most other peoples in the Europe of that day—undoubtedly accounts for some of the barbarity in their New World actions. It takes civilized men to teach refinements of cruelty to savages.

During their conquest of the New World, the Spaniards committed some atrocities that were on such a scale that they are horrifying to contemplate. But there is every reason to believe that Englishmen, Dutchmen, Frenchmen, Belgians, Germans, Italians, and Russians, given similar sixteenth-century opportunities, would have behaved as badly or worse. [The cruelty of Germans in Venezuela in the conquest period was strongly criticized by Spaniards; some indication that Nordics were possibly no more humane than Spaniards.] Spanish atrocities were severely castigated by a highly articulate, fearless, and powerful clergy, and by others who reported to a Crown consistently willing to listen, to legislate against, and to punish such criminality.[16] Such restraints were either absent, or were present but barely discernible, in the records of other European overseas empire builders until very recent times. And the truly terrifying inhumanity of twentieth-century civilizations, as evidenced by the torture and slave camps of the Russians, by the attempts at genocide by the Germans and other groups, and by the dropping of the atom bomb by Americans on Hiroshima, leaves no room whatsoever for any of these peoples to moralize about sixteenth-century Spanish behavior. Had Hernán Cortés dared to massacre noncombatant populations on anything like a twentieth-century scale, the Spanish Crown would surely have ordered his execution as a monstrous criminal.

Spaniards also sought gold and silver in America. What's more, they found and exploited fabulous mineral wealth in ways similar to those used by later Europeans and Americans in exploiting gold, copper, rubber, and oil. In the totality of man's history, with its records of gold, silver, and diamond rushes, and centuries-long seeking of profits in slave-trading and all other manner of exploitative activity in search of wealth, Spanish interest in New World riches seems logical enough, entirely normal, and not unique at all. By comparison with the pride, notable efficiency, and interest with which Englishmen, Frenchmen, Dutchmen, Scots, Jews, Germans, Anglo- or Italo-Americans seek the acquisition of material wealth, the Spaniard generally seems rather careless, and even disdainful, in such matters. He is (and was) more apt to have other goals in mind, risking his life or his goods on the turn of a card or the fate of armed conflict, bearing wealth and poverty (perennially the latter) with an equanimity that startles most foreigners. Ironically enough, a fundamental feature of modern Yankeephobic literature in Latin America is contempt for the preoccupation of people in the United States with material gain. To the Spaniard and his American relatives, this is, albeit hypocritically at times, a reprehensible brand of noncivilization.

The Spanish Centuries in America

The fact that Spain seriously and conscientiously governed a mammoth portion of the New World for some three centuries is usually lost sight of in our school texts and popular literature. Such faulty perspective arises largely from: (1) plain ignorance; (2) disproportionate attention to the more exciting conquest phase, with all its "blood-and-thunder" cruelties, gold-seeking, and sheer romance; (3) overshadowing attention given the Spanish American independence movement—it seems more like us, it is closer to our times, and the excitement of rebellion and warfare is involved, to say nothing of excellent opportunity for little homilies on freedom versus Spanish tyranny; (4) the distracting romance associated with piracy, international rivalry, and fighting in the Caribbean—Elizabethan Sea Dogs, Morgan, the buccaneers, etc.; (5) the blinding effect of United States power in more recent times, which throws our historical view of the American hemisphere out of focus by making our own past appear disproportionately large and important in comparison with any other; and (6) our interest mainly in the peripheral areas of the Spanish empire that came to be part of our own country.

To jump, as our schoolbooks so often do, from Cortés to Miguel Hidalgo; from Francisco Pizarro to José de San Martín and Bolívar; or from Francisco Vázquez de Coronado to the Alamo—with little between except a few sentences on Spanish tyranny, Father Junípero

Serra, restrictive commerce, Indian enslavement, and Inquisition censorship—is historical aberration on heroic scale. Furthermore, it is a grandiose injustice to Spain and a perpetual insult to Latin Americans. Thus, abysmal ignorance and pervasive distortion usually characterize our students' views of the Hispanic world.

This is no place for a resumé of Spanish American colonial history, and none is intended. But a few observations on some of the more common misunderstandings about this period should be helpful in appreciating how far the Black Legend type of writing has carried us off the track. Then, having done this, we can better comprehend the significance of the *furor loquendi, furor scribendi,* which got the whole aberration started.

The vast amount of polemical literature on Spanish conquest in America sheds but little light on the totality of Spanish action in America, for this controversial material pertains largely to the conquest decades, the first years of Spanish-Indian contact. This was, of course, the worst phase as far as harsh treatment of Indians was concerned. Las Casas deals exclusively with this and, since he is the best known, his polemical version of the conquest—ruthless, gold-greedy Spaniards versus innocent and peaceful savages—became, *ipso facto,* the most popular basis for characterizing (or, simply, dismissing) the subsequent centuries of Spain in America. This produced the impression that Spain's long rule was merely continuous conquest, an unending massacre and enslavement of Indians—a false perspective upon which a massive hispanophobic complex has been built.

The standard simplistic version of Spanish rule in America as a slavocracy, filled with tyranny, looting, bleeding taxation, and suffocating obscurantism, does not conform to the facts. Spanish rule through all this period was generally more benign than much or even most Spanish American government has been since separation from Spain. Had this not been so, Spain's rule would not have lasted as long as it did.

One of our leading authorities in such matters, Professor Lesley Byrd Simpson, writes:

> It seems to me that the average stature of the viceroys of New Spain [Mexico] was so great that no country to my knowledge was ever more fortunate in its rulers. New Spain had plenty of things the matter with it, . . . but it enjoyed a long life (three hundred years!) of relative peace, stability, and prosperity, in marked contrast to the squabbling nations of Europe. Some of the men who made this possible are worth our knowing.[17]

And an English scholar, Ronald Syme, recently implied something similar, in broader context:

In spite of the handicaps of geography and of distance, Spain was able to hold her wide dominions for three centuries and set upon them indelibly the stamp of her language, thought and institutions. That achievement deserves more honour than it has commonly earned—and a more searching investigation.[18]

The basic concept of Spanish Empire was not what we normally call "colonial" today. Rather was it designed as a number of overseas kingdoms officially coequal, under the Crown, with the several kingdoms of the mother country. In practice, Peninsulars usually viewed American-born Spaniards as inferiors, and this was the basis for continuous tension between "colonials" and Europeans—an important factor in the eventual wars for independence.

The coequal concept accounts for the virtually unstinted transfer of European culture to Spanish America and the generally successful effort to provide the American possessions with most of the mother country's civilization. Even more; one finds, at times, the curious paradox that taxation overseas was not as onerous as it was in some parts of the mother country.[19] One also finds that American life was often easier, or more prosperous, than in much of the mother country, where poverty was commonplace. In food availability, for example, Spanish Americans, of whatever level, were apt to fare as well or better than their European counterparts, Spanish or otherwise. Even the lower classes of Spanish America were likely to live somewhat better than much of the European peasantry.

There were, of course, many abuses of governmental authority, and all the many and varied evils of a vast bureaucracy, cholesterol of empire. Crimes of all sorts were committed, as one might expect in an empire of such size and long life. But there was also judicial machinery and legislation for punishment of abuses. The important point is that the norm was legality and law enforcement, just as in other civilized societies. In general, Spaniards did not try to impose upon America something hypocritically foreign or inferior to what they lived with at home. Taxation, municipal practices, university statutes, criminal and civil legislation, judiciary, artistic endeavors, social welfare agencies, commercial practices, etc., were, *mutatis mutandis,* close approximations of Spanish usage and norms in European territories. For example, in governmental and private welfare practices alone, there is abundant testimony to the comparatively advanced concern and practices of Spaniards in the New World. Moreover, this is a subject that merits much more attention and honor than it has received. According to a Mexican university professor of pharmacology: "Lima, Peru, in colonial days had more hospitals than churches and averaged one hospital bed for every 101 people, a considerably better average than Los Angeles [California] has today." [20]

The one great innovation was, of necessity, in Indian affairs. Spain's three centuries of tutelage and official concern for the welfare of the American Indian is a record not equaled by other Europeans in overseas government of peoples of lesser, or what were considered lesser, cultures. For all the mistakes, for all the failures, for all the crimes committed, and even allowing for Crown motives of practicality and self-service, in its overall performance Spain, in relation to the American Indian, need offer no apology to any other people or nation.[21]

Spain's Inquisition and her State-Church structure are usually blamed for an oppressive obscurantism that supposedly blighted the three centuries in America and entrenched so many of the ills that today beset Spanish American nations. Anti-Catholic prejudice in our own country makes this myth particularly attractive, and nineteenth- and twentieth-century Latin Americans are fond of reiterating it. But no scholar having acquaintance with Spanish educational and other intellectual achievement in America—e.g., Indian education, encouragement of literature, history, scientific investigations, university instruction—would subscribe to such a judgment. The Spanish record of some twenty-three colleges and universities in America, graduating 150,000 (including the poor, mestizos, and some Negroes) makes, for example, the Dutch in the East Indies in later and supposedly more enlightened times, look like obscurantists indeed. The Portuguese did not establish a single university in colonial Brazil nor in any other overseas possessions. The total of universities established by Belgium, England, Germany, France, and Italy during later Afro-Asian colonial periods assuredly suffers by any fair comparison with the pioneering record of Spain.[22]

In this vein, let us observe a few comments by Professor John Tate Lanning, of Duke University, our leading authority on the subject of Spanish American colonial culture:

> Up until a generation ago the view that all intellectual products of Europe were excluded from America by a zealous monarch and Inquisition went almost without question. No careful scholar would now pronounce upon the availability of books in America upon the exclusive basis of the estimable *Recopilación de Indias* or the *Index of Prohibited Books*. The bibliographical avenue of Enlightenment to Spanish America was at no time so thoroughly barricaded as the statutes and indexes indicate.

Again:

> An effective and relatively unhampered literary contact with the whole world of thought is implicit in the propositions defended in the [Spanish

American] universities toward the end of the eighteenth century. The censorship of the Inquisition, well established though it was in law, was even more than many other somnolent colonial institutions, essentially bureaucratic and ineffectual.

He also said:

A grandiose and tenacious injustice springing from the traditions and emotions of the early national historians [of Spanish America] is the sweeping condemnation of Spanish colonial culture as "three centuries of theocracy, obscurantism, and barbarism!" [23]

Along the way, let us notice also that barely more than one hundred persons were executed in Spanish America as a result of Inquisition action during its some 250 years of formal existence. This would seem, I think, to compare rather favorably, as these things go, with the torture and execution of Roman Catholics in Elizabethan England (130 priests and 60 laymen, or a total of 250 killed by the state if one includes those dying in prison). And estimates of deaths for witchcraft in the German states during the sixteenth and seventeenth centuries run well into the thousands.[24]

This, perhaps, is as good a place as any to add some words concerning the Spanish Inquisition, especially in the Americas. Not because this institution was tremendously significant in the total story of Spain in America—it was not—but because it has for so long been a focal point for anti-Spanish prejudice, and because it has been, and is, so little understood. As already indicated, the total number of executions committed in the name of the Holy Office in the Americas was very small. The use of torture was relatively infrequent and applied under strict regulations, with safeguards and conditions more enlightened than in most of the judicial processes of Europe during that day. Much of the Inquisition's jurisdiction embraced matters that are now handled by secular courts (e.g., bigamy, blasphemy, bearing false witness, and various brands of immoral behavior, such as sexual perversions). It must also be remembered that, in the sixteenth and seventeenth centuries (the period of greatest Inquisition activity), dissident religious practice was virtually synonymous with treason; this was true not only of Spain and her possessions, but of much of the rest of Europe also. Thus, crypto-Jews, crypto-Moslems, and Protestants were viewed by Spanish authorities as traitors or as subversive agents; these same people were found among those executed in the Americas.[25]

The Spanish Inquisition, in the Americas as in Spain, was subservient to the secular state. The Holy Office, with very minor exceptions, did not have jurisdiction over the American Indian. The censorship of books was largely concerned with religious literature and not significantly active in the main stream of belles lettres, scientific works, etc. As various scholarly investigations have shown, this censorship was never very vigorous or efficient, and therefore rested relatively lightly upon the totality of Spanish American culture. Avowed antagonists of the Inquisition usually admit that the institution was highly enlightened on the subject of witchcraft even while parts of Europe went homicidally berserk on the subject.[26] One of the greatest areas of Inquisition action was in discipline of churchmen (e.g., solicitation in the confessional), thus acting as a protective screen against behavior considered harmful to others in the populace.

The Inquisition's famous *auto de fe* was pageantry of high popularity, literally a public act of faith designed to reaffirm what we would today call patriotism. Loyalty to the faith was synonymous with loyalty to the Crown, state, empire, and Christendom, and Roman Catholicism was the great and popular universality of Christian Spain—much more so than was Protestantism in Elizabethan England or in William the Silent's rebellious Dutch provinces. In a milder form, our Fourth of July celebrations especially when they had that patriotic fervor of bygone days or later gatherings of the "I-am-an-American" type, filled a similarly popular desire for patriotic reaffirmation.

The Spanish Inquisition, as we shall later see, is a principal burden-bearer of the anti-Spanish legend, mainly for the following reasons: (1) its aims, methods, and power were wildly exaggerated and sensationalized within the general anti-Spanish propaganda of the sixteenth, seventeenth, and eighteenth centuries; (2) the institution's interest in censorship and Protestant heretics has been vastly overpublicized in relation to the totality of its work; (3) writings on the Spanish Inquisition are almost invariably of the sensation-mongering variety, lacking in objective scholarship, and above all, short in the use of comparative criteria so necessary in any fair understanding of the past; (4) the fashionable practice, especially since the eighteenth century, of automatic, or dogmatic, damning of the Spanish Inquisition, is mainly founded not upon knowledge but upon prejudice, sanctified propaganda, and the manifestly unjust but popular habit of using post-Enlightenment canons—rationalistic, moralistic, political, religious, humanitarian—as bases for judging pre-Enlightenment phenomena. In somewhat the same way that the Enlightenment scourged the "Dark" Ages, made "medieval" and "feudal" into terms of opprobrium, pummeled revealed religion and the Natural Law, so also "Spanish Inquisition" and "inquisitor" became modern synonyms for the cruelest of oppressions. Perhaps the unkindest and most revealing insult of all, in view of the Spanish Inquisition's enlightened views on witchcraft, is our present habit of using the terms "witch-hunting" and "inquisition" interchangeably.

It occurs to me at this point that in order to rectify Black Legend errors, one of the greatest services that scholarship could render would be to make a historiographically sophisticated and very complete study of the Spanish Inquisition widely available in the Western world. As an exercise in true enlightenment, a more interesting challenge would be hard to find.[27]

Near the end of the so-called colonial period, Spanish American universities and scientific and cultural institutes were strongly affected by the currents of European intellectual change. Intellectuals trained in such environments, therefore, acquired ideas that often led or contributed to their subsequent leadership of independence movements. And it was under the Spanish government's aegis and encouragement that such a cultural environment existed.

The substantial scholarly literature on American institutional development under Spanish rule continues to increase, but this fact usually comes as a surprise to many university students and intellectuals in the United States. It seems incredible to some that achievement worthy of later intellectual consideration could have taken place in an inquisitional Spanish-Catholic environment; but, if one applies a bit of logic to the situation, there should be no such astonishment. Spain, as should be well known, was enjoying a Golden Age during most of the first two centuries of her empire-building in America, and there was no reason for the mother country to withhold this intellectual activity from her colonies. And the answer is that she did not. Spaniards in America, and their progeny, had access to Spain's great intellectual achievements, and what's more, American universities were modeled on that of Salamanca, one of the most famous in Europe. Through the mother country came the intellectual currents of the rest of Europe. This was as true of the eighteenth century as it was of the sixteenth or seventeenth.

Almost all of Spanish and Spanish American history is a testimonial to the fact that people of Spanish descent do not long acquiesce to any tyranny that the majority, or even much of a minority, finds unbearable. Spain ruled in America for more than three centuries without professional soldiery or standing military forces except in a few places where they were needed mainly to repel foreign attack or guard against frontier Indian depredations. And in all that time there was not a single rebellion that indicated widespread dissatisfaction with the Crown's rule. There were, of course, local disturbances, conspiracies, and uprisings, which made some mark on this history; but in virtually every case, except the few strictly Indian rebellions, there were apt to be Peninsulars and Americans on both sides and the circumstances were local, with little or nothing to indicate significant separatist spirit. Even when Napoleon invaded the mother country, usurped the throne, and "shook the tree of independence" by pushing Spanish Americans to extraordinary measures of self-government, most Spanish Americans did not initially aim at separation from Spain; independence from the mother country was a slow-growing idea even in that heady atmosphere of crumbling traditions. Independence was almost an accidental outcome, and there were far more important factors in this achievement than any popular rebellion against Spanish tyranny or obscurantism. The strong anti-Spanish propaganda inspired within relatively limited circles did not achieve wide popularity until years of it and abrasive fighting had crystallized dogmatic hatred into war for independence. The war period and subsequent decades spawned a literature of justification with strong hispanophobic twists (see Chapter 6).

In summary, the evidence so far presented in scholarly monographs, articles, and in documentary publications, does not allow any fairminded observer to characterize those three centuries as a "tyranny," as uniquely "oppressive," as purposefully or generally cruel, or as "obscurantist." There is still much to be studied concerning those centuries, but it is already clear that they were too complex to fit such generalized epithets. Above all, it is completely fallacious to consider them as merely a continuation of the initial conquest patterns. Even if the terrible atrocities made famous by Bishop Bartolomé de las Casas were absolutely true and thoroughly characteristic of all Spanish conquest, it would still be an unpardonable error if such characterization should be applied to the whole three centuries, as is so frequently done. And the error of this practice is often compounded by uncritical acceptance of Las Casas' version of Spanish Conquest.

Bartolomé de las Casas, hero of hispanophobes from mid-sixteenth century to the present, is the person most responsible for our distorted views of Spaniards and their role in America. This Spanish bishop, so often sanctified in print through four centuries and enshrined today as the "saint" of anti-Spanish propaganda, did about as much as any one man could do to blacken the name of a people and nation—his own, at that. He surely did not plan it that way, since he could not have foreseen how his work would suit foreign purposes, but his writings are at the heart and center of the denigration of Spain. He is, incidentally, an excellent case study in the long-range damage that can be done by irresponsible zealotry, exploited by the propaganda mills of one's enemies.

Bartolomé de las Casas, Immortal Zealot

> *Las Casas was greatly responsible for creation of this somber picture of Spanish action in America. . . . The libels of Las Casas and the political use to which they were put [by Spain's enemies], mark the beginnings of propaganda in our epoch.*[28]

Spain in the sixteenth century produced a phenomenally large number of heroic figures. She also produced during the New World conquest a chain of events and controversies that were not only heroic but extremely bitter, a polemical flood commensurate in size with such a vast enterprise. It was the modern world's first great debate on how best to bear "the white man's burden," and this debate swirled around the fate of millions of newly discovered American Indians. This polemical process, though often passionately intemperate, in the style of Hispanic controversy, helped to produce an enlightened and generally benevolent tutelar legislation on behalf of the Indian. This debate, characterized by great freedom of speech, which included criticism of the Crown itself, must be viewed as one of the glories of Spanish history, a monument of self-criticism and meliorative humanitarian effort.

. . . The clash of arms was not the only struggle during the conquest. The clash of ideas that accompanied the discovery of America and the establishment of Spanish rule there is a story that must be told as an integral part of the conquest, and endows it with a unique character worthy of note. . . . The widespread criticism permitted, and even stimulated, by the crown really constitutes one of the glories of Spanish civilization. . . . It is to Spain's everlasting credit that she allowed men to insist that all her actions in America be just. . . .[29]

As so often happens in vigorous controversy, the moderate voices failed, relatively speaking, to register for history's benefit, though in practice they generally prevailed. The fundamental questions were: Should the American Indian be treated as a human being with reasoning power? If so, peaceful conversion to Christianity should be the Crown policy. Or, was the Indian in such a low state of culture that forceful persuasion and Spanish rule, including enslavement, if necessary, would be justifiable and legal?

Those who argued the former case, like Bartolomé de las Casas, went so far as to question the king's right to rule over the New World if he failed to protect Indian rights and use *only* peaceful persuasion (to be done, of course, by men like Las Casas). Thus, they challenged royal authority to the king's face, and their arguments were generally favored by the monarchy. Those who, like the great jurist Juan Ginés de Sepúlveda, espoused the opposite view upheld the king's right to rule in America, even if this entailed war or Indian enslavement. The battle of words ended as a draw, although subsequent Spanish legislation for Indian protection could be accounted rather more "lascasian" in concept than otherwise. Ginés de Sepúlveda did not get royal permission to print his views in Spain, but Las Casas published his arguments and propaganda in Seville in the early 1550s.

Indian slavery was definitely proscribed in Spanish legislation, and strong laws were enacted for Indian protection and welfare. But the king's authority remained, and moderately forceful persuasion to Christianity was the accepted pattern, although with restrictions. The sum total was a generally enlightened mixture of practicality and humanitarianism. The extreme positions, being more spectacular and more appealing to dogmatists, have commanded the most attention up to our own times. Depending upon the school of thought, the Indian has been regarded as a "noble savage" or as a "dirty dog." It was inevitable, however, that Las Casas would eventually far outdistance Ginés de Sepúlveda in popularity, for his doctrines were more in keeping with the humanitarianism of later times. Since Las Casas appeared to be a strong fighter in behalf of the "underdog" Indian, he was bound increasingly to be a hero of the noble savage school—especially when this concept became popular during and after the eighteenth century—without regard for the validity or practicality of his arguments.

The losers in this encounter were not the debaters, nor their subject, the Indian. Ironically, those who lost were Spain and the Spanish people, the very ones who deserve credit for the debate having taken place when and where it did. The tracts Las Casas wrote against Spanish iniquities were often so intemperate, so exaggerated, and so distorted that they stigmatized Spaniards with the brand of a unique greed and cruelty from that day to this. The Dutch, English, and French did not debate these matters on such a scale, and thus they escaped international exposure of their misdeeds. Self-criticism has never been such a notable characteristic of those peoples as it has been of Spaniards. Hence the very apt lines of Bartrina:

> Hearing a man speak, it is easy to tell
>   where he first saw the light of day.
> If he praises England, he will be an Englishman;

> If he speaks evil of Prussia, he will be a Frenchman;
> If he speaks evil of Spain, he is a Spaniard.[30]

Controversy over the merits and defects of Bartolomé de las Casas will assuredly go on forever, mainly because there will always be some who want to believe his total condemnation of Spaniards and others who recognize and roundly condemn the obvious prejudice and zealous excesses which guided his tongue, his personality, and his pen. There are those who worship Las Casas, overlooking the injustice of his methods in order to enshrine the nobility of his cause. And there are those who, for centuries now, have cared little about the cause, the methods, or the facts of the case, in their sheer delight with Las Casas as a propaganda hero of anti-Spain.

Although propagandistic fervor and distortion are much evident in Las Casas' historical writings, it is principally in his *Brevíssima relación de la destrucción de las Indias* that his choleric, intransigent, and intolerant zeal reaches its greatest height and fame. It is this tract that became the single most powerful weapon of Spain's enemies, the best known and most used source for foreigners writing on Spanish overseas actions and even for many foreign views of Spaniards, their history, and their character.

The Spanish friar and bishop, Bartolomé de las Casas, died in 1566 at the age of ninety-two and he was a contemporary of Columbus and of the first and greatest phase of the Spanish Conquest in America. He devoted the last half century of his life to the thesis that this conquest was a vast and cruel injustice, an "illegal" invasion by "wolves and tigers" against peaceful, innocent, and "noble" Indians. Las Casas advanced this description repeatedly before the Spanish court in his efforts to ameliorate Indian suffering as conquered people, and he was startlingly successful in obtaining legislative action designed to protect Indian lives and rights. The *Brevíssima Relación* was but one of the bishop's many passionate outpourings in this cause.

In the centuries of cliché-ridden emphasis upon Spanish iniquities, it is often forgotten that there were many others besides Las Casas who condemned and castigated cruelties during the conquest, and they were also Spaniards. Also, the remedial legislation was written and carried out by Spanish jurists and other officials. The sixteenth-century Spanish character contained within it the capability of harsh conquest, on the one hand, and on the other, the will to right consequent ill effects with zealous, idealistic, and often effective means, especially through Spain's religious and juridical processes.

The nine treatises Las Casas somewhat feverishly published in Seville in the 1550s were destined to exercise a phenomenally widespread and baneful influence upon evaluation of Spain's actions in America. This was and is particularly true of the *Brief Relation*. This propaganda weapon—for such it was and must be labeled—became a veritable bible for foreigners subsequently writing on the Spanish Conquest and rule in the New World. In spite of well-known errors, distortions, and general unreliability, the *Brief Relation* is still the handbook for those wanting to prove, or most willing to believe in, a unique Spanish depravity.

The story of Las Casas and his *Brief Relation* has been told in many places and in many controversies,[31] and it need not be repeated here: a very brief look at the setting and gist of the tract will serve.

The first climax of Las Casas' pro-Indian crusade, including a number of trans-Atlantic voyages and much pressure on court circles and rulers, came in the latter 1530s and early 1540s when he tirelessly and successfully lobbied for an overhaul of legislation to improve Indian conditions. Part of the outcome was the famous *New Laws of the Indies for the Good Treatment and Preservation of the Indians* (1542), which rocked Spain's American Empire to its foundations with violent controversy and even a rebellion of some of the conquerors of Peru. Among many other things, these *New Laws* struck at the bases of the *encomienda* system (Indian tribute granted to Spaniards, especially of the conqueror class) and reaffirmed the illegality of Indian enslavement. Though the Peruvian rebellion and the wise counsels of Mexico's Viceroy Antonio de Mendoza delayed enforcement of the *New Laws,* this legislation, nonetheless, served as a continuing goal of crown policy and most of the laws were put into force in succeeding years; they almost provoked a rebellion in the 1560s in Mexico. It is indeed a credit to that crown policy, strongly influenced by Las Casas and others of his Dominican Order, that potential loss of empire through rebellion did not deter the monarchs from what could be called a "pro-Indian" legislative goal, characteristic, generally, of most subsequent Spanish legislation in America. The Spanish crown, in the totality of its policies with regard to the Indian, produced a fascinating mixture of practicality and humanitarianism—an exceedingly rich area for study and certainly deserving of more honor than is commonly given it.

The second climax of Las Casas' crusade came in 1550–1551 when he engaged in crown-sponsored debate with Juan Ginés de Sepúlveda. Up to this time, Las Casas had not published his writings, though some circulated in manuscript. Now he did so, suddenly, in the space of a few months, and among them was the *Brief Relation*. The haste with which he published and spread his tracts remains something of a mystery. He may have wished more permanency and wider circulation for his views, or perhaps his publishers scented a bestseller and geared the work to be put out with exceptional speed. It could have been that Las Casas himself, already advanced in years, was in understandable haste to see his life's work thus projected. And, *¿Quién sabe?* maybe someone in Seville was highly impatient to speed the tracts on their way beyond the Peninsula.

Since Seville in the 1550s was a bustling maritime crossroads, with many foreigners, it is not difficult to imagine the abundance of facilities for rapid dispersion of the Las Casas tracts into European areas where an already cumulative hispanophobia would make them welcome. In the total European situation of this period (1550–1580), there was more than enough murkiness of plot and counterplot to suggest the possibility that the Las Casas tracts were methodically being spread as anti-Spanish weapons. Whatever the details, weapons they became—and quickly.

Las Casas in print was, of course, even more formidable than before, as he undoubtedly intended. From all sides, and especially from America, came bitter blasts to contradict him. His *Brief Relation* was quickly castigated as a tissue of distortions, exaggerations, overgeneralization, and outright error. In it he reiterated, *ad nauseam,* the story of villainous, completely depraved, Spanish conquerors versus the "noble savage," making all Spaniards inhumanly cruel and greedy for gold and all Indians peaceful and innocent. Out of this shameful potpourri came the outrageous figure of some twenty million Indians killed by the Spaniards during the conquest—a statistic that remains popularly believed to this day. With his pen, Las Casas destroyed more Indians than all his countrymen could possibly have killed. Professor John Tate Lanning puts it this way: "If each Spaniard listed in Bermúdez Plata's *Passengers to the Indies* for the whole half-century after the discovery had killed an Indian every day and three on Sunday, it would have taken a generation to do the job attributed to him by his compatriots." [32]

Las Casas did not allow for diminution of Indian numbers by disease, epidemics, warfare in which Indians willingly participated as Spanish allies in order to massacre traditional enemies, or the obvious lessening of Indian numbers through miscegenation.[33] Las Casas accused the Spaniards of killing more than three million on the island of Española alone, an area that probably could not have supported, with pre-Columbian agriculture, small trade, and small villages, any approximation of that number.[34] And Las Casas' obviously exaggerated figures are repeated uncritically even in our own century by writers who should know better.[35] In short, Las Casas simply did not let either the truth or historical sense interfere with his horrifyingly exciting story; and he threw in just enough circumstantial material to give his work a ring of authenticity. Short of accurate detail and entirely lacking comparative criteria, but long on impossible generalizations, Las Casas' work is believable only to the naïvely uncritical and those already convinced.

Unfortunately, historians and others often let the worthiness of Las Casas' cause interfere with critical evaluation of his work. Conceding the humanitarian worthiness of Las Casas' crusade one must also admit that Las Casas, intolerantly, was unable to find any kind words for any views that opposed his. He sweepingly denounced Spaniards with such intransigence, such untruth and distortion, such choleric insult, that he made them utterly unbelievable. Fray Toribio de Benavente, "Motolinía," famous missionary in Mexico, phrased it thus in writing to the king: "I am astonished that Your Majesty and those of your councils have been able to suffer for so long a man in religious garb [Las Casas] so offensive, restless, importunate, turbulent, pettifogging, disturbing, so bad mannered, abusive, injurious, and so lacking in tranquility." [36] In the last analysis, the thousands of conscientious Spanish officials and humble, realistic clerics who daily worked on Spanish-Indian amalgamation during three centuries, also deserve great credit for effective amelioration of the Indian lot.

For anyone sincerely interested in a fair appraisal of Spain's actions in America, the significance of Bartolomé de las Casas lies in the following: (1) he was correct in pointing out that Spaniards committed many barbarous acts in conquering and exploiting the Indians, but he was at fault in focusing attention *solely* upon the atrocities, and excluding other acts that would have given a more fair picture of *total* Spanish action; (2) he was, we must assume, sincere enough and he was certainly fighting for a worthy cause; (3) Las Casas, as propagandist, mistakenly stigmatized his own people with unique greed and cruelty, and in this he exhibited not only a meanness of spirit but a supreme disregard for historical perspectives and understanding of human behavior, basic prerequisites for good historical writing; and (4) his propaganda was accepted as *historical* fact and as the complete account of Spain's activities in America. It is this last point that has caused the greatest damage— the use of Las Casas as guide to a general view of the centuries of Spain in the New World.

Las Casas was violently attacked in his own time, and during the following centuries a substantial body of literature was produced which has sought to vilify him or simply to correct his distortions and beget sounder judgments on the Spanish conquest and its three-century aftermath.[37] The best ways to rectify the damage caused by Las Casas are: (1) constantly increasing knowledge derived from the vast documentation and scholarly writing on Spain in America; (2) an awareness of what Las Casas was trying to do, how he went about it, and how Spain's enemies used his work in propaganda; (3) to approach Spanish and Spanish American history and culture free of religious, racial, and other inherited prejudices and with application of the same criteria and standards of sympathy that we apply, for example, to our own history and its European backgrounds.

Spaniards, with abundant reason, have been sensitive to the total denigration penned by Las Casas and some of his emulators. But thoughtful Spanish scholars and hispanists of others lands ask only that Spain, Spaniards, and Spain in America be appraised and studied in an atmosphere of fairness—i.e., standards of impartiality used in judging other peoples and nations. They do not ask for creation of a "white legend," merely the elimination of the injustices of the black one.

The bitter blasts of Bartolomé de las Casas began to be spread in Europe precisely in those years (about 1560–1590) when the English were beginning to challenge Iberian monopolies in the New World, and the Dutch and English were entering upon long periods of conflict with Spain. This was also a time when Europe's interest in New World phenomena (e.g., wealth, geography, Indians) and tales of Spanish exploration and conquest there was awakening. The harsh coloring of the Las Casas indictment of Spaniards was made to order for propaganda designed to show that the Spaniards, because of cruelties and greed, were unfit to retain title to New World territories. Even more, this portrayal of Spanish depravity could be used to make Philip II, his officials, and his soldiery appear so monstrous that Europeans must perforce fight them to the death.

By the middle of the sixteenth century, even without the stimulation of a Las Casas version of Spanish iniquities, Spain had an abundance of formidable enemies, all the way from Constantinople to London to Lisbon. Spanish efforts to purify and reform her church, maintain the unity of Christendom, contain France, and preserve or enlarge dynastic heritages, had placed Spain at the European summit—but at the cost of some dangerously located fears, envies, and vindictive hatreds. There were already hispanophobic Europeans who would be delighted to exploit Don Bartolomé. Let us see why—and who.

Part ii

Growth of the Legend

Chapter 3

ROOTS OF HISPANOPHOBIA

> . . . mai parlava [Pope Paul IV] di
> Sua Maesta e della nazione spagnuola,
> che non li chiamasse eretici, scismatici
> e maledetti da Dio, seme di guidei e
> di marrani, feccia del mondo. . . .
>
> BERNARDO NAVAGERO [1]

The major outpouring of anti-Spanish propaganda began during Dutch and English conflicts with Spain in the decades after 1560. In this historic moment Spain and England, beginning to fight in American waters, headed rapidly toward an open break—a clash that was to be forever symbolized in the Armada story. The Dutch were simultaneously rebelling against Philip II's ways of governing his Low Countries patrimony. And England, fearful and envious of mighty Spain, sympathetically encouraged the Dutch rebels—and received from them a usable, rapidly increasing quantity of anti-Spanish propaganda materials.

Coincident and in concert with all this was the publication of the earliest foreign editions of Bartolomé de las Casas' tracts. The first foreign version of the *Brief Relation* was in French (1578), at Antwerp; it was quickly followed by one in Dutch, two in French (1579 and 1582), and the first English translation (1583). There was astute planning behind this concurrence of propaganda with war, as we shall see. There was also some hispanophobia in Europe's immediate past.[2]

For nearly a century a fertile seedbed of anti-Spanish writing and attitudes had been in formation. These were primarily related to the Spanish presence in Italy, Jewish-Spanish tensions, centuries of Hispano-French antagonisms, and Germanic antipathies stirred in the Lutheran Revolt. Dutchmen and Englishmen were, thus, relatively late in entering the current of hispanophobia, for certain stock attitudes were already prevalent in writings that were well known by the middle of the sixteenth century. In short, many of the propaganda weapons available for use against Spain were already in existence when the Spanish-Dutch and

Spanish-English conflicts began; these wars simply dramatized, crystallized, and gave enduring form to the Black Legend that was to reach us.

Italian Bases of the *Leyenda Negra*

> *Sobre todas las naciones contadas y sobre todas las demás que ay derramadas por el mundo, tienen este odio particular que emos dicho contra España los ytalianos.*
>
> GONZALO JIMÉNEZ DE QUESADA,
> *El Antijovio*, 1567 [3]

Beginning in the late thirteenth century, Aragonese monarchs extended imperialistic ambitions into the Mediterranean, successively incorporating Sicily, Sardinia, and Naples. As a consequence, Iberian soldiers and mercenaries were active on Italian soil through the fourteenth and fifteenth centuries. This Spanish action in Italy achieved a dominance in Italian affairs under King Ferdinand in the 1490s and early 1500s, when he thwarted French ambitions and invasions in that area. Along with this Aragonese intrusion, there was a significant Catalan trade competition with the Italians.

Thus it was that Italian views of Spaniards became preponderantly antagonistic. The Italians, as former rulers of the known world, were still feeding their egos on a cult of antiquity and had no doubts about their superiority over all other peoples. It was natural that the heirs of Rome of all classes, but especially the aristocracy and intelligentsia, would deeply resent and bitterly criticize such foreign intrusion, rule, commercial competition, and specific incidents of foreign behavior. Even when Spanish rule was of high order and mainly beneficial—as it sometimes was, even by Italian admission—it nettled Italian pride.

In early phases of this Hispano-Italian contact, several distinct features marked the growth of unfavorable views concerning Spaniards. The Swedish scholar, Sverker Arnoldsson, summarized it thus:

The intervention of Spanish monarchs and their soldiery—their victories and conquest in Sicily, Sardinia, and the Italian Peninsula—is certainly one of the important factors in explanation of the oldest Italian version of the Leyenda Negra. In all this, there is rooted the image of the hidalgo as a rustic, uncultured human type, barbarous and ridiculously ceremonious. Another factor is the competition of Catalan merchants with Italians, as well as Catalan piracy in Greek and Italian waters. Here is the basis for the view of the Catalan as treacherous, avaricious, and unscrupulous. A third factor is the migration of Spanish strumpets to Italy and observation of certain customs in the Aragonese-Neapolitan court; and also, the atmosphere around the Valencian Pope Alexander Borgia. In these things, there is founded the image of the excessively sensual and immoral Spaniard. A fourth factor is the age-long mixture of Spanish with Oriental and African elements, plus the Jewish and Islamic influence upon Spanish culture; this motivated the view of the Spaniards as a people of inferior race and doubtful orthodoxy.[4]

Until the opening of the sixteenth century, these antagonistic views of Spaniards referred mainly to Catalans, Aragonese, and Valencians, who constituted almost exclusively the Spanish presence in Italy. But after 1500 Castile more and more entered into the Italian scene and during the course of the *Cinquecento* it became leader of politico-military action in Italy, defender of Italy against Moslems, and, near midcentury, acknowledged leader of Roman Catholicism against the Protestant Revolt. Thus, Italian views of Spaniards, in the main antagonistic, were increasingly fashioned by observance of the Castilian as the "true" Spanish type.

The first half of the sixteenth century in Europe was deeply scarred by conflict between Spain and France, and much of the military action was on Italian soil. The result was a Spanish triumph, culminating in the Treaty of Cateau-Cambrésis (1559), by which the French monarchy renounced its claims in Naples, Milan, and Savoy. To the end of the century the bulk of Italy was either dynastically tied to Spain or was allied with Spain against such common enemies as Turks and Protestants.

Continuing conflict in Italy, involving large foreign armies, encouraged antagonistic Italian expression. And, since the most efficient and victorious soldiery was that of Spain, anti-Spanish feeling was particularly virulent. In spite of oft-expressed admiration for Spain's "Great Captain," Gonsalvo de Córdoba, and some other comments favorable to Spanish leaders and governors, the general tenor of Italian sentiment was hispanophobic. Over and above generalities, there were specific episodes that fastened upon Spaniards an opprobrium ringing down to our own day. The most famous of these was the sack of Rome in 1527.

A quantity of polemical and eyewitness literature has been published from that day to this blaming Spain for the cruelty, rapaciousness, and sheer barbarity of the sack of Rome and the lesser sack of Prato in 1512. In both episodes, Spanish soldiery were involved. In Prato, Spanish troops had intervened in a dispute between rival factions in the Florentine Republic, and in Rome, Spanish soldiery were mixed with Italians, Germans, and Burgundian-Netherland troops. Although the Prato case yields contradictory accounts about the amount of damage done, the excesses were clearly marked Spanish. The far more shocking sack of Rome is even more clouded with controversy—not about the damage done but about the share of blame attributable to Spaniards rather than Germans, Italians, or others. These events, though not unique in warfare then or now, contributed heavily to Italian belief that the Spaniard was an abnormally rapacious and dissolute soldier. This was one of the prices Spaniards paid for victory, for outstanding repute as fighting men, and for being on foreign soil. Since they were the dominant, and usually victorious, army in Italy, they were automatically disliked and often unfairly blamed for virtually all the specific tragedies that occurred in this long series of wars and feuds. But there is no case for any unique Spanish barbarity; Spaniards in Italy behaved like other victorious soldiery in similar circumstances.[5]

The long Spanish hegemony in Italy has been commonly accepted as specially marked by oppression, injustice, and heavy taxation. It also was generally blamed for Italy's economic decline. Modern historical investigations, however, have led to significant modifications—and even outright rejection—of these traditional views.

The imposition of Spanish justice, markedly impartial and benign as far as the general population was concerned, was bound to be unpopular among displaced or thwarted Italian aristocracy—the class most able and willing to broadcast in writing and otherwise an anti-Spanish attitude. Italians of the ruling classes resented a Spanish officialdom that did not hesitate to act against them in enforcing imperial justice. In this, Spanish officials incurred Italian antagonism in about the same way that Spanish Peninsulars in America were resented by Spanish American aristocracy (the Creoles). In Naples and Sicily, Spanish government was supported by the middle classes and it often defended them against excesses of the nobility. In America, Spanish officialdom was charged with enforcing the king's legislation on behalf of the Indian, and this inhibited the local aristocracy's exploitation of native peoples.

It can also be demonstrated that Spain did not impose onerous or uniquely oppressive taxation on her Italian lands; certainly not by the standard of times which were generally inflationary and made any taxation appear heavier than it actually was in comparison to the past. It is sometimes overlooked, too, that Castile bore a greater burden of taxation than the Italians for empire upkeep and defense of Italy against the Moslems. Thus, Spain, as in the case of the New World taxation, bled herself more than her overseas possessions for imperial maintenance, Comparison of economic conditions in the Italian areas ruled by Spain with conditions elsewhere in Italy during the same period, shows Spanish government in a generally favorable light, especially in matters of taxation, population increase, and general welfare. This can be stated categorically for southern Italy and Sicily, and probably for Lombardy. It must be borne in mind that this Spanish rule occurred in a period of almost continuous warfare, both internal and external, with all that this implies for economic matters.

Spanish leadership in defending Italy against Islam merits special attention. For one thing, this danger was very great in the sixteenth century. For another, it was primarily the excellence of Spanish soldiers, the energy of Spanish monarchs (Charles V and Philip II), and Spanish military and financial leadership and supply that saved Italy from being overrun or, at least, tremendously damaged by Moslem incursions. Finally, by much Italian admission—including even those Italians critical of Spaniards in other respects—this Spanish defense of Christendom was not only of heroic proportions but one of Spain's greatest contributions to Christian Europe. While the Italians criticized Spanish soldiery on their soil and Spanish leadership in governmental and military affairs— much as we are today criticized for troops, bases, and other influences in foreign lands—it must be borne in mind that Italians showed little inclination to maintain this defense against Islam without Spanish help and leadership.[6]

Despite all this and despite some favorable change of Italian attitude toward Spain when the Protestant Revolt made Spaniards and Italians allies against the new heresy, the general tenor of Italian literary expression throughout the sixteenth century was anti-Spanish. It is in this cultural, primarily literary, expression of their own *leyenda negra* that Italians contributed so heavily to the durability of the Black Legend. They made Spain pay, in the coin of what today would be called "world opinion," a great price for her victories in Italy.

Manifestations of anti-Spanish attitudes in Italian literature—a literature which, of course, was enormously influential in Renaissance Europe —are many and diverse. For one thing, literary form was given to wartime atrocities in which Spaniards were involved. Especially worthy of notice is the fact that Italian scholars expressed a general resentment at the destruction of their libraries and other cultural monuments—and Spain, of course, received most of the blame for this common concomitant of war. Secondly, many complaints about taxation in Spain's Italian dominions found their way into literature. And this occurred in an age when Italian individuals and aristocracy often failed to put Peninsular interests, such as defense against Turks, above local loyalties and rivalries.

Other complaints against Spanish administration, "very frequent and only in part justified," concerned the Inquisition. In Naples and Lombardy, resentment seems to have been based more on the view of the Holy Office as an arm of the Spanish secular state than upon fear of confiscations or the rooting out of heresy. In Sicily and Sardinia, where there were few heretics, antagonism seems to have been primarily directed against privileges of the *familiares,* honorary Inquisition titles carrying special privileges and some exemption from taxes. It is paradoxical that Italian literary attacks on the Spanish Inquisition were aimed at an institution dedicated to elimination of Jewish and Moslem influences that made Spanish orthodoxy suspect in Italian and other European eyes.

In some literary circles, bitterness against the impartial justice of Spanish administration, "without concessions to personal prerogatives," took form generally as an aristocratic resentment against foreign domination. Despite the fact that the general populace was usually benefited by this justice, literary expressions and aristocratic leadership certainly accounted for creation of popular resentment against Spaniards. This antipathy was nourished by the popular element, which was usually in closest contact with day-to-day behavior of Spanish soldiery.

Finally, "a general distrust" of the Spaniards accounted for a considerable literary hispanophobia in Renaissance Italy. As already indicated, Spaniards were suspect because their orthodoxy and culture were so infiltrated by Moslems and Jews. They were further suspect in the mirror of an Italian inferiority complex which was exceedingly touchy about foreign domination, especially in the more "Spanish" period of Philip II. Thus, for example, Italian military commanders were naturally bitter about predominantly Spanish leadership and attendant Spanish depreciation of Italian military qualities. "Spanish troops were not considered so much as protectors of the Italian territories as they were a kind of civil guard." The hypocrisy of the Italians became obvious when they failed to supply troops for their own defense.

Sverker Arnoldsson sums up the bases of Italian literary hispanophobia in the following words, and special note should be taken of the comment on the Venetian ambassadors, who are often used as primary sources for the history of this period and for observations on Spain and Spaniards:

The general odium which, for various reasons, was produced against Spaniards in the Italy of the Cinquecento, was manifested in many expressive ways. In this connection, the comments of the Venetian ambassadors must not be considered, for being themselves enemies of Spain, we can suspect that they attributed to their informants their own sentiments, or that they generalized impressions based upon conversations with persons holding their own opinions. . . .

Certain it is that individual Italians of the sixteenth century held a passionate hatred for everything Spanish, and they showed this hatred in the most expressive words. The best and most cited example is that of Pope Paul IV. In his bitter comments during the decade 1550–1560, we find all of the Italian inferiority complex facing the victorious, conquering and powerful neighbor nation. . . .

The insults of Paul IV express what many cultured Italians, during the height and decline of the Renaissance, felt toward Spanish power: the sorrow that their own country—land of the great civilization of antiquity and heir of Rome—should be dominated by a people of inferior quality in culture, religion, and race. The Spanish hegemony in Italy was, for those holding this view, a moral and cultural catastrophe. The literary attacks against Spaniards assumed, at times, the genuine characteristics of cultural opposition.[7]

Although Spain was thoroughly in the Renaissance current and a European leader along several lines (e.g., jurisprudence, philology, classical studies), and was linguistically and in other ways influential in Italy itself, Italians, thoroughly narcissistic in the mirror of their own past, heaped literary insult and hot coals of caricature upon Spain and Spaniards, and the effects are still influential. In facing Spanish political and military dominance, Italians felt a strong need to cover their own humiliation by scathing denigration of the foreign influence. This situation, as Arnoldsson himself points out, can be compared with some Europeans' reactions to the great power wielded by the United States today. It also can be compared with Latin America's literary Yankeephobia, which often takes refuge in flattery of their own cultural and spiritual qualities and achievements to counterbalance the material power of the United States.

Thus, Italians fulminated against the "barbarity" of the novel of chivalry, an extremely popular Spanish literary genre with an influence roughly equivalent to the present global spread of United States westerns or detective novels. The Italians delighted in portraying the Spaniard as rapacious, cruel, and, above all, haughty. They caricatured the bombastic, proud Spanish captain in various ways in their literature and they stereotyped him in their *commedia dell'arte*. They fastened upon Spaniards a reputation for treachery and trickery. In short, Italians literarily stabbed and stigmatized Spaniards in about the same way that many throughout the world have caricatured, damned, and ridiculed us. It did not matter so much that Italians sometimes found admirable qualities in the Spaniard (e.g., military excellence, astuteness, dignity); what counted was the preponderantly black picture that was painted at a time when Italian literary expression exercised great influence in the intellectual circles of Europe.

The crowning insult that Italians heaped upon Spaniards was to criticize them for their Jewish and Moorish characteristics and consequent "bad" Christianity. It was the Italians, especially, who originated and widely disseminated this part of the general *leyenda negra*. There was enough truth in this allegation to make excellent anti-Spanish propaganda. But it was also an unfair blow, for two reasons: first, the Jewish and Moslem cultures in the Iberian Peninsula had contributed much to general European culture; and secondly, Spain was at the very time of this strong Italian criticism doing her best to purge her Christianity through Inquisition, expulsion, and reformation. It can also be demonstrated that in this period Italy (especially Rome, Ferrara, Venice) was usually one of the safest refuges for Jews escaping the Spanish purging process. Ironically, Spain was later damned for her intolerance and bigotry in treatment of Jews and Moslems.

The presence of Jewish and Moslem blood among Spanish soldiers in Italy was held by some writers—and evidently by much popular opinion—to explain some of the barbarities in the sack of Rome and Prato, especially the despoliation of churches and other religious buildings. The epithet "marrano" (crypto-Jew) was often hurled at Spanish soldiers in Italy. Also, Jews in the Italian drama of that day were almost always portrayed as being of Spanish origin. The racial and religious impurity of Spain and Spaniards not only led to Italians' depicting Spaniards in their literature as abnormally barbarous and with "oriental" traits, such as general immorality and sexual perversion, but also encouraged, for political reasons, the view that Spaniards were heretics by nature and, thus, not to be trusted. Arnoldsson sums up this paradox:

Precisely in the period in which Spain was trying to extinguish, by force, Judaism and Mohammedanism; when she was forcing Moslems as well as Jews to either accept Christianity or depart from the country; this is precisely when Italians began to call Spaniards "marranos." And at the same time that Spaniards were embarking upon the Schmalkaldic War and other long warfare against Lutheranism or Calvinism in the Low Countries, in France, and in England, exhausting her resources in these struggles, Spaniards were called "heretics" and "Lutherans" by many Italians.

This ridiculous accusation of heresy against Spaniards is simply a picturesque circumstance in the history of the Black Legend. More important for the subsequent growth of the Legend was the word "marrano" and the concept it contained that the Spaniards were close relatives and, in great part, descendants of Moors and Jews. This myth of the racial "impurity" of the Spaniards was spread ever wider. And also, in connection with it, the idea that there was something inherently "impure" or "bad" sexually in the Spanish people.[8]

One of the greatest Italian hypocrisies in damning Spain and Spaniards was the wide propagation of the idea that the sexual immorality and general viciousness of the Spanish were unique. The early belief in Valencian immorality, the naturally large number of Spanish prostitutes and courtesans in Italy, the atmosphere around the Spanish Borgias, and the lively sexual propensities of soldiers campaigning abroad, contributed to this picture of a unique Spanish depravity. But it must also be remembered that these insults were hurled by Renaissance Italians who were themselves famed for loose morality and general viciousness, often pointed out as strongly characteristic of that people and time. If there was anything unique in Spanish immorality in sixteenth century Italy, it would certainly take an Italian of that day to recognize and label it: *ladrón juzga por su condición.*

Origins of the Germanic Black Legend

> . . . *Stecht in die Spanisch Sew und Hund vie in die Frösch und lert sie Rund, was heiss, die Deutschen pochen!* [9]

The Spanish soldier, already famed as the best in Europe, made his first significant appearance in Germany during the Schmalkaldic, or Spanish War (1546–1552), when the Holy Roman Emperor Charles V fought the German Protestants. As in the case of Italy, the greatest antipathy toward Spaniards came from their role in warfare. In Germany the religious conflict gave added cause for hatred by midcentury. However, even before the Schmalkaldic War, the German peoples had developed some antipathy toward the Spaniard, based partly on Hispano-German personal and commercial relations, partly on anti-Jewish views, the beginnings of religious schism, and Italian influences.

Early German visitors to Spain, in the fifteenth and early sixteenth centuries, seem to have been unfavorably impressed by the tolerance and favoritism accorded there to Jews and Moslems. They were also disagreeably affected by the Spaniards' avarice, trickery, immorality, pretentiousness ("as great as that of Englishmen"), and small size and dark coloring. Furthermore, there had been occasional conflicts of German and Spanish commercial interests. Some of these early unfavorable impressions of Spain became incorporated in the *Cosmographia Universalis* of the great German cosmographer, Sebastian Münster, and thus achieved a sizable intellectual audience throughout Europe.[10]

More important for later strengthening of the Black Legend in Germany and in Holland was the decided suspicion of Spain by Germans because of their incipient nationalism and often bitter anti-Jewish feeling. In the fifteenth and early sixteenth centuries, a powerful surge of German patriotism was stimulated by the disdain of Italians for German cultural inferiority and barbarism, which led to a counterattempt by German humanists to laud German qualities. Some of this was stimulated by disdain for the immorality and decadence of the Italians. The Spaniards, of course, received their share of insults because of their Italian ties and their Jewishness. The strong anti-Jewish attitude of Martin Luther was linked with his suspicion that Spaniards desired to impose their universal rule upon Germany as part of a supposed advance to world domination. Ulrich von Hutten and Luther, probably the two most influential German writers of the first half of the sixteenth century, thought Germans were racially superior to Italians, Spaniards, and Jews. When this attitude spread, and became linked with antipapal sentiments, firm foundations for a German-Protestant hispanophobia were laid. In Luther, it reached the absurd length of prophesying that an alliance of Turks and Spaniards would attempt to subjugate the German fatherland.[11]

The harsh hispanophobia of Martin Luther, spread by his followers, paved the way for anti-Spanish polemical and popular outbursts as soon as Spanish troops entered the Schmalkaldic War, just after the death of Luther himself. Given the fact that Luther was one of the strongest molders of German popular opinion in his century, it was inevitable that his hispanophobic sentiments would find wide popular acceptance in the heat of this warfare, exacerbated as these sentiments were by deepening religious cleavage. Through popular songs and propagandistic writings, this animosity was hurled at Spanish soldiers and, more important, it was popularly attached to the idea that Charles V was trying to impose a foreign (Spanish) domination upon the German "nation."

In popular song and pamphlet, Emperor Charles V was made to appear as not just a leader of one faction of the German religious struggle, but as an enemy of Germany who had the satanic support of Spanish troops. The Spanish-Italian-papal links were made abundantly clear—to the point that Catholic Germans were considered traitors to their "fatherland." It can, therefore, be said that German nationalism, in the crucial moments of its origins, was partly founded upon anti-

Spanish propaganda. This was later even more true with Holland and England. Its role in the formation of German nationalism gave permanence to the German "Black Legend," buttressed by racial overtones and anti-papal sentiments.

The German version of the Black Legend, crystallized in the Schmalkaldic War, was widely diffused because of the special circumstances of that war. Charles V, by virtue of being at once Holy Roman Emperor, King of Spain, and ruler of much Italian territory, was unable to develop any popular, propagandistic force to combat attacks based on German patriotism and on racial and cultural antipathy toward southern Europeans. Thus, the cause of Charles, because it was identified with Rome, could not identify itself with the German people. And, since he was also King of Spain, fears of Spanish universal domination, already awakened, were spurred on to become a bitter hispanophobic propaganda. And there was always that concomitant of war, the hatred of foreign troops on one's own soil. The World War II British comment on American soldiery as "overpaid, oversexed, and over here" expresses it succinctly, except that Spanish and other soldiers in sixteenth-century Germany were apt to be *under*paid, with consequences easily imagined.

In the second half of the century, a further accumulation of factors contributed to growth and spread of this German *leyenda negra*. Thus, although many Germans were able to profit commercially from certain policies of Philip II, this was probably more than offset by inconveniences and irritations that Germans encountered in contact with Spanish ports. Also, Philip's suspension of payment to creditors in 1557 damaged some German banking interests (e.g., Fugger), and a few years later specific circumstances of the Spanish-Dutch fighting sometimes stimulated Hispano-German antagonisms. In addition, German views of Spain and Spaniards were affected by such events as the Saint Bartholomew's Massacre in France (1572), Spanish origin of the Jesuits, an outburst of anti-Inquisition propaganda, further publication of Luther's anti-Spanish views, colonies of Protestant Netherlanders in Germany who had escaped Spanish victories in the Low Countries, and various other episodes of Protestant-Catholic warfare.

Of particular importance in crystallizing the Black Legend was the concentration at Frankfurt/Main of Protestants and Jewish refugees from Spain. In this city, a veritable propaganda mill came into being, with emphasis upon such popular reading matter as anti-Inquisition blasts.[12] In passing, it should be noted that Frankfurt was later to be a significant publishing and distributing point for Las Casas' *Brief Relation* (see Chapter 4).

In sixteenth-century development of the German Black Legend, one notable feature stands out: the strong German propensity to consider the Spaniards a race apart, and definitely an inferior one. They constantly linked Spaniards with despised Italians and Turks, emphasized their Jewishness, and reiterated the dark color of Spaniards ("they eat white bread and kiss white women with much pleasure, but they are as black as King Balthasar and his monkey"). German travelers in Spain in the late part of the century remarked upon the frequency of Spaniards' marriage with "black and dark women, who come from the Indies and the Island of Saint Thomas." This view of Spaniards as a dark race apart was much abetted by growing Dutch propaganda against Spaniards, which over and over again described them as *marranos*.[13] It is in this aspect particularly—one that is notable today among Dutch, Germans, and the Nordic type generally—that the rise of the German Black Legend differs somewhat from that of the Italians. It is here that one can most clearly see the roots of that Nordic superiority complex, which comes to us especially by way of English literature.

Jews and Spaniards

In the century prior to England's clash with Spain, a significant degree of hatred grew out of conflict between Christianity and Judaism in Spain itself. To a large extent, Jewish hatred of Spaniards in this period mingled with that of Moslems, Italians, and Protestant-German-Dutch combination. And Jewish words and actions against Spain became a feature of the later Dutch-English-American Black Legend. The immediate and best-known causes of this Jewish antipathy were, of course, the Spanish Inquisition (1480) and the Spanish edict of expulsion (1492). But the story is much more complicated than that, even though most Jewish writers and continuing common belief maintain a relatively simple anti-Spanish picture of this conflict.

Let us admit that this is a delicate matter. The very misleading term "antisemitism" is so carelessly, or malevolently, tossed about these days that it virtually has no meaning except as a convenient rock to hurl in anger—but, like a rock, it can hurt. Furthermore, Jewish antagonism toward Spain has been stimulated more recently by certain aspects of the Spanish Civil War and its reverberations through World War II. Spain's guilt-by-association with Germany and Italy before and during World War II, summarized in Israel's stated reason for voting against Spanish entrance into the United Nations in 1950, is a revealing part of this story.[14]

All this is understandable enough, given the atrocities committed against the Jewish people, but their impassioned opinions hamper the writing of fair and unbiased accounts of Spain. Jewish emotion, when aroused by historical memory of Spanish Inquisition and expulsion, exaggerates and distorts, and certainly gives little shrift to the Spanish side of the story. In this, Jewish writers are aided by a popular opinion, much created by themselves, which has for centuries influenced writing upon these themes. And Jewish authors, especially in more recent times, have had much the best of it in spreading their side of the Jewish-Spanish story in the Western world.

Delicate matter or not, this subject must be discussed, for it is a fundamental part of the Black Legend's growth and dissemination.

Long before Spain attempted to expel its Jews, and even before there were significant anti-Jewish demonstrations in Iberia, other countries—notably England (1290) and France (1306)—had ordered expulsion. Persecution of the Jews had become a popular European activity. This should be compared with the fact that Jewish power, influence, and numbers were far greater in Spain during the Middle Ages than anywhere else in Europe. In such light, Christian Spain deserves some degree of recognition for unusual restraint in the face of what other Europeans obviously viewed as provocation. During the Middle Ages Jews in the Iberian Peninsula were able to attain a cultural and material prosperity and political, economic, and religious influences far beyond anything even remotely comparable elsewhere in Europe. In short, the Jew achieved a true golden age in medieval Spain. When expulsion was finally ordered, a dozen years after the Inquisition had begun to search out and castigate the crypto-Jew, it marked an official end to the greatest age of power and well-being that the Jewish people had known since the Diaspora.

I call this an "official" end only, for it must be quickly pointed out that many Jews continued to live in Spain and her dominions either as genuine Christians or as crypto-Jews. These so-called Conversos occupied positions of power near the throne itself; engaged in commerce and financial affairs; and were even officials in the Spanish Inquisition, slave traders, churchmen, etc.[15] It is a grave error to ignore this Jewish continuity in Spain, but this highly significant feature of Spanish history is often ignored in favor of concentrating upon the more sensational stories of Inquisition torture and expulsion. Jews, and other writers of anti-Spanish tendencies, have preferred to focus attention upon these

Spanish crimes as a means of demonstrating Spanish cruelty and bigotry. The usual groundwork for this is a morality of later centuries applied to fifteenth- and sixteenth-century historical situations, without that sense of justice so essential to historical interpretations. Or, sometimes more simply, it may come from the well-known Jewish propensity for cultural replenishment out of martyrdom.

Even a moderate understanding of Jewish influence in Spain during the fifteenth century—and the ways in which European Christians viewed such things in that age—leads inevitably to the conclusion that there is a highly respectable Spanish side to this story. Jewish writers, such as Cecil Roth and the influential, deeply hispanophobic Heinrich Graetz, point with pride to the unique prosperity and power of their people in the Spain of that day. Many another writer, then and since, has borne witness to this historical fact.[16] [Approximate subsequent equivalents would be the material and cultural strength of Jews in Holland during the seventeenth century (when Amsterdam became known as the "Dutch Jerusalem"), in England during the nineteenth and twentieth, and in the United States and Germany during the present century.]

The words of Cecil Roth, in his *History of the Marranos,* illustrate this point and certainly indicate some of the need, from a Spanish-Christian view, for firmness in dealing with the Jewish problem.

[The Conversos] formed in the organism of the state a vast, incongruous body which it was impossible to assimilate, and not easy to neglect. . . . It was, however, notorious that [the Conversos] were Christians only in name; observing, in public, a minimum of the new faith while maintaining, in private, a maximum of the old one. . . . There was a similarly large body [of Conversos] inside the fold [of the Christian church], insidiously working its way into every limb of the body politic and ecclesiastic, openly condemning in many cases the doctrines of the Church and contaminating by its influence the whole mass of the faithful. Baptism had done little more than to convert a considerable portion of the Jews from infidels outside the Church to heretics inside it. . . . It was natural, and indeed pardonable, that all the pulpits resounded to impassioned sermons calling attention to the misconduct of the New Christians [i.e., crypto-Jews] and urging that steps should be taken to check them.[17]

And Louis Israel Newman, in his *Jewish Influences* . . . , shows Jewish action of the kind that would certainly disturb a pious Isabella: ". . . the backsliding and Marranos silently 'judaized' the doctrines of the Church from within." [18]

The strength of Jewry in fifteenth-century Spain was an important basis for anti-Spanish criticism in other parts of Europe, as we have already seen in Italian and German attitudes. English, Dutch, French, and the Papacy also observed this phenomenon and made it a racial and religious basis for their suspicions of Spain.[19] An approximate modern parallel, that of critical foreign views of the strong Jewish cultural, political, and commercial influences in the United States, is well known and should help us to understand the fifteenth-century Spanish situation.

Spanish monarchs up to and including Ferdinand and Isabella, and even some later kings, consistently showed favoritism toward Jews and *Conversos,* even when the latter's Christianity was suspect.[20] But the majority of the Spanish people, witnessing this and other evidence of Jewish-*Converso* influence—their posts as tax collectors; notable ostentation by wealthy Jews; blasphemy and ridicule of Christian practices; the insulting epithet "Marrano" hurled by foreigners at Spain and Spaniards; the ineradicable historical memory that it was Jews who had significantly contributed to the success of Moslem invasion and who were often strongly tied to this traditional and dangerous enemy of Spain and Christendom; the bitter anti-Jewish writing and oratory of some *Conversos* themselves; and simply the numbers of Jews daily discernible in the population—could, and did, view the situation with antagonism. And on some occasions, they were stimulated into mob attacks upon Jews. If there was anything uniquely Spanish in all this, it was not intolerance or bigotry, but rather a notable forbearance in comparison to the ways the Jewish problem was handled elsewhere in Europe.

The Inquisition that Isabella established in Castile in 1480, for all the criticism—including papal strictures—against it, was an obvious necessity and solution, though reluctantly undertaken. Any other monarch in the Europe of that time, faced with similar conditions, would probably have employed measures much harsher.[21] The Castilian Inquisition was designed to eliminate the possibility, or likelihood, of a Jewish "state within the state" and, in this, the Inquisition was an arm of monarchy and a defense against treason. With similar goals, sixteenth- and seventeenth-century England captured, tortured, and executed Jesuits and other Catholics; and eighteenth-century monarchs, including Spanish and Portuguese, expelled Jesuits with much "enlightened" approbation. The near success of Jewish conspiracy and rebellion against Inquisition establishment, both in Castile and Aragon, bears eloquent testimony to the need for such a step. And European Christendom heartily approved Ferdinand and Isabella's action and was relieved that they were finally doing something to stop the cancerous influence of Judaism.[22]

The Inquisition was intended to eliminate subversion of Christian moral and religious customs by secret Jews who were active at virtually all levels of national life. The Inquisition was not designed to try or punish Jews who openly adhered to Judaism or those who had sincerely accepted Christianity. The secret practice of Judaism under a false front of Christianity, with attendant subversion, was considered treason by a minority against the majority and against prevailing laws. This view of subversive minority action is a respectable legal one in our own century and country.[23] There was nothing unique about Spanish expulsion of Jews or punishment of crypto-Jews, except that Spain's problem was far larger than that of any other European nation of that day; and, incidentally, her processes for resolving the problem were more juridically enlightened than were likely to be found elsewhere in contemporary Europe for a similar situation.

It is one of the tragedies of the Jews that they have often suffered the greatest hurt from their own people, and thus it was in the Spain of Inquisition days. Men of Jewish blood were active in the Spanish Inquisition, energetic in fomenting anti-Jewish hatred, and held positions of power when the Spanish Inquisition was established and during the time of its greatest influence and action. And it has been asserted, with considerable logic and evidence, that any "unique" intolerance in Spaniards (built rather heavily upon the story of their treatment of Jews) was primarily a fifteenth-century development, which at least partially could be ascribed to the intransigency shown by Jews themselves.

In this vein, notice the perceptive words of Salvador de Madariaga, one of Spain's most sophisticated intellectuals and certainly one who could not fairly be tarred with the epithet "antisemitic."

To many Jews and non-Jews the idea that Spanish intolerance may well be in part at least of Jewish origin will no doubt sound paradoxical; what of the Inquisition? they would ask. And if then the answer were that the Spanish Inquisition was, for a considerable part, a Jewish-inspired institution, the paradox would be complete. That intolerance was by no means a typical Spanish feature until the fifteenth century can be easily proved. The Spaniard of the years between 800 and 1400 was not intolerant.

Not, at any rate, to the degree which later was to distinguish him. Intolerance does not become either general or persistent until the fifteenth century. And it takes these two features from the Jews.

For what in fact the Jews bring to the Spanish character, during that century when they begin to influence it deeply, is a consistence and a persistence it had not possessed before. . . . The Spaniard stood in no need of any Jew as to ferocity or civil war. But, despite time-honoured ideas, he did perhaps borrow from the Jew a dogmatic motivation for them, and certainly the persistence needed to maintain strong institutions to that effect.[24]

With the approaching end of Moslem politico-military resistance in the late 1480s, Isabella became increasingly aware that she would have to deal with orthodox Judaism as well as the crypto-Jew. The affinity of Jews and Moslems was too close and too traditional for Spanish safety; the fall of Granada would probably be followed by Moslem attempts at reinvasion (it was certain there would be, and there were, retaliatory raids on the Spanish coast), and the Jews would surely serve as spies and collaborators of the Moslem attacks on Spain, which they did. And there was always the popular, heightening clamor against Jews, to say nothing of the deep Christian piety of an Isabella who had long been worried and offended by the presence of so many followers of the Mosaic law. The result was, in 1492, the edict of expulsion of all Jews who refused to accept baptism as Christians.

An overabundance of bathetic nonsense has been written and spoken on this subject of Jewish expulsion from Spain. For one thing, the numbers of those expelled are often exaggerated.[25] For another, this action is often grossly exaggerated as a principal factor in the decline of Spain.[26] Third, the expulsion is often exploited as evidence of unusual Spanish bigotry and intolerance, without bothering to study conditions in the Peninsula at that historical moment or to make any comparison with views and actions in other European territories earlier, then, and later. Even a little objectivity in studying and appraising this matter leads inevitably to a moderate judgment of this Spanish action and even some sympathy for it, although twentieth-century humanitarianism cannot, of course, condone specific instances of hardship resulting from the expulsion order. But a twentieth-century judge must also take into account the crimes of his own times with similar objectives. Along this line, it is not even necessary to recall such horrors as Russian and German genocidal actions. Let us just remember the kind of thinking that went into our own treatment of a supposed Japanese "fifth column" [the Nisei] at the outset of World War II. And another case, with ironic overtones, is illustrated by a press report dated November 7, 1961: "No Arabs—Israel's Parliament has again rejected any return of Arab refugees of the 1948 war as impracticable and as equivalent to readmission of potential fifth column!"[27] This was precisely the danger that Spaniards saw with the Jews, and the whole story of Israeli treatment of Palestinian Arabs might lead one to the conclusion that Spain behaved toward Jews in ways far more modern than medieval.

The pros and cons of Spanish treatment of the Jews are almost hypnotically fascinating, today as yesterday. There is a strong romantic streak in this story, as Cecil Roth aptly observes. The relations between the two peoples were characterized by considerable passion (since Jews and Spaniards are passionate peoples); and a centuries-old tension between them was a result of their having lived together for so long that each strongly influenced the culture of the other. This tension is a bit like the antagonism of brothers or cousins who instinctively know where insults will hurt most. Undoubtedly, this accounts for much enduring Jewish interest in Hispanic culture and the Spanish nation. It also accounts for Jewish reiteration of anti-Spanish prejudices. The fact that the persistence of Inquisition officials in tracking down and punishing Jewish enemies of the state can be attributed to a mixture of Jewish-Spanish exploitation of combined knowledge of Jewish customs, beliefs, and dodges, such as the use of aliases, certainly heightens the poignancy, the tragedy, and thus the drama of the whole subject.

The main point of all this, in connection with the Black Legend theme, is that the century after 1480 saw the creation, or intensification, of hispanophobia among the Jewish people. It came at a time when Jews were becoming very active in the rapidly growing printing and publishing industry.[28] After leaving Spain, many went to such areas as Italy, the Moslem dominions, the Low Countries, Germany, and France where there was increasing receptivity to anti-Spanish propaganda and action. In their new homes, Jews eagerly engaged in whatever might damage Spanish commerce, or whatever aid they could give to Moslem projects of revenge for the Granadine defeat. And Jewish scholarship and propensity for theological disputation happily helped fan flames in the Protestant Revolt, which caused Spaniards such anguish.[29]

This century of Spanish-Jewish crisis, which saw important restrictions imposed upon Iberian-Jewish power and influence, came at a time when Spain was creating the world's greatest empire with virtually unlimited commercial horizons. Jews have never forgiven Spain for this restriction of their opportunities. This is one of the reasons for the noticeable spite in subsequent Jewish writings emphasizing the role that Jews played in the remarkable rise of Dutch and English capitalism, which were in competition with Spanish commerce. And there is obvious Jewish satisfaction in pointing to the activities of their own people (usually Marranos) in aiding or stimulating political, military, and commercial attacks by Dutchmen, Frenchmen, Englishmen, and Turks on Spain.[30]

It is, of course, quite pointless to argue about whether Jews or Spaniards were right or wrong at any given moment in these developments. Spanish Inquisition and expulsion were calamities for Jews who did not become Christians, but it is not at all clear that this way of handling the Jewish problem was, in light of alternatives, significantly harmful to Spain or a serious factor in Spanish decline. It is similarly pointless to debate about the formation of the Italian and German black legends on any such basis. They were historical developments, actions, and counteractions thoroughly understandable in the texture of their times. They help explain the existence and strength of anti-Spanish attitudes in various parts of Europe during the latter half of the sixteenth century, when the Dutch and English struck out against Spain.

France and Spain

A fourth very significant area of anti-Spanish feeling, France, antedates all others and is most obvious. For a thousand years and more, contiguity of the two peoples stimulated mutual dislike. Again, this is not a matter of right or wrong, but of the facts of historical development, similar to Franco-Prussian animosities, United States-Mexican abrasiveness, or Jewish-Arab hostility.

Since the beginning of Moslem domination in Spain, with its brief military projection into France and its threat to Europe by that route, Frenchmen have viewed Spaniards as a kind of barbaric-Oriental extension of Africa. This was exacerbated through the Middle Ages and into modern times by conflicts over territory along the Pyrenees. And this culminated in the great imperial rivalries of the fifteenth and sixteenth centuries, in which Spain successfully thwarted French ambitions in Italy, virtually surrounded France in a dynastic-military vise, and sometimes was involved in France's bloody religious strife.

In addition, Frenchmen resented, along with the Dutch and English, Iberian monopoly in the New World and sought to breach it. During the eighteenth and nineteenth centuries, France exercised powerful dynastic and cultural influences over Spain, and traditional enmity between the two peoples was aggravated by the bitter Napoleonic interlude. The Spanish fight against the troops of Napoleon, symbolized in the famous "dos de mayo" (May 2, 1808), brilliantly immortalized by Goya, hardened hatreds long entrenched. And in our own times, passions stirred by the Spanish Civil War reopened old wounds, as France became a strong base for propagandistic and other intervention in that struggle.

The significance of these historical antagonisms in development of the *leyenda negra is* obvious and, therefore, needs but passing reference here. Intense Spanish-French rivalry and clash of arms in the first half of the sixteenth century, coming after centuries of conflict, made France a natural center for anti-Spanish activity. The first significant foreign threat to Spain in the New World, in the form of piracy, was launched from the ports of Brittany. Later, French travel literature and French leadership in the eighteenth-century Enlightenment was of enormous significance in hardening a generalized European disdain or even hatred toward Spain and Spaniards. From the late seventeenth century to our own times, French cultural hegemony in Europe and the Americas set, *inter alia,* prevailing patterns of anti-Spanish prejudice. [If Latin America were to displace the United States as dominant power in the Western Hemisphere, as France displaced Spain on the Continent, it is easy to imagine, given Latin America's entrenched Yankeephobia, what would then become the prevailing interpretations of United States history and culture.]

In any discussion of the Western world's attitudes toward Spain and Latin America, France must be constantly borne in mind as an intellectual and propagandistic center and disseminator of a vast amount of hispanophobia. This is obviously significant when we recall that during the last two centuries, Latin American and United States intellectual leadership has been much influenced by French cultural fashions.

In summary, the bulk of anti-Spanish feeling preceding entry of the Dutch and English into the lists against the Spanish colossus originated in Spain's imperial actions beyond her own borders, embracing a hodgepodge of dynastic and religious motives. Secondarily, it grew out of some international economic rivalries and antagonisms characteristic of this beginning period of European capitalism. Thirdly, a mixture of social, cultural, and "racial" antipathies, which were mostly the predictable concomitants of warfare, caused the first stirrings of the Nordic superiority complex. Finally, there was the special Jewish hispanophobia, embedded in the spirit of the times and intimately related to measures that then seemed logical and necessary for the safety of Christian Spain.

As these various anti-Spanish attitudes formed and grew in Europe, Spanish occupation of her newly discovered transoceanic territories was proceeding apace. In its own peculiar way, Spanish conquest in the New World created another facet of the Black Legend, and this merged with the already existing anti-Spanish patterns.

As we have seen, conquest of the Americas produced an outburst of typically Spanish self-criticism, masochistic and nearly suicidal in tendencies and results. The timing of Spain's conquest was perfect for causing the greatest possible damage to its reputation. The polemics that occurred between Discovery and the end of the sixteenth century created an abundance of bitter words and material ready for foreign exploitation when the Dutch Revolt began and when England and Spain finally came to open war on the seas. The sons of Spain, while building a vast and envied empire, uninhibitedly fashioned weapons for endless defamation of the Spanish character. Dutchmen and Englishmen showed no hesitancy in using these and earlier propaganda weapons against mighty Spain.

Chapter 4

THE PAPER WARS

This leads me to fear that the history of my exploits, which they tell me has been printed, may be the work of some magician who is my enemy, in which case he would have set down one thing in place of another and, mingling a thousand lies with a little truth, would doubtless have amused himself by relating many things that have nothing to do with the true sequence of events. O envy, thou root of endless evils, thou cankerworm of the virtues! All the other vices, Sancho, have in them some element of pleasure, but envy brings with it only vexation, bitterness, and rage.

Don Quijote, part II, chapter 8

By about 1560, Spain had all the enemies that it could handle—and then came more. Starting in the 1560s a cancer of rebellion began to grow in the Low Countries. It was compounded of the Protestant heresy, political ambitions of local nobility, assertion of "medieval freedoms," antipathy toward the Spanish foreigner, Spanish errors in government, French and English encouragement, and the printing press. Above all, the printing press was the greatest single weapon in popularizing rebellion in the Low Countries, in damning established government, and in winning interest and support from abroad. That is why the term "Paper War" has been so appropriately applied to the early decades of the Dutch Revolt.[1]

The years immediately after the accession of Elizabeth in 1558 also saw official confirmation and completion of the English religious schism —a trying major problem in diplomacy, religion, and war for Philip II. The Anglo-Spanish antagonisms of those decades begat another "paper war" that was to have important damaging effects upon Spain, especially in the hardening of England's "anti-Spain" brand of patriotism and, eventually, the Western world's antipathetic views of Spain and Spaniards.

Dutchmen Strike at the Spanish Colossus

Dutch restiveness under Philip's rule did not start as a popular uprising. It was planned and carried out by a small league of local nobility—disgruntled, anxious for power, and much influenced by some of the heady tenets and plots of the relatively new Protestant movement. At first, the leaders of this rebellion were so few in number and so lacking in military strength that they found it difficult to make their cause a widely popular one. Indeed, they long feared to expose their Protestant predilections, since the great bulk of the population was still loyal to the Roman Church.

In efforts to widen the popular base of the revolt, leaders of the league, especially William of Orange and some of the men close to him, hit upon the expedient of printed propaganda. From the start, propaganda pamphlets were definitely aimed against Spanish governors and the Roman Church. In the earlier years the conspirators did not dare to openly rebel against the lawful monarch, Philip of Spain, but hurled their weapons of plot and propaganda at his ministers of government, the Inquisition, or at Spaniards in general. So dangerous was the game they played and so subversive of dynastic legitimacy that their partial success, in the form of the Dutch Republic (confirmed after some eighty years of struggle), seems a miracle indeed, and certainly merits the tributes paid to their courage, astuteness, and patience. Much of that miracle can be attributed to their adroit, if often unscrupulous, use of the printing press.

Even among the Catholics of today's Netherlands, who are now forty percent of the population, it would be difficult to find any denial that the aim of this revolt—independence from the Hapsburg-Spanish monarchy—justified the means (rebellion against monarch and church stimulated by a minority). Even with partial eventual success (much of the area remained in the Catholic-Spanish orbit), the Revolt is wholeheartedly viewed, in present-day Holland, as a worthy endeavor and an eventual good; it was long ago sanctified in a proud national tradition, like our "Spirit of 'Seventy-Six." However, almost any modern historian must inevitably curse the confusion wrought by the deviousness of plot and the intemperate viciousness of propagandistic verbiage on both sides. Some of it will never be straightened out satisfactorily; certainly not by any such deep, one-sided prejudice as that of a John Lothrop Motley.

This is, of course, no place to attempt improvement upon the excellent Dutch, Spanish, and other historians who have in recent times tried sincerely and effectively to find the truths about the long, bloody, and wordy conflict between Dutchmen and Spaniards.[2] And certainly I shall not recite details of that struggle. It is my intention here merely to indicate the main lines of propaganda attack upon Spain, principal themes that became imbedded in the Dutch mind and thence spread to other peoples; some of the relationship between this anti-Spanish propaganda and that which originated elsewhere; and, finally, some indication of the significance of this propaganda in forming attitudes popular in our own times.

At the outset, it should be made clear that William of Orange and his co-conspirators consciously and purposefully made anti-Spanish propaganda a major weapon for popularizing rebellion and gaining sympathy and aid elsewhere in Europe. A recent Dutch author phrases it thus:

From the beginning of the revolt the Prince of Orange took a great interest in the pamphlets as a measure of opposing Spain. . . . The aim of the . . . pamphlets was in the first place to stir up hatred of the Spaniards and their institutions. A modern work on the Eighty Years' War describes the intention as follows: "The enemy had to be depicted black as the Devil for the sake of the waverers and doubters, who were always the majority of the population that had to be won over. Many pamphlets are concerned with this ignoble but necessary business." Contents and form of this type of pamphlet were designed for popularity. The small size also indicates that they were destined for a simple public.[3]

The propaganda pamphlet which had the widest spread and deepest, most enduring hispanophobic effect, was Orange's *Apologia* of 1580, a reply to Philip's proscription of him as rebel. But for at least a dozen years prior to this outburst, the lines of propaganda attack against Spain had been emerging. They were very much the work of Orange himself, aided by such "ministers of propaganda" as Jacob van Wesenbeke and Marnix van Sainte Aldegonde. In content, the principal features were:

1. Avoidance of direct attack upon the king, preferring rather to place blame for oppressive government upon his ministers (Granvelle, Alba, and Don Juan of Austria). Thus, the idealized Orange, in the Dutch national anthem, *Wilhelmus van Nassouwe,* puts stress on avoidance of direct attack, as part of his self-justification motif: "Before God and his great might I will testify that, while I have at no time repudiated the King, I have had to

obey God, the Highest Majesty, as justice bade me." [4] There were, however, some direct attacks upon Philip during this period. [5]

2. Tremendous exaggeration of the power and actions of the Spanish Inquisition, reaching the absurd length of calling Philip its captive and even blaming the Holy Office for planning the Dutch revolt in order to encompass destruction of the Netherlands. The Spanish Inquisition was not imposed upon the Dutch provinces, but fear of it was constantly stimulated for propaganda purposes. Even if apocryphal, Philip II's famous comment to the effect that there was no need to transport the Spanish Inquisition to the Low Countries since their own Inquisitors were severe enough, indicates the religious climate of those European times. [6]

3. Beginning of the strong, pervasive theme of a unique Spanish cruelty, by citing specific instances in the Low Countries and by frequently mentioning Spanish killing of Indians in the New World. These references were based on Las Casas' writings and often cited him by name. The Las Casas figure of twenty million Indians killed became standard among the Dutch, along with the exaggerated figure of 18,000 executions by Alba's so-called Council of Blood. [7]

4. Emphasis upon the theme that Spaniards aimed at conquest of all Europe and the world, an idea apparently taken from German usage. [8]

5. Invidious comparison of Philip with his father, Charles V. This was a way to strike at Philip indirectly, especially reproaching him for not visiting the Netherlands and personally attending to matters there, as had his father. The pamphleteers usually ignored the fact that Charles himself had initiated much that they complained about (e.g., suppression of heretics); Charles was not only conveniently dead, but being born and educated in the Low Countries, he could not be tarred with the hispanophobic brush. [9]

6. Beginnings of irresponsible use of the Don Carlos theme, sometimes making it appear that it was Philip's Spanish counselors who caused his son's imprisonment, then attributing this act specifically to the Inquisition. Don Carlos thus begins his immortal role as a hero of hispanophobia. He became a political martyr to Netherlanders because of his supposed sympathy for and connection with the leaders of Dutch rebellion.

[The death of Philip's son and heir, Don Carlos, is still clouded by lack of evidence. However, the son was clearly deranged and physically abnormal, and his reluctantly undertaken confinement by the father was obviously justified. The main controversy revolves around whether Philip II actually ordered the death of the son, and though the evidence is unclear, it seems most likely that Don Carlos died as a result of his own excesses. To understand this story in its Black Legend context, it suffices to know that the enemies of Philip, especially those in the Low Countries and Protestant circles generally, quickly accused him of murdering his son. They were especially diligent in assuring the world that Philip did this because Don Carlos wanted to place himself in alliance with those in the Low Countries who were rebelling against Philip. Thus, the mystery of Don Carlos' death, in conjunction with the rebellion in the Low Countries, the known efforts of rebels in Holland to contact Don Carlos, and the pathetically inept attempts of the latter to conspire against his father, provided excellent propaganda weapons with which to defame Philip as a cruel monster. Thus unjustly, without even a thought for Philip's side of the case, Don Carlos became a hero of Protestantism and a perpetual symbol of Philip's inhumanity.

William's *Apologia* of 1580 goes one step further and makes Philip II the murderer of Don Carlos to clear the way for "incestuous" marriage with his niece.[10]]

7. Adroit use of the theme of unique Spanish treachery, partly emanating from the Egmont and Hoorne executions and probably also an inheritance from German and Italian literature. This theme was strategically emphasized whenever negotiations with Spain were in the air. Refinement and more extensive use of this motif came in the early part of the next century. There is a noticeable similarity in Dutch and English stress on Spanish treachery.

The Dutch pamphleteers, emphasizing Spanish perfidy, made much of the thesis that Spaniards were under no obligation to keep faith with heretics —"Haereticis non est servanda fides" ran the phrase—and thus could never be trusted. There was much hypocrisy on both sides, and only a fool would have put full trust in negotiated agreements, unless, perhaps, there were built-in protections or other factors making treachery impossible.

8. Propagandistic usage of the Saint Bartholomew's Massacre as a symbol of Spanish perfidy and cruelty. In Dutch hands, this event became a "slogan" far out of touch with the truth of the matter. Even though the Spanish government had nothing to do with the massacre, Dutch pamphleteers insisted on Spanish responsibility and even associated it with supposed plans to reintroduce the Inquisition into the Low Countries.[11]

9. Beginnings of the fundamental theme that Spanish governors in the Netherlands, especially the Duke of Alba, were merely tools, or mouthpieces, of the Pope. Thus, all acts of Spanish government that the Dutch considered tyrannical were purposefully linked with Roman Catholicism, killing two birds with one propaganda stone. In this aspect of Dutch pamphleteering, one can most clearly see the subsurface conspiracy against the Roman Church—using all disgruntlement with foreign overlordship as a smoke screen for overthrow of the Church. This also foreshadows English emphasis upon the Spanish-Rome theme and general merging of anti-Spain with anti-Rome, of which more is said later.

Both sides of the Dutch-Spanish struggle were composed of all shades between extremes of political and religious idealism and the most sordid of motives. Both sides resorted to propagandistic exaggerations in pamphleteering, the Spanish-Catholic side taking it up when the effectiveness of rebel efforts began to be apparent.[12] However, the rebel-Protestant propaganda began earlier, was more persistent, widespread, and successful. Anti-Spanish, anti-Catholic propaganda became in Dutch hands widely and deeply imbedded in the general Protestant tradition, the result of effective linking of the Dutch Revolt with French, English, and German interests. And that part of the Netherlands that eventually achieved independence, uncritically absorbed as an integral part of its nationality the deep hispanophobia, with all its distortions, that was so successfully propagated in the early years. This propaganda, in short, became Dutch popular history. From the stirringly idealistic national anthem, *Wilhelmus van Nassouwe,* through the proud and self-righteous hatred in the Sea-Beggar songs, and the excesses of the most unscrupulously exaggerated anti-Inquisition pamphlet, the anti-Spanish theme rang clear and strong.

By far the greatest of the propaganda pamphlets was William's *Apologia;* it is a milestone in the total story of the Black Legend. Not only did it reiterate themes already in existence, including some from Italian and German traditions, but it invented new libels and gave new twists to existing ones. The pamphlet was translated into the major European languages and widely disseminated. The monarch's proscription of William is a relatively typical outlawing of a rebellious subject, often enough practiced by kings or other authorities and generally considered a prerogative of sovereignty, or chieftainship. But Orange's reply was an imaginative departure in the art of waging rebellion and war, a dramatic mixture of self-justification with the gossipy kind of personal slander, all made into a circumstantial whole for wide popular appeal. If we except the personal libels against Philip, it could be called a forerunner of that peculiar species, the "Paper" that modern governments are fond of issuing to assert the rightness of their causes.

In tracing the growth of specific anti-Spanish distortions, the *Apologia* is a point of departure for a number of main themes. For one, Orange was the first to publicize widely the accusation that Philip II had ordered the murder of his own son, Don Carlos; Antonio Pérez, the traitorous secretary to Philip, later, as renegade, repeated this charge—and it was followed by French embroidery on the theme and its entrenchment as a classical theme in literature (see Chapter 5). For another, Orange accused Philip of incest in marrying his niece. He further accused him of having assassinated his wife, Isabel of Valois, for this reason. As if this were not enough, William accused his king of bigamy, insisting that Philip was married to Isabel Osorio and had children by her at the time he married the Infanta of Portugal, and of adultery since he had relations with another woman after marriage with Isabel de Valois. The obvious pettiness and irrelevance of all this does little credit even to a rebellious prince in desperate straits, whatever the political idealism he sought to justify. But, even worse, Orange sought to blacken the entire Spanish people in the supposed image of their monarch. The unproven or irrelevant slanders of Philip were at least directed against a single man who could attempt specific defense; the slandering of a whole people in such a widespread document can never be entirely undone.[13]

In his generalizations, William damned all friars and inquisitors, stigmatizing all Spaniards as haughty, greedy, fanatical, cruel, vengeful, disdainful of anything foreign, and brutally lacking in culture. He was possibly even less discriminating in his epithets than were the Germans and Italians whom he partially echoes. But the charges were astutely chosen for widest possible appeal through Europe; it was a formidably effective propaganda weapon. As a Lutheran of German birth and connections, William automatically won Protestant plaudits; as a rebel against Spain he was naturally favored by Frenchmen; and as subverter of Spanish dominion so near to Albion's coasts, he was bound to win English sympathy.

William of Orange thus became the first great political hero of hispanophobia, author and disseminator of much of the classical Black Legend. David against Goliath, Protestant rebel against Catholic colossus, Nordic versus Spaniard, champion of "Liberty" against "Tyranny." How could the giant in this fight possibly protect his image? How can anything be successfully said for his side? [How can a huge and powerful United States achieve wide popularity in any argument with the head of a small country, like Cuba's Castro?]

The assassination of William (1584), coming soon after the *Apologia,* made him a martyr of the independence effort and unassailable folk-hero of Dutch nationalism—a theme, of course, which constantly renewed the flow of anti-Spanish pamphlets. Virtually coincident with this, the Dutch began to take interest in the cause of the Portuguese pretender, Dom Antônio, in his grievance against Philip II. The Dutch then began to view Portuguese dominions as fair game for attack and seizure, since they were now (after 1580) ruled by the hated Spaniards. As is well known, this concept of Portuguese holdings paved the way for Dutch acquisition of an overseas empire, an expansion that was squarely based upon an anti-Spanish psychology rooted in earlier pamphleteering and fighting.

Incidentally, utilization of the Dom Antônio cause for anti-Spanish pamphleteering was not confined to Dutch writings, but was used elsewhere in Europe and Islamic areas to stir anti-Spanish action. There was even some Jewish use made of Dom Antônio, and vice versa, in mutual anti-Spanish interests.[14] Dom Antônio's vain claim to the Portuguese throne was not as good as that of Philip II, but it was good enough to interest Spain's enemies as a source of propaganda and cause for potential action.

After the *Apologia* and death of William, anti-Spanish pamphleteering by the Dutch increased not only in quantity but in boldness and intemperance of language. The breach between rebel leaders and Spanish king, which had been only mildly expressed in earlier years, was henceforth clearly stated. The martyrdom of William, the open declaration of independence by the States General (1581), and the already cumulative effect of earlier propaganda, hardened the lines of anti-Spanish tracts, songs, and other literature. Dutch participation in defeat of the Spanish Armada, in 1588, further encouraged the anti-Spanish cause. Successes on the seas, heightened trade interest intruding into the Spanish-Portuguese dominions, and everincreasing bitterness of the Protestant-Catholic conflict were all contributing factors in the entrenchment of an exceedingly malevolent propaganda against Spain and its people. In the decades after 1580, hatred of Spain and Spaniards became a basic, national Dutch characteristic.

The extremes of this hatred, in printed form, are easily illustrated; and its abundance makes easily imaginable the kind of language in common use but undignified by print. A few examples will show the main themes and principal devices of this propaganda.

From a pamphlet of 1587 reprinted in 1608, entitled *Necessary Considerations that all good Lovers of the Fatherland must consider maturely on the proposed Treaty of Peace with the Spaniards:*

And if we might think that the king of Spain . . . was not also burning against us with a fierce desire of the most cruel revenge that ever was: So we might perceive the contrary from knowledge of his natural actions and of the Council that he uses, that are known by the whole world . . . as the one by his Inquisition exercises the most extreme cruelty and also has cruelly killed his son under pretext of the slightest disobedience and his wife to set free his inclination to adultery . . . If one thinks that these are mere words read what the Spaniards have written of their Indian actions where they themselves tell how merely out of lust or to make themselves execrable they have murdered millions of people who have never angered them nor done them wrong and on whom they had no right of mastery whatever.[15]

Notice the repetition of the *Apologia*'s libels and the adroit use of Las Casas.

From *The Spanish and Aragonese Mirror* (1599):

In which one may see clearly . . . to what end . . . tend the designs of the Spanish soldiers . . . in the Westphalian District . . . where they have committed more cruelty and tyranny than the Turkish enemies of Christendom have ever done.[16]

[Making Spaniards more cruel than Turks was a common propaganda technique also found often in Italian, German, and English writing.]

A parody of the Paternoster (1602), a common device, is even stronger.

Take revenge, take revenge Oh God, on this cursed rabble that every-where, to your sorrow, keeps the world in disturbance, violating your Holy Word. Punish them for their unbelief, Curse them on earth as in Heaven. . . .

Deliver us, God Almighty, of these raving dogs. Of this damned race which is more given to wickedness than all the Turks together. And see whether we complain rightly because they thus take, Plague them!, our Bread.[17]

Noticeable here is the insinuation that Spaniards are not good Christians, a theme dating back to Italian and German beliefs, as we have seen.

For popular appeal and ease of repetition, rhyme was frequently used, as in the 1611 Dutch edition of Las Casas' *Brief Relation*. The following is from rhymed couplets of 1603:

Thus appearing from the deeds of the Duke of Alba, who, like a tyrant, came to reign ruthlessly over us. The Bloody Edicts he has planted every-where, so as to ruin all the land, as they did to Peru and the Indians. . . . This Spanish monster slyly attacks you. As they murdered the Indian lords, they have also killed many of your princes, so as to further tyrannize over you; which they did not spare, as they showed in Zutphen, Naarden, and also Harlem.

As long as you keep the Spaniard in the nest; as long as he builds fortresses in your towns that, like a pest, infect the whole country; as long as you quench the bloodthirsty Spanish desire. So long you remain like the Indians, unfree. So, drive away the Spanish tyranny! [18]

A curious twist on the Indian theme occurs in a 1605 pamphlet warn-ing Netherlanders against rumored articles of peace spread by the Spaniards:

. . . they will labor to obliterate all signs and remembrance of the freedom of the Netherlands, to put an end to your mother tongue and introduce the Spanish language, . . . as indeed they cause the Indians to speak Spanish.[19]

A 1606 attempt at comical verse, titled *A Demonstration that a Good War is Better than a Sham Peace,* includes, along with repetition of Las Casas, the older German themes of Spanish attempts at universal dominion and alliance with the Turks against Christians:

The Spaniards seek nothing else than to make themselves Monarchs of all Christianity; and rather than let us live in peace, they would tolerate the great Turk to attack with violence a great part of Christendom.[20]

[The sheer hypocrisy of this is easily seen in Dutch diplomacy which, on occasion, aimed at encouragement of Turkish attacks upon Spain, whereas there is no instance in which Spain encouraged Moslem attack upon Christian Europe; rather, Spain was the constant shield of Europe against this threat.[21]]

A small versified tract, apparently of 1608 or 1609, throwing together the Dom Antônio cause, the Sicilian Vespers, Bartolomé de las Casas, and Antonio Pérez, illustrates about as well as any not only the vitriol of the attacks upon Spain, but also the standard anti-Jesuit corollary of the common format of the pamphlets:

New, Clear Astrologer Spectacles, for the strengthening of many dim eyes that cannot see well the obscure Jesuit's Comet-star, recently appeared in the north-west. After the Roman Indication called LIBERTAS. By a lover of truth and of the National liberty.

> But when a fierce Eagle lusts after the prey
> It fights almost all bird-animals
> And also is nobody's friend. Such cruel vultures
> The Spaniard has hatched of a Basilisk-nature
> Who with his cruel face not only alarms
> But kills man and beast.
>   It is not all patrimony, his seventeen realms;
> The Kingdom of Lisbon he has stolen from Don Antonio;
> The Kingdom of Sicily, taken by a VESPER-murder.
> Some of them have been given him by the Pope, out of love,
> and the poor Natives murdered and chased away.
>   And how many hundreds of thousands he has killed in the Indias;
> Read Bartolomé de las Casas, who described it amply.
> But read Antonio Pérez; there you will find the conclusion!
> How they try to deck out the Spanish bride
> With the plumes of other birds to embellish their raven.
> But, although she seems somewhat beautified, she is black by nature.[22]

Not only did impending, rumored, or actual negotiations with Spain bring forth a spate of anti-Spanish pamphlets in the Netherlands, but when pacts were actually consummated—as in the truce of 1609—a rash of "doubters" and "warners" appeared in print, invariably stressing Spanish duplicity, Bartolomé de las Casas, and the evil relationships of Rome and Spain. Illustrative of this kind of scurrility is the following:

The Testament, or Last Will of the War of the Netherlands. Such as, lying on her Death-bed in The Hague, she has had it written down and sealed the second day of February of this Year 1609. By Somebody of Truthful Tongue.

> I, Daughter of Lucifer, from a Devilish family . . .
> From Spanish seed born out of the Inquisition,
> On the other side of the Pyrenees;
> Baptized on Tiber's border, accommodated in the Netherlands,
> With Roman Whore's Milk fed from childhood up. . . .
>   For the Inquisition and New Bishops are introduced;
> For the Council of Blood preys on the Blood and the goods of many.

My rule is spread and the revengeful mind
Satiates me fiercely with Fire, Gallow, Wheel, and Sword.
These, out of gratitude, I bequeath to my most powerful Patron,
Philip, King of Spain,
The heavy burden of his and his Father's sins,
    These, I leave to him God's terrible wrath
And righteous judgment, that he always has sworn by,
Over the innocent blood unjustly spilled
When once Las Casas' will be proved.[23]

This brand of propaganda seems, perhaps, a bit crude to the educated, twentieth-century mind. But it is the kind of verbiage which, stimulating and stimulated by war, can shape literatures, establish traditions, and determine the content of future schoolbooks. That is why even today's well-educated Dutchman, from childhood, knows that Spaniards are inherently and uniquely cruel, are benightedly Rome-ridden, by nature treacherous, and certainly not in the same efficient class as more advanced Nordics, like himself. It takes but a minimum of conversation with today's Dutchman to find this out. It is true, however, that some fair-minded Dutchmen of today admit the existence of this deep-seated and ineradicable prejudice born of the independence struggle and attendant propaganda.[24]

But propaganda for persuasion of the masses does not just grow, like Topsy; the anger and hatred of the populace need to be inflamed, guided, and constantly fed, lest they lag. Some reasons for the astonishing success of Dutch propaganda against Spain have already been indicated, but even restless Dutch burghers needed intellectual guidance to move them toward a thoroughgoing and enthusiastic break with Catholicism and toward rebellion against a legitimate monarch. Thus, in the background of the propaganda of hate, as seems ever the case, intellectuals of one sort and another provided the biblical and classical allusions, the translations, the sonnets, the poetic attempts, the fundamental ideas, and the continuity from other parts of Europe.

The Low Countries by 1560 had already become a vortex of: radical Protestantism, of high and low intellectual levels; great interest in printing; university excellence; Sephardic Jewish commercial, cultural, and religious interests—first at Antwerp, later in Amsterdam; English and French intrigue; sundry other activities, which attracted the interest and presence of diverse intellectuals. Many of these were, in the spirit of the times, much taken with religious controversy over and above other cultural pursuits.

Thus, William of Orange's most famed "minister of propaganda," Marnix van Sainte Aldegonde, was a noted scholar "inspired by . . .

hatred of popery and zeal for the Reformation," and as early as 1570 he was the author of a famous anti-Catholic blast called *Beehive of the Holy Roman Church.* "In this virulent pamphlet Dutch prose was for the first time employed for the purpose of bitter satire, and this by a man who was at home in French and classical literature." Sainte Aldegonde's personal library contained works showing Black Legend influences from other parts of Europe.[25] Lucas de Heere, painter and well-known poet of Ghent, was writing in the 1560s, until he had to flee to England because of his Protestantism. The poet Jonkheer Jan van der Noot was "conspicuous among the most zealous Calvinists" in the 1560s, and in English exile "manifested as bitter a hatred of Catholicism as did Marnix himself." (After Parma's reconquest of Antwerp, however, van der Noot returned to Catholicism.) Abraham Ortels (Ortelius), whose *Theatrum Orbis Terrarum,* published in Latin in 1570 and in Dutch in 1571 (and various other languages) was, like the famous publisher Plantin, a secret member of a heretical sect.[26] Marcos Pérez, a Spanish Jew, was an active leader of the Protestant community in Antwerp. There were also French and English residents, observers, and intriguers (e.g., Sir Thomas Gresham) contributing to the ferment.

If there ever was a wonderfully vigorous combination of anti-Spanish, anti-Catholic intrigue mixed with intellectual potency, the ferment in the Low Countries during the time of William of Orange was that indeed. The international connections of Low Countries intellectuals and powerful merchants antagonistic to Spain and to Catholicism ranged through Huguenot France, Elizabethan England, Lutheran Germany, Renaissance Italy, Spain, and Portugal, the Moslem realms, and even into the New World.[27]

With all this, in addition to the great talent for pamphleteering shown by the Dutch, it is not surprising that the anti-Spanish motif became thoroughly entrenched in Dutch letters. This was to reach even greater heights in the next century, the Golden Age of Dutch culture. An example or two will illustrate the point.

The early seventeenth-century poet, Daniel Heinsius, notable for his "tone of vigorous patriotic pride," was author of the famous line, "Wherever you [Spain] are not, there is our fatherland." [28] And the anti-Catholic and anti-Spanish Heinsius tragedy, *Auriacus sive Libertas Saucia* (1602), was notable on the Dutch stage in the most heated years of Dutch-Spanish military conflict. The great Dutch poet, Joost van den Vondel, born of Baptist parents, "spokesman of his country" for a half century after 1612, was of "patriotic enthusiasm" until about 1630. He was, of course, anti-Spanish in his writings. In about 1641 he became a Catholic convert.[29]

The clearest manifestation of the fundamental anti-Spanish theme in Dutch culture is to be found in the great collection of popular songs known as the *Geusenliedboeck*. They appeared in collected form probably as early as 1574 and were frequently published thereafter; there were well over thirty editions prior to 1688. This is "anti-Spanish, anti-Catholic resistance poetry," representing the "national awakening" in the latter half of the sixteenth century; "partly political, partly religious, of very unequal merit" but exceedingly popular—and a beloved Dutch heritage even today.[30] A similar song collection is the one commonly known as Valerius' *Gedenck-clanck*, first published in the early seventeenth century with illustrations to fit the songs; the anti-Spanish vitriol, as basic Dutch heritage, runs all through this.[31]

The present small-power status of the Netherlands should not lead us to undervalue the significance of Dutch contribution to the Western world's hispanophobia. Dutch views of Spain today, while an interesting example of the exceedingly deep impress of centuries-old, wartime propaganda, are relatively unimportant in fashioning opinions that will determine major events or cultural attitudes. But Dutch propaganda in the sixteenth and seventeenth centuries played a fundamental role in forming a general hispanophobia in the Western world. This propaganda was purposefully spread throughout the continent during a critical and formative period of European opinion. It was interrelated with earlier Italian and German intellectual and popular attitudes, and it was significantly related to the development of similar propaganda in England, the source of most of our own literary, political, and religious inheritance.

England versus Spain: Words and War

In the century after 1560, England developed many Protestant characteristics (imposed mainly from the top), a strong nationalistic patriotism, the beginning of an overseas empire, and a very vigorous national literature. In the first three of these achievements, Spain, by virtue of its hegemony in Europe, its vast empire, and championship of the Roman Church, was the principal enemy of England. This enmity was reflected and traditionalized in English literature. The fact that "an instinctive hatred of Spain was regarded as an important element in Elizabethan patriotism," [32] and that this patriotism was closely linked with overseas colonization as a challenge to Spanish monopoly, meant that our own cultural foundations were firmly rooted in this "tree of hate." And our British ancestors in America brought westward some of the bitterest, most intolerant fruit of the violent Protestant-Catholic struggle—attitudes firmly hispanophobic.

By inheritance, then, we acquired England's heroes and villains, her war propagandas, and her prejudices. We can sympathize and rejoice with Francis Drake as he singes the beard of the "Spider of the Escorial" or heroically trounces a Spanish Armada—but we almost never hear of Lepanto, and only accidentally, usually in the Columbus story, know that Spaniards toppled Moslem Granada, two very significant events in Western history, and great Spanish achievements. We easily condone or even applaud Elizabethan duplicity and piracy (early linked with the trade in Negro slaves), for the end—blows against Spain— obviously justified the means. But a Machiavellian Ferdinand or a devious Philip II simply confirm our fundamental conviction that Spaniards are inherently treacherous (we usually do not understand either Machiavelli or Spanish history). A rascally prevaricator like Captain John Smith is one of our folk-heroes, but we simply refuse to understand a Cortés, much less allow him the full measure of his greatness.

It takes but a small resumé of the relative Spanish-English positions in this century and a few illustrations from English writings to show why and how this anti-Spanish hatred became such a basic part of our inheritance.

England, of course, was intimately concerned with the Dutch-Spanish struggle that blossomed in the 1560s for two main reasons: (1) Spanish rule in such a strategic spot would be a greater danger to England than would a weaker Dutch control, or continuing conflict; and (2) English leadership, playing a nip-and-tuck game of turning England Protestant, was sympathetically linked with the anti-Catholic subversion centered in the Low Countries. Thus, there was a flow of exiles, spies, some aid from England to the Dutch rebels, and anti-Spanish, anti-Catholic propaganda exchanges across the Channel. Anti-Spanish, anti-Catholic pamphlets and news crossed the water for translation and publication with a rapidity betokening purposeful collusion, and this is reflected in the libraries of England and the Netherlands today. Closely related to this was the connection of English leaders with the Huguenot movement in France, for this was also tied into the activities of William and other conspirators and rebels in the Low Countries.

Within England itself, a determined Protestant leadership managed to stave off the Catholic threats, in which Spain was usually involved, until the 1580s. Then, as Spain became more obviously a military threat (as distinct from the strictly religious one), even English Catholics tended to join the growing national patriotism, much as had happened earlier in Germany. National unity in the face of the Armada definitely handicapped the Spanish-Catholic cause within England, though the Protestant-Catholic conflict was not yet ended. The Armada episode greatly stimulated English patriotism and made the anti-Spanish theme outrun the anti-Catholic one, though both continued closely linked.

The Catholic danger was feared well beyond the death of Elizabeth in 1603 and repressive measures were continued. But the Spanish aspect of the threat was felt mainly in such episodes as the proposed "Spanish Marriage" of the 1620s (which brought forth some virulent anti-Spanish propaganda) and complications attendant upon the Thirty Years' War, where Spanish hegemony in Europe was finally ended (the 1640s) and Dutch independence confirmed. Along the way, Catholic plots, real and unreal—e.g., the famous Gunpowder Plot of 1606, propagandistically then traditionally linked to Catholic conspiracy, furnished fuel for anti-Catholic, hispanophobic propagandists.[33] The ascendant Puritanism of the Cromwellian interlude allowed unrestrained publication of such anti-Spanish writing as that of Thomas Gage and a timely new English edition of Bartolomé de las Casas' *Brief Relation*. Finally, the so-called "Glorious Revolution" of 1688 put a direct descendant of William of Orange upon the English throne, and this ended the major phase of Protestant-Catholic struggle in England. But, by this time, there was no end to the literary status of Spain as England's traditional enemy. More than a century of propaganda pamphlets, war, and international plot and counterplot had seen to this. The unceasing flow of words in England, as in Holland, had indelibly stigmatized Spaniards as Lucifers incarnate.

The propaganda barrage against Spain did not get under way, significantly, until the 1580s. It is true enough that there were some pamphlets and other writings showing sympathy for the Dutch cause against Spain, and there were assuredly enough nonprinted epithets growing out of the strained relations between Spaniards and Englishmen on the seas and in the West Indies. Also, Richard Eden had published, in the 1550s, translations of such authors as Sebastian Münster and Peter Martyr, thus implanting in English minds some observations on the cruelties of Spanish Conquest in America.[34]

But it was a quick pile-up of events, starting around 1580, that loosed the explosive mixture of fear and defiance that was henceforth to feed English hispanophobia. In 1580 Drake returned from his cocky, 'round-the-world challenge to Spain; William issued his *Apologia* (quickly translated into English); and Philip II successfully claimed dominion over the vast Portuguese Empire, which placed England's oldest ally within the Spanish orbit and made the Spanish Empire more than ever frightening in size. During the next few years the Portuguese Pretender, Dom Antônio, fled to England (1581), the first English edition of Las Casas' *Brief Relation* came off the London press (1583), and William was assassinated (1584). Also, increasingly frightening news concerning Spain's build-up of mighty sea forces began to enter England. During most of the decade, England was tense, fearful, yet defiant of Spain. In singeing Philip's beard, England went beyond mere piracy; it attempted American colonization in these years, and Drake raided Santo Domingo and Cartagena. And, as climax, came the almost miraculous triumph over the Spanish Armada, in 1588.

The first English edition of Las Casas was clearly intended to stir hatred of Spain, a goal made crudely and endlessly obvious in its introduction.[35] The "passionate Protestant" promoter of English patriotism and expansion, Richard Hakluyt, issued his famous *Discourse on the Western Planting* (projected colonization in Virginia) in 1584, at a moment when "hatred of Spain was reaching the point of hysteria."[36] This, his important publication of English voyages and his other writings over the next few years thoroughly reflected and promoted hispanophobia. In Hakluyt's pamphleteering and in his more solid work, hatred of Spain is artistically mixed with exhortations to emulate Spain in order to stir English patriotism toward heroic deeds. Hakluyt's is surely one of the most significant patriotic propaganda efforts in English history.[37]

Two very bitter pamphlets of 1589 and 1590 illustrate an intertwining of French and English propaganda efforts against Spain. As so often was the case in Dutch writing, the wording is vulgarly intemperate and quite apparently intended for wide, popular appeal, coming as it did on the heels of the Armada defeat.

[We must] learne to despise those magnificent *Don Diegos* and *Spanish Cavalieros,* whose doughtiest deedes are bragges and boastinges, and themselves (for the most part) shadowes without substance. . . . What humanitie, what faith, what courtesie, what modestie, and civilitie, may wee thinke to finde amongst this scumme of Barbarians? [My assertions can] be cleared by conference of their manner with ours, that is, of their vices with our vertues, of their vile viliacquerie, with our generositie. . . . The comparing of our conditions with those of this mongrell generation. [The Spanish Nation is] unfaithful, ravenous, and insatiable above all other Nations. . . . The nature and disposition of the Spaniards, in whom may be seene together incorporated, a craftie Fox, a ravenous Wolfe, and a raging Tygre. . . . [The Spaniard is also] an uncleane and filthie swine, a theevish howlet, a proud peacocke . . . a legion of divels. . . . [Columbus] would never have undertaken this voyage, if he had thought that the men whome hee brought thither . . . should straightwaies be transformed into Lions, Panthers, Tigres, and other savage beastes. . . . O Turkes, O Scithians, O Tartarians [rejoice, for Spain's much greater cruelty makes yours look so much less]. [The author of this pamphlet gives credit to the famous Venetian, Guicci-ardini, for some of this characterization of the Spaniards.]

[Spain] is and ever hath bene the sinke, the puddle, and filthie heape of the most lothsome, infected, and slavish people that ever yet lived on earth. . . . This wicked race of those half Wisigots. . . . This demie Moore, demie Jew, yea demie Saracine. . . . What? shall those Marranos, yes, those impious Atheistes reigne over us kings and Princes? . . . [Those Spaniards with] . . . theyr insatiate avarice, theyre more than Tigrish cruelty, theyr filthy, monstruous and abominable luxurie . . . theyr lustfull and inhumaine deflouring of their matrones, wives, and daughters, theyr matchless and sodomiticall ravishings of young boyes, which these demi-barbarian Span-iardes committed. . . .[38]

A violently hispanophobic preacher and pamphleteer, Thomas Scott, would echo this sort of epithet a generation later, in the 1620s, when he urged England to war against "those wolvish Antichristians" instead of accepting the "Spanish Marriage." But by that time refinements had been made in British propaganda techniques. Lascasian clichés on Spanish cruelty and greed were accompanied by closely woven argu-ments concerning Jesuits, Inquisition, relations between the Dutch and English against their common enemy, the Pope as Antichrist, Rome as Babylon, Spanish aims at universal dominion, etc. ". . . Where the *Spaniard* comes, he sets himself downe like an absolute and tyrannical Lord, silencing all Lawes but his owne, which are those of the *Medes* and *Persians;* yea, as those of *Drace* written in blood . . . there is as much trust to their promises, as to the *Moores* their Kinsmen and late Countrimen." [39]

Scott wrote and printed a number of his tracts in Holland, and this undoubtedly accounts for some of his propaganda themes and phrase-ology. England sometimes became too hot for him, as when delicate Spanish-English negotiations were under way or his exceedingly violent anti-Catholicism set enemies on his trail. But Scott was undoubtedly popular, and he wrote and published anti-Spanish vitriol rapidly and in quantity. In his thorough linkage of anti-Spain and anti-Rome, he did much to popularize the synonymity of those hatreds in the English tradition.[40]

Such pamphleteering was paralleled through the Elizabethan period and beyond by a vigorous anti-Spanish motif in English literature. Thus Thomas Middleton's dramatic satire, *A Game of Chess* (1624), almost exactly paralleled pamphleteer Scott, in its satirization of the proposed "Spanish Marriage," Spanish Ambassador Gondomar (long a favorite butt of anti-Spanish writing in England), the Count-Duke of Olivares, and the general of the Jesuits. The Spanish were painted all black and invariably were defeated when the heroes "discovered" their wicked plotting.[41]

"Spanish personages, of course, are scattered up and down the Elizabethan drama, but for the most part they are caricatures and 'drawn with an unfriendly pen.'" Among these caricatures are: the perversion of the Spanish Lazarillo in Middleton's *Blurt Master Constable;* Jonson's Don Diego in *The Alchemist,* "an intentionally ridiculous, affected and bombastic falsification"; and Fletcher's lecherous poltroon, Prince Pharamond, in *Philaster.* Dramatists and others not only ridiculed and blackened the Spaniard of their times but they even turned to the past, developing some anti-Spanish themes whose only relevance was as vicious propaganda. Thus, in Peele's *Edward I* "is contained one of the most cruel and unjust perversions of historical truth of which our drama was guilty. This is the outrageous transformation of the charitable and estimable queen Eleanor of Castile into a monster of craft and wickedness." Although the dramatists rather generally represented Philip II "with dignity and respect" in the sixteenth century, some then (and later, many) fastened upon him the blame for the anti-Protestant persecutions of so-called "Bloody" Mary, his wife; this has become unjustly fixed in British tradition and is about as difficult to eradicate as it is to arouse any sympathetic understanding of Queen Mary herself.[42]

The plays of Thomas Heywood are examples of the hispanophobia so prevalent in the English drama of the period. They have been thus described: "the Diegos play a fairly important and not at all flattering role in Heywood's dramas. First and last, they are tyrannous, cruel, lascivious, and bloody."[43] The *Dick of Devonshire,* which provides the epigraph at the beginning of this book, seems to have been of Heywood's authorship.

As one might expect, given the patriotic interest of the English in the sea fighting against Spain and in overseas trade and colony-planting, the English drama concentrated heavily upon the cruelty and injustice of Spanish actions in America. The Dutch had emphasized Spanish misgovernment, the behavior of Spanish soldiers, and had slandered the Spanish monarch, etc., for Dutch propaganda was largely established in a period antedating any significant overseas interests. The English in the period of which we speak, however, were much taken with the possibilities of defeating Spain on the seas and in the Indies. Their hispanophobic writing reflects this in several of their main themes, most of which are today regularly read in our elementary and high schools (see Chapter 7):

1. The Las Casas picture castigated all Spaniards in its main theme—greedy Spaniards versus innocent savages. The English constantly used these distortions in their literature to justify their capture of Spanish treasure and to portray their own virtues by contrast with Spanish villainies. The fond cliché of Indian friendliness toward Englishmen was advanced to demonstrate the ease with which Spanish rule in America could be overthrown by Englishmen. The theme was extended to form part of a larger picture of English moral, racial, and religious superiority over the Spaniard.[44]

2. Exclusivity of Spanish imperial trade restrictions was often and bitterly condemned. Englishmen naturally did not like such policies, for they were kept out by them—they called it Spanish "insolence." Francis Bacon, in his famed *Considerations Touching a War with Spain,* roundly condemned such exclusion and used it as justification for English raids on Spanish treasure in the Indies.[45] [This unrelieved condemnation of Spain's exclusivist trade policy is nearly always present in our schoolbooks, usually without any attempt to judge it in light of its times or to understand that Spain possibly had some very good reasons for such a policy, such as keeping out piratical and heretical Dutchmen and Englishmen. Other European colonizers overseas engaged in similar policies when they had opportunities at all similar to those of Spain.]

3. The Pope's "unfair" division of the overseas world between Spain and Portugal provided grounds for a double English propaganda blow against Spain and the Pope. [The Portuguese, whose Tordesillas treaty of 1494 with Spain was far more the real basis for the division than the papal decision, are seldom mentioned in this connection. They were, after all, England's traditional allies—and, in any case, the English were more interested in intruding into Spain's West Indies.] The English, erroneously enough, scoffed at papal authority in the matter. They bitterly resented Spanish prior discovery of America and even went to the length of inventing an earlier English discovery. The subject was so painful that there was some hindsight literary castigation of Henry VII for having lost such a golden discovery opportunity.[46]

4. Even when English writers departed from the "noble savage" theme to make remarks critical of the Indians, the Spaniards were not left unscathed. They were either damned as virtual cowards for

having attacked such low-quality people, or the Indians were said to merit the horrible fate of being ruled by Spain, since their vile habits deserved nothing better.[47]

5. A basic threat through all this was the Englishman's blatant assurance of his complete superiority over the Spaniard in every way. Understandably, this theme rapidly became stronger after defeat of the Armada. The gloating sometimes reached the point of dangerous overconfidence. And for all that the Armada defeat was a superb achievement, it is almost invariably overrated in English tradition as the end of Spain on the seas and the beginning of England as "mistress of the seas"—a view that is constantly reiterated in our own schoolbooks and other writings.

With pen and printing press, Elizabethan Englishmen parlayed defeat of the Armada, Bartolomé de las Casas, and a large envy into a vast, hypocritical, and unqualified superiority complex over the baser, less efficient, and more cowardly Spaniard. This was certainly a stimulus for empire building and not entirely unlike some Spanish attitudes in defeating Moslems, discovering, exploring, colonizing, and Christianizing a New World, with the helpful conviction that they were chosen by God for such important tasks. But the new, quickly solidified tradition of hate toward the inferior Spaniard distorted history and confused historians; grossly unfair to Spain and Spaniards since the British "tree of hate" bore so much evil fruit in the Western world; and very deceptive to many generations of English-speaking schoolchildren whose education has inherited the nearly unbridgeable gap of misunderstanding between Anglo and Hispanic cultures and peoples.

The printing press, as utilized by the Dutch and English during the century after 1560 was, as we have seen, wondrously fertile in vilification of Spaniards. Now, let us notice an important development anent the Las Casas theme near the end of the sixteenth century.

The significance of England's Richard Hakluyt in energizing English patriotism by playing on anti-Spanish attitudes has already been indicated. What is less generally known is the close relationship between Hakluyt and the Fleming Theodore De Bry, an engraver, printer, and bookseller residing in Frankfurt. This city, let it be recalled, was in the sixteenth century a thriving center of anti-Catholic publication; and De Bry was of the heretical persuasion.

In 1587 De Bry went to England, where he came under the influence of Hakluyt. From this point on, the De Bry-Hakluyt relationship shows in the parallelism of their lines of publication; both produced important series on discovery that were large in concept and scope, and, *inter alia,* strongly anti-Spanish in flavor. In the case of De Bry, this led to a development that was to have enormous significance in propagation of the Black Legend by means of Las Casas' *Brief Relation*.

In 1598 the De Brys of Frankfurt issued an edition of the *Brief Relation* with a new twist. The work contained seventeen engravings illustrating specific episodes of purported Spanish torture and killing of Indians, as described in Las Casas' text.* These pictures were extremely gruesome, obviously catering to the general public and its common appetite for horrors. From this time on editions of the *Brief Relation* often contained all or some of the De Bry engravings. And the pictures themselves were dignified by separate publication,[48] thus indicating their original propaganda aims.

The De Bry engravings reflect not only the artist's complete lack of knowledge of the American Indian (the natives look like bald-headed, plump imitations of Titianesque subjects), but also one of Las Casas' own great weaknesses—failure to appreciate or delineate the important differences among Indians themselves. To Las Casas and to the house of De Bry, the American Indian was a faceless abstraction created by the former for propaganda and by the latter for both propaganda and profit. But the significance of the De Bry engravings is that from then to now they have heightened enormously the popular appeal of Las Casas' chamber of horrors. These engravings continue to appear from time to time in otherwise respectable publications.[49]

Dos Palabras on Target Spain

Although the Dutch might call them "raving dogs," a "damned race which is more given to wickedness than all the Turks together", and in England they were cursed as "scumme of Barbarians . . . whose doughtiest deedes are bragges and boastinges," the Spaniards of those early modern times were enjoying a truly great golden age of intellect and empire. In the epithetical barbs of those olden hispanophobic

* Beneath each of the ten reproductions of the De Bry engravings is my translation of those sentences in Las Casas's *Brevísima relación* (Frankfurt, 1598) which seem to have served as inspiration for the original. With some deletions, I have thus followed the system of presentation used by Rómulo D. Carbia in his *Historia de la leyenda negra hispanoamericana* (Publicaciones del Consejo de la Hispanidad, Madrid, 1944).

PWP

I

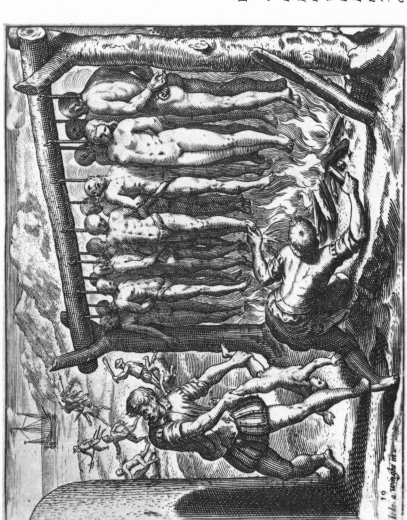

"[The Spaniards] took babies from their mothers' breasts, grabbing them by the feet and beating their heads against rocks. . . . They set up long gibbets from which they would hang the Indians, thirteen at a time (thus honoring Our Redeemer and the twelve apostles), with their feet almost reaching the ground. They would then build fires underneath and burn them alive."

II

"When the [Cuban] cacique was bound
to the post, a Franciscan friar . . . told
him some of the matters of our Faith,
which the chieftain had never before
heard. . . . The padre told the cacique
that if he wished to believe these things,
he would go to Heaven . . . but if not,
he would go to Hell and suffer eternal
torment and sorrow. The cacique . . .
asked the friar if Christians went to
Heaven, and was told that the good ones
did. The cacique, without further
thought, said that he did not wish to go
to Heaven but to Hell, so as not to be with
Spaniards or see such cruel people."

III

*"From Cholula [the Spaniards] went to
Mexico. Montezuma sent to meet them
thousands of presents and lords and
people, making merry along the way. At
the entry to the causeway of Mexico
. . . he sent to them his own brother,
accompanied by many great lords and
wonderful presents of gold, silver, and
clothing. And at the city's entrance,
Montezuma himself came, in a litter of
gold, with all his court, to receive them,
and accompany them to the palaces
which he had ordered readied for them."*

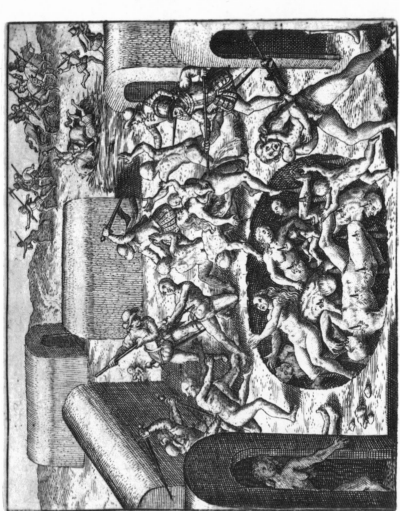

IV

"The Indians [in Guatemala] dug some holes in the roads and filled them with sharpened stakes to pierce the bellies of the Spaniards' horses; the holes were covered with turf and weeds to disguise them. The Spaniards fell into these holes only once or twice, then they decreed that any of those Indians caught alive should be thrown into those same pits. They then cast into those pits pregnant women, women newly delivered of children, and old people, as many as they could until the pits were filled with Indians impaled on the stakes. . . . The rest they killed with lances and daggers and threw them to their war dogs who tore them up and devoured them. And when they captured a lord, they honored him by burning him alive."

▼

"This [Spanish] tyrant, when he went to
war upon any towns or provinces, had
the habit of taking with him Indians
already subjugated, to make war upon
the others. Since he gave no food to
these ten or twenty thousand Indians, he
permitted them to eat all captured
Indians. His camp was thus a shambles
of men's flesh, where, in his presence,
children were killed and roasted, and
men were killed solely for their hands
and feet, which were considered the
daintiest morsels."

VI

"The Spaniards gave this Indian king the torture of the strappado; they put burning grease upon his naked belly; they put upon his feet bolts which were fastened to a stake and tied his neck to another stake, and two men held his hand while others set fired to his feet. From time to time, the Spanish tyrant came to tell the king that he would thus be slowly tortured to death if he did not give up the gold. And so they did, killing the said lord by torture."

VII

"This great tyrant [Nuño de Guzmán, in Jalisco, Mexico] burned towns, captured caciques and tortured them. He made slaves of all he took. He carried off infinite numbers in chains; women newly delivered were forced to carry burdens for the evil Christians and thus could not carry their infants because of the hard work and weakness of hunger. Infinite numbers of these were cast aside on the road and thus perished."

VIII

*"As these cursed Spaniards went with
their war dogs hunting down Indians,
men and women, it happened that a sick
Indian woman who could not flee from
the dogs, sought to escape being torn
apart by them, in this fashion: she took
a cord and tied her year-old child to her
leg then hanged herself from a beam.
But the dogs came and tore the child
apart; but, before the creature expired,
a friar baptized it."*

IX

"Another time the captain sent this same cruel man . . . into the Province of Bogotá, to find from the inhabitants who was the lord who succeeded the one he had put to death. This cruel captain went over many leagues, capturing all the Indians he could; and, since they did not tell him who this lord was, he cut off the hands of some and threw others to the dogs who tore them to pieces. He did this to men and women alike, and thus destroyed very many Indians. On one occasion, at the fourth watch of the night, he came upon some chieftains and many Indians, who were peaceful and had been assured by the word of this same captain that they would not be harmed, and thus they emerged from their hiding places. This captain then treacherously seized them, made them stretch their hands out on the ground, while he himself, with his sword, cut off their hands, telling them that he gave them this punishment because they would not tell who their new lord was."

X

"The use [the Spaniards] made of the Indians was to send the men to the mines to bring out gold, which is very cruel work; and the women were put on the farms, to plow and cultivate, which is very difficult even for the strongest of men."

Carbia points out that this engraving, in the De Bry edition, also bears these words: "[The Spaniards punished lagging workers] by whipping them . . . until they were almost dead. And even this was not enough, for after such cruel flogging they would drip hot lard into their wounds. . . ."

propagandas, target Spain is not even slightly recognizable—it is completely incredible, in fact—to the minds of men then and now acquainted with the superb cultural achievements of Spain between 1492 and 1680.

This was the Spain that was cleansing and reforming its Church well before Luther, and thus felt no need of a Protestant Revolt or of sectarian hairsplitting with sword and civil war. And ahead of the rest of Europe, Spaniards had created a vigorous, systematized, modern idiom—the Castilian tongue—which went in tandem with a revitalized Church to form twin pillars of great intellectual and imperial achievement.

Iberia was the land which, with its novel of chivalry, first "democratized" literature, so to speak. And from the pens of Castile came the novel of realism (*La Celestina* of the 1490s and the picaresque *Lazarillo de Tormes* of the 1550s), and, in most ways, the novel itself, especially in Miguel de Cervantes. In philology and linguistic scholarship generally, Spain was a sixteenth-century leader, much stimulated by the multitude of new languages found and studied overseas.

This was the land and people creating literary characters and concepts of timeless fame and universality—Don Quijote, Sancho Panza, Don Juan, Calderón's *Life is a Dream* and the most exalted literary expression of the concept of honor. Its superb poets and playwrights were creating a national drama that was a marvel of the continent and which provided guidelines for the later French theater of Corneille and Molière. The names of Lope de Vega, Tirso de Molina, Juan Ruiz de Alarcón (born in Mexico), and Calderón—the "big four" of drama during the Spanish Golden Age—when added to those of Cervantes and such poets as Luis de Góngora, and Francisco de Quevedo constitute a pantheon of literary genius of which any people at any time could be justly proud. Then add to these the uniquely Spanish contributions to literary religious mysticism (e.g., San Juan de la Cruz and Santa Teresa) and the truly prodigious and innovative output of histories, chronicles, biographies, the varied literature of exploration and conquest, didactic and religious works—and the resultant panoply of names and titles indexes an intellectual flowering seldom equaled or excelled in other lands and times.

The Iberian Peninsula in this age was also leading Europe in the advancement of jurisprudence, creating basic principles of international law, and producing outstanding jurists along every line. It was a land that simultaneously produced the great humanist friend of Erasmus, Luis Vives, and the military genius known to Europe as "The Great Captain," Gonsalvo de Córdoba. And, in the decades when Dutch and English pamphleteers were most vigorously using the tarbrush to paint Spaniards as a "filthie heape of the most lothsome, infected, and slavish people that ever yet lived on earth," Spaniards themselves were painting their way to eternal glory. It was the age of El Greco, Zurbarán, Ribera, Velázquez, and Murillo—and Goya in a later, declining Spain would round out a picture of Spanish excellence.

In these same decades the great Spanish musicians, Antonio Cabezón (the "Spanish Bach," before Bach) and Luis de Victoria were outstanding contributors to the musical eminence of Rome, and superb composers and instrumentalists were at work in the Peninsula itself. A mestizo, Garcilaso Inca de la Vega, born in Peru of a Spanish father and an Inca mother, was in Spain writing his way toward literary immortality with his famous works on the Incas and the Spanish conquest in Peru. And a beautiful *criolla,* Sor Juana Inés de la Cruz, born in Mexico at about the time when English literary denigration of Spaniards reached new heights in the Cromwellian period, was destined to become the first major and possibly the greatest of New World poetesses.

The people whom the anti-Spanish pamphleteers were so thoroughly damning were also enjoying global primacy in geographical knowledge and experience, in navigational sciences—its great maritime "university" at Seville was a leader and innovator in cartography, trained generations of highly expert navigators, and had archives that were a vast storehouse of scientific knowledge and geographical reporting. In the sciences of metallurgy and botany especially and in the general observation of nature, Spain was producing a quantity of scholars and writers who are still accorded recognition for their basic contributions to knowledge.

It was this Spain, a deeply civilized land of grand cultural flowering, that was hidden from view by the "tree of hate" so purposefully nourished in the vitriol of pamphleteers who gave to their own and many subsequent generations a picture so false that it seems impossible that anyone could have believed any of it. This, in spite of the knowledge we have of how eagerly such portrayals of "the enemy" have been swallowed by war-stimulated populaces in more recent times.

However, men of education and of enlightenment are supposed to know better—and usually, the lies and other frauds of wartime propagandas are in due course exposed in such circles and their most pernicious effects erased or ameliorated.

But, as we shall see, the propagandas against Spain were fated otherwise.

Chapter 5

THE ARROGANCE OF ENLIGHTENMENT

It is not truth but opinion that can travel the world without a passport.

SIR WALTER RALEIGH

The virulent propagandas and prejudices of the anti-Spanish legend that spread through Europe after 1560 might have come to rest upon history's slag heap had it not been for two significant developments. Spain, though it lost European primacy in the Thirty Years' War (1618–1648), remained a great power, mainly as a result of the continuing vastness and wealth of its overseas empire, which never ceased to attract envy and attack. Also, a new age of Reason, Tolerance, and Enlightenment, following hard on the heels of the earlier poisonous pamphleteering, intellectually enshrined anti-Spanish beliefs and dogmatized their tenets.

From about 1650 until well after the opening of the nineteenth century, Spain unforgivably remained an empire of great size and consequence and, equally unforgivably, a colossus of Roman Catholicism in an age that took as one of its intellectual guidelines a disdainful skepticism of revealed and hierarchal religion in general and of the Roman version in particular. The vaunted tolerance of leading intellectuals of this age definitely did not include any sympathy for a Catholic Spain; the propaganda of the preceding century was continually warmed over, chewed, and spat out to the greater vilification of the land of Philip II and the Inquisition. Bartolomé de las Casas, Philip, the Don Carlos story, Antonio Pérez, the Spanish Inquisition, were seldom accorded any critical evaluation; instead, they became symbols of the ignorance and lack of reason that Enlightenment was supposed to scourge. The relatively few attempts to apply critical analysis were drowned in the popularity of the famous penmen who led the new intellectual fashions and who, almost to a man, denigrated Spain along the lines created earlier. For the new prophets, Spain served as ideal Devil, so to speak, for their pungent wit.

During most of this period, Spain and England found themselves either at war or in precarious truce, thus keeping alive the anti-Spain brand of patriotism. And Frenchmen, for all the evils their own country was suffering and for all that they failed dismally in their efforts to rival the grandeur of Spain overseas, relished the hispanophobic barbs thrown by their intellectuals. Even some Spaniards, influenced not only by sincere concern over their country's institutional weaknesses but also by foreign intellectual fashions, became increasingly critical in their writings, in the tradition of Spanish self-depreciation.

Dutchmen, thoroughly embittered by the long struggle against Spain, became intransigently hardened hispanophobes, as was the case with many Englishmen, including many of those who settled in North America. And always near the heart of any action against sinister Spain and its deep Catholicism were to be found energetic Jews, mainly Sephardic, gladly serving as printers, publishers, and intelligencers. The enemies of Spain, now clearly dominating the printing press and Western intellectual styles, were thus still numerous and active. Spain had become, for large numbers of Europeans, a traditional enemy and remained uncritically accepted as such.

The Legend's Rendezvous with History

The history of Spain and Spanish America, especially as written by non-Spaniards in the seventeenth and eighteenth centuries, is an excellent illustration of the alliance of legend and history. History, of course, is never written with perfect objectivity, and it is peculiarly susceptible to the biases of religion and politics [also, in more recent times, to certain economic and social dogmas], and to man's tendency to stress the marvelous or the sensational. In the centuries of which we now speak, there was unusual stress upon the writing of history in terms of large, prototypal figures, who came to personify national or religious traits either admired or hated by the authors. Thus, a truly unsavory Henry VIII of England was cleaned up a bit so that he could cut a finer figure as a paladin of Protestantism. On the other hand, Philip II, far more an expression of his people's spiritual and material traits and goals and a more deeply civilized human being, came to personify the "intolerant" spirit of Catholic Europe. The William and Philip juxtaposition of good and evil was similarly strengthened in these centuries.

In somewhat the same way, twentieth-century historical writing tends to intolerant extremes in describing and interpreting the "Left" and "Right." The writing of history, being far more an art than a science, inevitably reflects prevailing prejudices and fashions—and the acceptable histories are usually those written by the victors in war. France, increasingly victorious in war and diplomacy, came to supplant Spain as the strong power on the continent, and England began to rival, then finally outdo Spain in seaborne activity. The iconoclastic literary fashions of the one and the Protestant intolerance of the other hardened into dogma the caricature of Spain as exemplar of religious evils and as eternal symbol of error and unreason. [On a smaller scale, a parallel might be found in the entrenched acceptability of the victorious and very self-righteous Northern interpretations of United States history since the Civil War.]

The seventeenth-century Black Legend hardened around several basic themes. The figure of Philip II, handled with at least some respect in his lifetime even by the Dutch and the English, evolved in the seventeenth century as the prototype of Spanish cruelty, immorality, obscurantism, and treachery. Such roots as Orange's *Apologia* and the "exposé" taken to the lands of Philip's enemies by his traitorous and none too savory secretary, Antonio Pérez,[1] gained literary popularity throughout Europe. Pérez's bestseller success caused his hate-ridden picture of Philip II to be accepted unquestionably as an "historical" source—a wonderful drama of Spanish court intrigue and immorality, with Philip as villain and Pérez himself as a persecuted political martyr. The discriminating historian, of course, discounts the Pérez views for he was, after all, in disgrace with his patron and a traitor to his king. An Antonio Pérez view of Philip II and Spanish politics of that day might be likened to a portrayal of congressional mismanagement of the American Revolution by Benedict Arnold for avid readers in England. Antonio Pérez wrote the kind of snappy stuff that mightily pleased the anti-Spain, anti-Philip audiences in Europe. His version has continued in vogue, making it difficult for those who attempt to study and portray Philip with greater objectivity to gain an audience.[2] Along with Pérez went repeated editions of González Montaño's reputed "inside story" of the horrors of the Spanish Inquisition and the inevitable *Brief Relation* of Las Casas.[3]

By the end of the seventeenth century the Don Carlos story, with embellishments by Antonio Pérez, had won its way to classical literary standing in Europe. Built upon the accusations of Orange, expanded by Pérez, and embroidered by successive French authors, each with a variation on the manner of Carlos' death, it crystallized into a historical novel in the hands of the French "romancer and pseudo-historian," César Vichard Saint-Réal, whose *Dom Carlos, Nouvelle Historique,* was published in Amsterdam in 1672.[4] Don Carlos became a popular, classical, and idealistic martyr, a victim of the cruelty and immorality of Philip II. This theme and its variations thrilled, horrified, and fascinated successive generations who came across them in historical writing, drama, the novel, and in pictorial art. The Dutch reprinted Saint-Réal's *Dom Carlos* three times in the first half of the next century, when literary figures were no longer interested—a fact "doubtless to be explained in terms of Dutch patriotism." [5]

Although the French, Dutch, Italians, and English were much obsessed with the Don Carlos story, it was in German that it achieved immortality. "At the culmination of these predominantly sentimental or liberal works stands Schiller's justly famous sentimental and liberal drama, *Don Carlos, Infant von Spanien,* completed in its blank verse form in 1787." [6] Schiller made the Marquis of Poza the hero of the drama, nobly mouthing the ideas of liberty and tolerance that Schiller himself, a true son of eighteenth-century Enlightenment, espoused. The most odious figure in Schiller's hands was the Inquisitor-General, constantly and cruelly pursuing the heresies attributed to the Marquis of Poza and the tragic figure of Don Carlos. As the last scene unfolds and Isabel of Valois is dying of poison, Philip II turns his own son over to the Inquisitor with the famous words: "Grand Inquisitor, I have complied with my duty, now comply with yours." [7]

Schiller's *Don Carlos* has enjoyed tremendous success in the world of Western thought, not only because of the fame of the author but because the work, as a literary creation, excels in its dramatic and poetic qualities. It is perennially popular, too, because the Marquis of Poza's "enlightened" ideas express the aspirations made popular in the eighteenth century and enduring to the present time. But as history, the *Don Carlos* is an absurdity; it was based on the Saint-Réal romance and the tremendously biased and otherwise faulty Robert Watson version of Philip II. No Spaniard or other European of the sixteenth century could have spouted Schiller's brand of enlightenment. The figure of Philip II is that same odious and gloomy fanatic who forever appears in the writings of foreigners. Schiller's highly stereotyped versions of Spanish cruelty and inquisitorial fanaticism have exercised far greater influence than the judicious historians who have conscientiously tried to find and present the truths concerning Philip and his

Spain. Also, the enormous popularity of Verdi's opera made it even more difficult for the Western world to appraise with fairness the facts of a sixteenth-century Spanish case.

Other significant seventeenth-century developments of the anti-Spanish theme were in the areas of historiography and travel literature, which was blended with what passed for history. Along with continuing pamphlet material (some of which, like the *Brief Relation,* Thomas Scott, and the Dutch tracts, through repetition, came to have a reputation for authenticity), anti-Spanish views were spread widely throughout compilations of miscellaneous history, geography, eyewitness travel accounts, and large historical works of generally wide reputation and influence. In the first category, that of the heterogeneous compilations, falls much of the work, already mentioned, that originated in the previous century—such as Benzoni, Hakluyt, De Bry, Eden, etc.—and which continued to be popular in the seventeenth in fragments or in whole, especially under the stimulus of vigorous English, Dutch, and French overseas ambitions.[8] These collections were published repeatedly and often contained the De Bry or similar engravings, graphically illustrating the cruelty and fanaticism of Spain. And, like the calculated "big lies" of our own times, they acquired wide reputations as the purveyors of truth about Spain. Unfortunately, most of the more influential writing of later times was based upon this exciting storytelling. Thus, for example, the Benzoni version of Spanish ousting of the French from Florida—definitely anti-Spanish—became the commonly accepted version of Parkman and other nineteenth-century historians and of our schoolbooks in that century and this one.

In the opening decades of the seventeenth century, Hakluyt and Eden, Purchas, the De Bry series of voyages, and others, were current in Europe, and they all contained the thesis, supported by selection of their materials, that Spanish conquest and rule in America were uniquely iniquitous. Their authenticity was confirmed by writers who followed and repeated them. This is not to say that all the fragments published in such compilations were of anti-Spanish flavor, for these and other compilers often included material of the most varied sort, but titles, editorial comments, and selection of fragments, generally fostered—and often flatly expressed—anti-Spanish views.[9]

But, for all the French, German, or English compilations of this type, it was definitely the Dutch who led in the publication of this travel-history-geography literature during the seventeenth century. The mere fact of this Dutch leadership would be enough to assure maintenance of the anti-Spanish bias, for by the opening of the century it was a basic tenet of their national patriotism. Also by this time, Dutch naval strength and the wide diffusion of Dutch shipping, under the aggressive auspices of the East and West Indies Companies, made inevitable a large interest in this kind of literature, heavily flavored with hispanophobia. It was a golden century of Dutch literature, printing, and empire-building—and many of the Dutch literary and military blows were aimed at Spain. Holland, especially Amsterdam, was during this same century the home of a vigorous population of Sephardic Jews, actively engaged not only in the flourishing printing industry but also in a worldwide commerce and intelligence activities that were bitterly antagonistic toward Spain.[10]

Probably the most famous and influential of the many writers of Dutch origin was Jan Laët, who became a director of the Dutch West India Company in 1624 and who made a journey to the New World in an official capacity. His *History of the New World, or Description of the West Indies,* first appeared in Dutch, then in Latin and French during the years 1630–1640. Laët is still a well-known and oft-used source, and he enjoys a wide reputation for the appearance of strict objectivity which he presents. However, his choices of phrase and adjective in many small, not normally noticed ways reflect the patriotic Dutchman in belittlement of Spain. And Laët became a basic source for later writers who absorbed from him a definitely Dutch view of things Hispanic.

Of more importance to our own literature and traditions was the rascally Thomas Gage. His bitterly anti-Spanish, anti-Catholic *The English-American,* served to fan hispanophobia in the seventeenth and eighteenth centuries far more than the comparatively serene Laët. Originally published in English in 1648, his work was soon available in French editions (Amsterdam, 1676, 1695–6, 1721). So intemperate were his anti-Catholic strictures that his latest editor thought it best to omit some of his absurd calumnies, so as not to offend today's readers.[11] Gage's purpose in writing was to encourage and aid English attack on the Spanish New World empire by exposing the fact that Spain maintained no appreciable military force overseas and, therefore, the Americas could be easily and successfully invaded by Englishmen. To strengthen this thesis, Gage stressed the great benefit to humanity that would result from the replacement of Spanish rule with that of more virtuous Protestant Englishmen, a concept we have seen before.

Gage must also bear the responsibility for furthering, if not originating, some of the widespread prejudices that afflict strongly Protestant views of past and present Latin America. For one thing, he stressed the Catholic clergy's immorality. In the Puritanical atmosphere triumphant in the England of Gage's writing, he professed himself shocked, for example, that Spanish churchmen whiled away some of their leisure time in gaming. He also commented distastefully on the hypocritical ornateness of religious ceremonies and the clergy's parasitical living off alms. Gage either failed to understand much of what he saw in the Hispanic World or he deliberately twisted his comments to fit the needs of a renegade Catholic anxious to gain prestige and preferment among his new, Puritan coreligionists; probably some of both, but with more of the latter. In any case, his words have all the sound of a present-day fundamentalist [Protestant] missionary in the lands of Catholic Latins. To the moralistic, self-righteous Gage, as to his modern counterparts, any and all efforts to undermine Hispanic-Catholicism were entirely excusable, for the ends, Protestant-based enlightenment, justified the means thereto.

[The whole subject of Protestant missionary views of Spain and Spanish America, à la Thomas Gage and later, is indeed an intriguing one from the standpoint of influentially entrenched and extremely dogmatic hispanophobia. This is very noticeable in our own society, but is also strong in such north European countries as England, the Netherlands, and those of Scandinavia. It is, of course, impossible to measure the extent of such influence upon our ways of thought, or even upon our policy-making. But, from considerable personal experience and some knowledge of Black Legend growth, I would assert that Protestant missionary attitudes and propaganda have played a very important and largely harmful role in shaping our attitudes toward Hispano-Catholic culture.]

Closely related to the popular stream of travel-geographic-historical publications that, in whole or in part, touched upon and almost invariably distorted Spanish history and Spain's overseas enterprises, was the work of Bartolomé de las Casas. Of his *Brief Relation,* there were at least thirty-four editions between the end of the sixteenth century and the middle of the eighteenth. Fourteen of these were Dutch (all seventeenth century), six were English, six were French, three Italian, two German, two Latin, and one Spanish. And the other Las Casas treatises of 1552, in similar vein, went through at least sixty-one printings in the same period, including some twenty-four Dutch versions and at least eighteen in French.[12] Clearly, Las Casas was a consistent bestseller, beloved alike of printers and propagandists in the century or so leading into full flowering of the Enlightenment. Between about 1600 and 1800 Las Casas became, without significant critical analysis, firmly ensconced as the most popular authority on the nature of Spanish action in America. A few examples will show not only the propagandistic use of Las Casas but also his increasing stature as the authentic source for the writings of reputable and very influential historians and sundry literary lions of the age.

The tenacious hold of Las Casas on the European mind is more clearly seen in some of the notable historical works of the eighteenth century that treated the Spain-in-America theme. Such a work was the fourteen-volume *General History of America after its Discovery* . . . , by Antoine Touron, published in Paris between 1768 and 1770. The fact that Touron was a Catholic churchman seemed to lend an air of authenticity to his treatment of a theme so largely concerned with the spread of his church; but his sources were few, and his main inspiration proceeded from Las Casas. Touron mentions Las Casas frequently and in laudatory terms, and in places he even uses Las Casas' vocabulary and phraseology. His thesis, similar to that of Las Casas, affirms that the principal obstacles to proper Christianization of the American Indian were to be found in the cruelty and disorder of the conquistadores. Significantly, Touron was not the only cleric of the eighteenth century and later who aggressively pushed the themes of Las Casas. Ecclesiastical authors, notably French and Italian, using Las Casas and his zeal, have contributed enormously to the distorted view that the good missionaries were the only upholders of humanitarianism during Spanish Conquest and rule. This is a distortion, stemming directly from Las Casas, which calls for more critical evaluation than it has yet received.[13]

Let us point to another extremely influential work of the latter eighteenth century—Marmontel's *Les Incas ou la destruction de l'Empire du Pérou,* which appeared in 1777 and went through a number of subsequent editions. It became well known to the leaders of Spanish American independence. Marmontel made no secret of the fact that his main source was Las Casas, and he painted a picture of innocent natives and ruthless conquerors strictly in the vein of his source. But he adds to it his own eighteenth-century philosophical reasoning: that religious fanaticism was the cause of the evils of Spanish Conquest and governance in America.[14]

The Las Casas influence continued strong in England. The 1656 edition of the *Brief Relation,* entitled *The Tears of the Indians* . . . , immediately preceded and provided the basic source for William Davenant's famous drama, *The Cruelty of the Spaniards in Peru* (London, 1658). And the new edition of Las Casas coincided with the push of Puritanism into the Caribbean in the form of Cromwell's "Western Design." Though this English attack on the Spanish Empire enjoyed but a relatively small success (mainly, the acquisition of Jamaica), it can be viewed as a strong reflection of a kind of Lascasian-Gage-Puritan build-up of English moralistic force, used to bolster the imperial-commercial objectives against Spain. Davenant's *Cruelty of the Spaniards,* which enjoyed much popularity along with the 1656 edition of Las Casas, is an early forerunner of the type of propaganda that stimulated the moralistic urges to defeat "cruel" Spain in our war of 1898—which included, as we shall see, a timely propaganda edition of Las Casas in New York.[15]

The 1656 English edition of the *Brief Relation* is an excellent, quite typical, example of the use of Las Casas for propaganda against Spain. It is dedicated to His Highness, Oliver, Lord Protector, laying:

> prostrate before the throne of Your Justice, above Twenty Millions of the Souls of the Slaughter'd Indians . . . the cry of [their] blood ceasing at the noise of Your great transactions, while You arm for their Revenge. . . . There is no man, who opposes not himself against Heaven, but doth extol Your just Anger against the Bloudy and Popish Nation of the Spaniards, whose Superstitions have exceeded those of *Canaan,* and whose Abominations have excell'd those of *Abab,* who spilt the Blood of innocent *Naboth,* to obtain his Vineyard. And now, may it please your Highness, God having given you a full Victory over Your Enemies in this land, and a fix'd Establishment, by the prosperous and total quelling of those pertinacious Spirits; certainly there is no true English-man who doth not lift up his eyes to heaven with Thanks to Almighty God, that you have made the Land so happie, as to be the Admiration of other Nations, who have laid themselves at your feet for Alliances, as knowing your wonderful Successes both by Sea and Land. Pardon me, Great Sir, if next my zeal to Heaven, the loud Cry of so many bloudy Massacres, far surpassing the Popish cruelties in *Ireland,* the Honour of my Country, of which you are as tender as of the Apple of your own eye, hath induced me, out of a constant Affection to your Highness Service, to publish this Relation of the *Spanish Cruelties;* whereby all good men may see and applaud the Justness of Your Proceedings. . . .

The title of this edition similarly reveals its intent: *The Tears of the Indians: Being an Historical and true Account of the Cruel Massacres and Slaughters of above Twenty Millions of innocent People; Committed by the Spaniards in the Islands of Hispaniola, Cuba, Jamaica, &c. As also, in the Continent of Mexico, Peru, & other Places of the West-Indies, To the total destruction of those Countries.* Written in Spanish by *Casaus,* an Eye-witness of those things, And made English by J. P. London, 1656.

This propagandistic use of Las Casas is worth attention as a kind of forerunner of the "paper" warfare used by England and ourselves in later times. England used it, for example, against Napoleon and against the "Hun" of World War I. It is similar to our own propaganda against Spain in the 1890s. The above introduction to Las Casas leads the reader to think that Las Casas is describing a total edifice of Spanish rule in America and that the cruelties of the conquest period are totally characteristic of Spaniards and all their overseas enterprises (and even their iniquities in Europe). This is, as I have said, the fundamental fallacy of the Black Legend as it pertains to Spain in America.

Our ancestors established themselves in America during the seventeenth century, and this colonization process was nourished by their hatred of Spain and their desire to break the Spanish New World monopoly. The 1656 and other editions of Las Casas were soon found in abundance in the libraries of our founding fathers and became part of their mythology (demonology?). The English view of Spain as the traditional enemy, and the uncritical acceptance of Las Casas, became basic parts of our colonial heritage.[16]

Continuity of Jewish-Spanish Conflict

Before pursuing the Black Legend further into the years of Reason and Enlightenment, a few words must be said about the continuing thread of Jewish antagonisms and action against Spain.

Seventeenth-century Spanish Inquisition activity in ferreting out crypto-Jews is the last important phase of this purging process. Continual residence of the Jew in Spain and Spanish America meant corresponding protraction of his inquisitorial difficulties. Accordingly, Jews in some numbers continued to seek refuge elsewhere, and they carried with them bitter memories. This accounts for the increasing strength in influence and numbers of the Sephardic community in Amsterdam and, to some extent, elsewhere in Holland. It also accounts for the successful reentry of Jews into England, not officially sanctioned, but tacitly recognized and condoned.[17]

Concomitantly, Jewish action against Spain was intensified. Amsterdam, their strongest center in northern Europe, was not only a satisfactory place for the *Marranos* to invest capital and manage far-flung commercial networks (which included strong relationships with coreligionists remaining in Spanish and Portuguese territories),[18] but it also became a lively Jewish cultural center. It revolved around a general increase of interest in Hebrew studies, the very large number of Jewish printers operating in Holland during that century, and a significant flourishing of Jewish-Iberian literature.

The Sephardic Jews went to Amsterdam "because Amsterdam was

the enemy of Spain and because its star was in the ascendant." The Dutch city was reaching into the Americas and the Far East, and the republic being created in Holland in the early seventeenth century "was frankly and openly after gold, considered the main assurance of economic security for a nation." ". . . The most highly respected merchants reaped their profits by promoting what was nothing less than piracy, permitted and encouraged by the government." [19] This description, incidentally, was written by a Jew, apparently to explain the sharp practices of his own people within this Dutch atmosphere. It is a description that also fits the England of Elizabeth I and later. (Spaniards, too, had some interest in gold; but this was more sordid, as everyone knows.)

The Jew in Amsterdam, in addition to engaging profitably in commerce (spices, precious stones, tobacco, sugar) and virtually monopolizing the trade in some colonial products of Spain and Portugal, found himself in a congenial spot for writing and publishing works against Spain and the Catholic Church—and also against some of the prevailing forms of Protestantism. So much was this true that in midcentury the Amsterdam government felt obliged to issue an edict "forbidding Jews to publish pamphlets against Protestants and Catholics. It appears, however, that the edict went unheeded." [20] Printing was one of the activities most heavily engaged in by Jews in Holland and, when one reflects that Holland then, "probably produced more books than . . . all the other European countries put together" [21] (including, you will recall, a great amount of literature concerning the New World and by far the largest number of reissues of Las Casas), and was a most active center of the publication of Protestant works and of those expressing general enmity toward Spain, it is easy to imagine the enthusiasm with which the Spanish-Portuguese *Marranos* entered into the process of publishing anti-Spanish writings.

The Jewish historian, Newman, provides us with an interesting example of this printing-press base in the Low Countries.

No more striking proof of the contributions of Marranos to the progress of religious reform within the bosom of Christianity can be found than the fact that Marranos in Holland from their headquarters in Antwerp disseminated the Anti-Papist writings of Luther in Spain in order to weaken the hold of the Church on the religious life of the nation which a few decades before had exiled its loyal [sic] Jews.

On another occasion, this author puts it a bit stronger:

. . . the Marranos of Amsterdam sought to disseminate Luther's writings in Spain with a view to break the sway of the Catholicism which had brought them so much suffering.[22]

And Davies, in his *Elseviers,* rounds out the picture:

> Spanish and Portuguese Jews offer a striking illustration of how exiles pro-
> moted [the book] trade. In the seventeenth century and until 1732 there
> were three hundred and eighteen Jewish printers in Amsterdam, almost all
> of whom were of families exiled from Spain and Portugal. Of these, the best
> known are the Rabbi printers Menasseh ben Israel and Joseph Athias, but
> many others conducted business on a large scale, and Amsterdam became
> the European center for Hebrew printing.[23]

The seventeenth century in both England and Holland saw extensive
utilization of Jewish intelligence facilities and individuals in launching
damaging blows against Spain in particular and against Portugal while
under Spanish rule. The Sephardic Jew was, of course, animated by a
deep spirit of revenge; and he continued to have secret and effective
contact with friends and relatives in Spanish-Portuguese possessions
and in the lands of Moslem antagonism toward Spain. These intelligence
resources were put to the use of England and Holland (probably also,
at times, of France), and certainly to Moslem advantage. There were
close relations between the Sephardic communities of Constantinople,
Salonika, and Dutch Jewry and between the Jews of Amsterdam and
those of Morocco. The Jewish Dutch-Moroccan tie-up helped supply
Morocco with munitions to be used against Spain, and a Jewish Moroccan Ambassador to Holland, Joseph Palache, was at one time admiral
of a Moroccan pirate fleet "directed against Spain." [24]

An extension of this intelligence work was the close relationship
between Dutch Sephardic Jews and the establishment of their people in
England at midcentury, near the eve of the Cromwellian push against
Spain's West Indies. Cromwell effectively utilized, as had Elizabethan
England's Cecil before him, the services of Jewish spies; they knew
the languages and had the secret contacts so valuable in making attacks
effective. The Sephardic Jew was quite willing to ingratiate himself with
the English in this way, for it facilitated settlement of his people in
England and constituted some revenge for what his people had suffered
in Iberia.[25]

Before the end of the seventeenth century Jewish action against Spain
had crystallized along three main lines: (1) large and highly influential
activity in printing and publishing, with strong anti-Spanish characteristics; (2) personal action in trade and in intelligence to help Spain's
enemies in war and diplomacy; and (3) active belief in and promotion
of the blending of anti-Rome with anti-Spain, to make the two channels
of thought and action virtually synonymous. This last was not a Jewish
monopoly, by any means, but the Sephardic Jew had particularly good

foundations for it, and the merging of the hatred of Papists and Spaniards in the Dutch-English atmosphere was highly congenial to the Jew.

The Legend Becomes Enlightenment

As already indicated, the Black Legend might have faded away had it not been that Spain continued as a great and envied empire and had not the Enlightenment carried the older hispanophobia into the new intellectual fashions.

Unfortunately, the exhilaration engendered by such discoveries as man's perfectibility, superiority of nature's laws over tradition, and the infallibility of Reason, called into being a less admirable aspect of human nature, that of intellectual arrogance. The sages of the century, the celebrated wits, quickly perceived that even a Golden Age Spain and, more obviously, a Catholic Spain in decline, could not possibly fit into the new ways of thought, and they wasted no tolerance or compassion on the wrong side of the Pyrenees. Spanish aspirations—political, economic, social, or religious—seemed such an "unreasonable" mixture of benighted earthiness and mystic idealism that they could not possibly be in step with the new age. (Of course, the common man in England, France, Germany, Italy, and the Americas hardly fitted the new order either, but his intellectual leaders flattered him into thinking that he did, and certainly in comparison to backward Spain.)

Spain had reached the summit long before the new Reason made its appearance, and she could not maintain the heights forever. The rising power of the politico-philosophical agents of the new and refurbished ideas came from nations that had supplanted Spain as a continental leader, and condescension, or worse, was the characteristic pose in commenting upon a seemingly enfeebled, decadent Spain.

If Spain did not usually retaliate and defend her aims with the printed word, it was because she was far too busy managing her own empire, or she did not realize the seriousness of the case being built against her, or she simply believed that her causes were good enough to stand on their own merits. If it took our own country much too long, in a world of faster-paced propaganda, to face up to its need for press and public information agencies to effectively explain and defend our own goals and traditions, it seems difficult to blame Spain for a similar failure in an age when propagandistic resources were still in their relative infancy.

To the wits of the eighteenth-century Enlightenment—"apostles of tolerance and reason"—declining Spain was living proof of the errors of a bygone age. Spain in the eighteenth century held firmly to her religious tenets and even maintained loyalty to her kings, and these were viewed as indisputable signs of decadence. It is a bit like the Victorian stuffiness which we scoff at today, or the unenlightened white Southerner who has for so long been the butt of Yankee wits in our country. The avant-garde always knows best and, while preening their own wit, they revel in impressing the sheep who follow their intellectual fashions. In addition, there are always Encyclopedists to alphabetize the dogmas.

To be most effective, such wit needs a big target that all can see, a target whose obvious evils can serve, like the De Bry engravings, to harden doctrinaire articles of faith that are easily understandable to the slower-thinking clods being cued in. And the enlightened Europe that looked at target Spain in the eighteenth century was led by a new order, managed by opinion-makers riding high in the lands of Spain's bitterest enemies.

As might be expected, Las Casas and his *Brief Relation* continued to serve as source for all those writers who, not wishing to seek out the heart of the matter of Spanish historical action by means of such tedious work as documentary research or by logic because it might confound preconceived notions or disturb propaganda aims, yet wanted to aim barbs at Spain and her Catholicism. If Las Casas was not used directly, then works which had been based on him were always ready at hand. Additional German, French, and English editions of the *Brief Relation* saw the light of day. More importantly, the harsh words of Las Casas were already so well engraved in the memories and historiography of Europe that there was hardly need for more editions.

In other contexts, too, the Black Legend of Spain's past and present had bases for strong revival in the eighteenth century. For one, France and England were increasingly anxious to expand their empires in the New World and thus wrest from Spain the riches of her overseas possessions. For another, the old juxtaposition of cruel Spanish conquistador and innocent Indian savage had an enormous fascination for the new *philosophes*. The picture painted by Las Casas was used to invigorate the supposedly new portrait of the noble savage, the undefiled man in a state of nature who became the darling of Rousseau and Chateaubriand and a host of others. To make the picture fully credible, it was essential to preserve Las Casas' thoroughly evil white men bent on the ruthless destruction of innocent aborigines.

The scoffing at Christianity and religion in general—a vigorous anticlerical and often agnostic or atheistic tendency of the times—utilized the Spanish Conquest and rule in America, and also inquisitorial Spain, to show the destructiveness and oppression of hierarchical religion at its supposedly worst, most intolerant form, that of Catholic Spain and Spanish America. It did not seem to matter that French writers often had to publish their works outside France because of the dangers in their own country, while some of them circulated quite freely in Spanish dominions. "Nearly all the great works by which French eighteenth-century creative literature is remembered had to be printed either outside France or under a feigned imprint." [26] While Raynal's *Histoire des Indes* was prohibited in France, it was being widely read in Spanish America and became "the gospel of the emancipators and liberators of America." [27]

The declining strength of the Spanish Empire, more an article of faith than an actual fact—for its American portion was now larger than ever, and its government was active in promoting political, economic, educational, and ecclesiastical reforms much in keeping with the Enlightenment—was used as a warning to others of the disastrous effects of Church-State intimacy and consequent obscurantism and oppressiveness. Such homiletic exploitation of poor old Spain is still around: "Sometimes [Norman Cousins' trails] lead only into murky corners, such as last month's warning [January, 1961] to U.S. space-program planners of the dangers of pushing into the unknown. Spain and Portugal tried exploring the unknown five and a half centuries ago, recalled the *Saturday Review* direly, and look where they've ended up." [28]

A few examples of this eighteenth-century intellectual sneering at Spain will show how slavishly it followed the now traditional Las Casas and the standard distortions of the Inquisition, Philip II, and the Don Carlos story, and the libels of Orange and Antonio Peréz. Thus, the great Voltaire, in his *Essai sur les moeurs et l'esprit des nations,* writes of the "reflexive cruelties" of the Spanish conquerors and their general excess of cruelties, without any attempt to establish comparative criteria or deduce logically, as such a great mind should have done, that humankind (even Spaniards) never consists of peoples or classes who are entirely cruel or of whole peoples who are all out of step with their own times. When Voltaire stigmatizes Philip II as authorizing the extermination of the American Indian, and then goes on to comment that "never has there been issued an order so cruel, nor one more faithfully executed," he is writing malicious nonsense and even outdoes Las Casas in substituting fiction for fact.[29] And when Montesquieu, always anti-Spanish, writes that Spain, "to preserve America . . . did what even despotic power itself does not attempt: destroyed the inhabitants," [30] he, too, is penning arrant falsehood that bears no resemblance to the authentic story of Spanish occupation and rule in America.

Montesquieu does not stop at this; he grandly synthesizes Spain in Mexico, in these terms:

What good might not the Spaniards have done to the Mexicans? They had a mild religion to impart to them; but they filled their heads with a frantic superstition. They might have set slaves at liberty; they made freemen slaves. They might have undeceived them with regard to the abuse of human sacrifices; instead of that they destroyed them. Never should I have finished, were I to recount all the good they might have done, and all the mischief they committed.[31]

Montesquieu, as Juderías points out, knew nothing of Spanish actions in America except what came from Las Casas and his followers. For all his greatness in other directions, Montesquieu was here writing on a subject about which he knew nothing. But his opinions, like those of Voltaire and many others, counted for much—traveling the world "without passport" simply because he was a great name in the intellectual circles of his times and later. (This seems rather like some of our famous professors who, without any significant knowledge of Spanish or Cuban history, obstinately and with great air of authority, know the answers to why men such as Franco or Fidel Castro acted as they did; just as they also carry at the tips of their tongues definitive judgments on the Spanish Inquisition and Philip II, with no real knowledge of either. Scholars deeply concerned with things Hispanic often have doubts; but twentieth-century imitators of Voltaire and Montesquieu have no doubts at all.)

But it was a man of lesser fame who made the Las Casas version of Spain and Spaniards a bestseller of the latter part of the eighteenth century. The ex-abbé Guillaume Raynal, with his famous *Philosophical and Political History of the Colonization and Commerce of Europeans in the Indies,* repeated all the standard calumnies against Spain in America. He directed his philosophical fury against the Catholic Church, the Inquisition, the conquistadores, and everything else that did not accord with the benevolence and tolerance that he preached but did not seem to practice. Raynal, in his story of New World colonization, showed himself a typical freethinker of his time, and this accounted, of course, for much of his popularity, plus the fact that his view of Spain and Spaniards perfectly fitted the prejudices already popularized. Raynal's work was publicly burned by the executioner in Paris in 1781 —a rather lively version of Bostonian censorship, with about the same results—but it circulated in supposedly obscurantist Spanish America, and it was popular with the founding fathers of our own republic. It was rehashed Las Casas, with an Enlightenment twist, and it had many addicts and emulators.[32]

Since Europe's eighteenth-century intellectual leaders were so characteristically hispanophobic, it is not strange to find that belletristic literature, from this time until the period of nineteenth-century Romanticism and beyond, followed the same pattern. The Gothic-Romantic versions of inquisitorial Spain constitute one of the most shameful chapters in perpetuation of the Black Legend. Since they were horror tales designed to reach wide audiences of a type that had already soaked up a century or two of the wildest misinformation on the subjects of Catholicism and Spain, they contributed immensely to a fixing of lurid and lugubrious prejudices in the popular mind. It is not too large a step from these tales of Inquisition and gloomy, secretive monks, with "no idea of accuracy, and shocking blunders . . . over the simplest details," [33] to hushed whispers about secret preparations in Catholic churches for the great takeover, when Al Smith would become president of the United States; and horrifying pictures of Inquisition tortures were paraded in New York to thwart the Smith candidacy.

Unfortunately, Gothic-Romantic exaggerations in popular literature had roots in seemingly historical materials. Thus the *History of the Conspiracy of the Spaniards against the Republic of Venice in the year MDCXVIII,* translated from French to English in 1675 (under title of *A Conspiracie of the Spaniards against the State of Venice*), and its second edition in 1679, became in England "deservedly famous and popular" as the base of Otway's "tragic masterpiece," *Venice Preserv'd: Or, A Plot Discover'd.* This play was originally produced at Duke's Theater, Dorset Garden, on February 9, 1682, and "kept the stage" until 1845, with revivals in 1876, 1904, and 1920.[34] Along the lines of this popular, fantastic tale, the English reading public (as also the French, German, and Dutch) during some two centuries was repeatedly thrilled and delightedly shocked by the wildest exposés of the sinister goings-on in the gloomy settings of Catholic monasteries and nunneries, with Spaniards as the actors in much of this villainy. The famous ambassador to London, Gondomar, becomes a "desperate and murderous villain" in the Gothic novels; and "the Holy Office often assumes terrific features in these romances." [35]

While it may be true that there was no militant Protestantism in all this, some Protestant clergy did take a hand. Thus, "Maturin (the Reverend Charles Robert, of French Protestant stock and bitterly anti-Catholic), in *Melmoth the Wanderer,* 1820, has some extremely detailed and lurid descriptions of what he conceived monastic life in Spain to be, and in his last romance *The Albigenses*, 1824, he writes with the most deep-rooted prejudice and an entire disrespect for history." And a William Henry Ireland, a lesser name than Maturin, "indulges in grossest caricature. . . . In *Gondez the Monk*, 1805, we have the wildest and most outrageous melodrama, as, for example, in the scene when the yelling spectre of the Little Red Woman, a damned witch, appears before the full tribunal of the Holy Office to ding the villain monk to perdition." And the same author's three-volume *Rimualdo, Or the Castle of Badajos*, "is a fine type of the extreme Terror Novel . . ." [36] Perhaps it was not "militant Protestantism," but it amounted to the same thing when it came to blackening Spain in general and Catholic Spain in particular.

Along the way, a couple of famous literary figures from the land of Enlightenment laudably enough risked trips to Spain to see for themselves. In the course of their Iberian tourism, both Alexandre Dumas and Théophile Gautier visited the Escorial, lair of the "Demon of the South," Philip II, and titillated their readers in similar vein.

Dumas: "The day dawned grey, overcast with cloud, and I was glad, for that seemed to me the right light in which to see the Escorial. . . . Approaching it, one realises the insignificance of Man in the face of its gigantic bulk. A great door yawns, then shuts, behind you, and though you are merely a casual visitor, if you are aware of what freedom means to you, you shudder as though you were fated never to leave this place. . . . No one would call it beautiful. It evokes not admiration, but terror. Even Philip himself must have shuddered when his architect handed him the thousand keys of this monument conjured up by his inflexible spirit. . . . The chapel is admirable; perhaps the only place in the whole edifice where one can breathe freely. Pray if you like, but the chapel will give no response, returning no more echo than would a dungeon of the Holy Inquisition." Concerning the foot-stools in Philip's room: "They are both folding stools . . . and on both the powerful heel that oppressed half of the world for forty years has left a mark that remains clearly visible and almost threatening." [37]

Gautier: "The first thing that struck me was the vast quantity of swallows and martins circling the air in countless numbers, and filling it with their shrill, strident cries. These poor little birds seemed scared by the deathly silence reigning in this Thebaid, and were making an effort to introduce a little noise and animation. . . . Twenty paces from the door, you scent an indefinable odor, icey and sickly, of holy water and sepulchral vaults, from which blows a draught laden with pleurisy and catarrh. . . . When we returned to Madrid there was a stir of pleased surprise among our friends, who were glad to see us still alive. Few people come back from the Escorial; they die of consumption in two or three days, or if by chance they are English, they blow their brains out. Luckily, we have strong constitutions. . . ." [38]

The popular fiction writer cannot, even now, resist the theme of Catholic Spanish villainy. Rafael Sabatini's *Torquemada and the Spanish Inquisition,* popular a generation ago and still used as a source by some writers, is but a few steps removed from the Gothic-Romantic tribe. And Samuel Shellabarger's horrifying version of the Inquisition, in the opening pages of his bestseller, *Captain from Castile* (and in the movie version) is not even a small step from Sabatini. The theme of Spanish-Catholic Inquisition villainies has exercised an irresistible fascination for writers of fiction from the seventeenth century until now, for it is ready-made melodrama of terror, appealing to wide audiences enjoying the sensational, especially when it fits preconceived notions.

The anti-Spanish prejudices, dogmatized in the eighteenth and early nineteenth centuries, heightened several curious ironies which, when realized, inject some poignancy into the total picture. The pummeling by the political, philosophical, and literary leaders of the day coincided precisely with the time when Spanish government and intellectuals were drawing up large plans for imperial reform on a scale and of a type commensurate with the ideals of the Enlightenment—and a scale hardly approached by imperial England, France, Holland, or Belgium even in later times. But Spain, even in this, could not win. One of her secret investigations, designed to provide bases for reform, was exposed and used by her enemies to confirm the standard picture of total evil in the Spanish system.[39] An approximate equivalent would be the global spread of information in our Congressional investigations on organized crime, for example, in order to stigmatize the whole of our national life.

Ironically also, many Spaniards, always supremely critical of their own institutions, in the Lascasian vein, were, under the influences of foreign criticism, beginning to accept almost uncritically foreign attitudes about their own country. This was to be intensified during the nineteenth and twentieth centuries, and it led to some strong reactions against the Black Legend. Spanish imitation of France, partly due to the intrusion of the French-Bourbon dynasty, partly due to widespread European acceptance of the leadership of French culture, and partly due simply to a very characteristic Spanish readiness to praise the foreign and belittle their own, marked a kind of inferiority complex of the type that sometimes moves with popular currents.[40] It could be likened, perhaps, to the general American (Latin and Anglo) cultural inferiority complex which so handicapped appreciation of the American scene in the nineteenth and early twentieth centuries, because it was always under the shadow of European—especially French—superiority and leadership. The flocking of Latin- and Anglo-American expatriates to Paris up to recent times has been one concrete expression of this. And some present American intellectual readiness to accept, often uncritically, European belittlement of our own ways and institutions, somewhat parallels the earlier Spanish case.

Spanish management of her vast empire toward the close of the eighteenth century assuredly left much to be desired, and there was, of course, much in the Spanish way of life that would be even more incompatible with our twentieth-century thought than it was with the Enlightenment. But if this could be said of Spain, it could also be said of France, to judge by the causes of and the bloody course of the French Revolution. And, of a certainty, some of our most respected patriots had some nasty things to say about the England of those times. It took Napoleon, we must not forget, to pick up the pieces of the savage Revolution and to mobilize the physical and patriotic power of France, just as it took a stern military leader rather than witty intellectuals to stave off the disaster that faced France just a few years ago. Also, it required two wars with us and much rebelliousness and dissatisfaction in Canada and elsewhere in the empire before England learned some of the fundamentals of benign imperial government. Prejudiced disparagement of Hispanic institutions past and present, especially in the atmosphere of today's "decline of the West," has a hollow ring when it comes from Frenchmen, Englishmen, Dutchmen, Germans and Americans.

With the Spanish-American revolt against Spain, occurring mainly between 1810 and 1825, came a new wave of anti-Spanish propaganda, revival of Las Casas in bright new Enlightenment dress, and formulation of certain Latin- and Anglo-American dogmas, which lived on to shape Western world views of Spain, Spaniards, and Spanish America. Many of the clichés of our own times, forever repeated as we go through spasms of fumbling which we call Latin American policy, were coined in a witch's brew of cumulative Black Legend and Spanish American propagandas and prejudices relating to that area's struggle for independence.

Chapter 6

OF MATRICIDE AND AMERICAN DOGMAS

> *El progreso consiste en desespañoli-*
> *zarse.*
>
> FRANCISCO BILBAO,
> in *Evangelio Americano* [1]

Spanish America Adopts the Legend

The wars for Spanish American independence are still described in classrooms and popular literature, here and in Latin America, in terms of heroes-and-villains. That this is so can be much attributed to the thoroughness with which the separatist causes exploited the anti-Spanish Legend. The patriot leaders, with great passion and more than a little hypocrisy, hurled Las Casas and the cruelty, tyranny, and obscurantist themes against Mother Spain. Then, with the winning of independence, Spanish America's leadership, intellectual and otherwise, sanctified the Black Legend to justify the achievement. In addition, many influential Spanish Americans, enthusiastically embracing a liberalism that made the terms "Evil" and the "Old Order" synonymous, made rejection of their Spanish heritage a basic tenet of the New Age. The doctrinaire and dogmatic opinions in this process, often applauded and abetted from abroad, remain to this day a fundamental American aberration in education, international relations, domestic politics, and social ideologies.

We in the United States can recall how long it took to bring some semblance of objectivity to the classroom and to popular juxtaposition of Patriots and Tories in the story of our own Revolution. And our struggle for independence, in its main military phase, lasted only about five years—much less in time and with less shedding of blood and verbiage than the Spanish American conflict. Even after a century, some of the antagonisms of our Civil War are still fairly lusty and give promise of continued existence, though we have often lulled ourselves into thinking that they were safely swept under the carpet. Thus, we should be able to understand the continuation of passion and unreason in Spanish American popular views of their own "civil war," for that was what their independence struggle amounted to. There were Spaniards, Spanish Americans, churchmen, and all shades of Indians and mixed bloods on both sides at any given moment or place. Simplistic interpretations are based on ignorance or the unhistorical opiate of national patriotism.

The Spanish American independence struggle, in addition to being longer and bloodier than ours, was cursed by the importation and exploitation of an essentially foreign brand of very anti-Spanish Black Legend, built up in the Western world over the previous two and a half centuries. At the time of the wars, the Legend, as we have seen, had received fresh impetus and respectability in the Enlightenment. To leaders of the Spanish American separatist movements, it did not matter that their use of Las Casas and the rest of the hispanophobic Legend was essentially matricidal, counter to the fundamentals of their cultural heritage and quite a nasty denigration of their own ancestry. It was a strong weapon, popularly approved in the Western world, and it was eagerly grasped and vigorously wielded to stimulate the rebel cause and then, afterwards, to crown its victories.

Even before the Spanish conquest in America had run its main course (by about mid-sixteenth century), antagonisms between American-born Spaniards (the so-called Creoles) and those of the Peninsula were noticeable. This tension of American versus European, largely rooted in Creole desire to manage exploitation of New World resources (including native labor) against royal legislation and officialdom's restrictions, was a continuing characteristic of succeeding centuries. (This had its parallels, incidentally, in the build-up of American planter and commercial aristocracy versus mother country controls in the story of our own colonial period, or in the Algerian *colon* mentality, or among Dutch Indonesians.) However, it must be emphasized that this tension was mainly evident among the minority of "white" Americans, and not by any means all-pervasive there. Even after the nineteenth century opened, there was no sign that the majority wished to remove the sovereignty of the Spanish crown. Like our own independence movement, rebellion was stimulated and led by small minorities, mainly within the Creole class.

Among the American Spaniards, something other than the longstanding Creole-Peninsular tension had taken root by 1800. Spanish governmental encouragement of reforms, educational and otherwise, plus relatively easy circulation of the new philosophies of the Enlighten-

ment, gave Creole and Peninsular intellectuals abundant access to the
Freemasonry, anticlericalism, and general skepticism of the newer ideas.
These new trends of thought included the doctrinaire view of Spain as
the "horrible example" of obscurantism and backwardness, and the
vigorously renewed Lascasian portrayal of Spanish cruelties during the
American conquest. With characteristic Hispanic enthusiasm, some of
the Creole intellectuals (Francisco de Miranda, Simón Bolívar, and
Mexico's Hidalgo are wellknown examples) embraced the strongly
French Enlightenment and, along with it, some of the Black Legend
view of Spanish iniquities. With grandiose disregard for historical facts,
this Creole leadership—and some Peninsulars, too—took up the
cudgels of the Black Legend to accuse Spain of unmitigated cruelty,
tyranny, and obscurantism in its conquest and rule of the Americas.
It was a vast hypocrisy, but it fitted popular intellectual currents and it
provided incipient leaders of rebellion with wonderfully effective propaganda arms against the mother country.

The literature of the Spanish American independence movements
abounds in denigration of Spain, with the ideas of Las Casas, Raynal,
Marmontel, Voltaire, Rousseau—the now classical Black Legend—setting the style. Memorials and manifestos, designed to stimulate a patriotic cause and dissatisfaction with Spanish rule, were strongly characterized by emphasis upon Spanish depravity. The hymns and other
poetic outbursts, propagandistic letters and pamphlets, and so forth,
were so passionately intemperate in blackening Spain that it is a wonder
that they were effective.[2] But it was a civil war, often intransigent on
both sides, with many bloody episodes, and a builder of hate as only a
civil war can be, compounded by Hispanic passion in language and deed.

In the process, like the sixteenth-century Las Casas they so often
quoted and lauded, patriotic leaders did great violence to history and
stained their own culture with the tar brush of the Black Legend. Even
though their best scholars clearly see, and try to undo, this damage,
it is a tragic irony that Spanish Americans, generally accustomed to
denigrating Spain in patterns propagated by the independence movement,
foster, thereby, not only foreign belittlement of their own culture but
also a kind of cultural rootlessness in artificially rejecting, with the
language of Cervantes, the land of Don Quijote and Sancho. This is very
notably the case in Mexico and some other countries where the cult
of Indianism exercises great educational and political influence.

Nor is this all. The decades after the achievement of independence
saw continuing vilification of Spain and Spaniards, kept alive, in part,
by some conflicts with Spain itself.[3] Through the nineteenth century
and even to the present the alliance of Black Legend distortions with

anticlericalism and even anti-Catholic aspects of doctrinaire liberalism popularized the harshest views of Catholic Spain. Freemasonry, for example, continues as an important purveyor of this kind of thought in Spanish America, an influence not always understood or appreciated in our own country, where Masonic views and activities are less passionately embraced and are of less political and intellectual influence.

Anti-Spanish prejudice became characteristic of liberalism in the bitter clash of forces over religious, political, and educational issues in nineteenth- and twentieth-century Spanish America. So-called "de-hispanization" became a popular creed and was considered the solution for sundry Spanish-American ills. Three centuries of Spanish rule became a favored whipping boy of those trying to remedy such ills.[4] (In recent times, United States imperialism is frequently accorded the scapegoat role.)

Closely allied to these developments was the vigorous growth, in the latter nineteenth century and continuing with even greater force into our own times, of what is commonly termed *"indigenismo,"* or "Indianism." Briefly defined, this is a cult of emphasis on Indian America over the Spanish heritage, naturally in much and often bitter disparagement of the latter. This way of thought has its roots, of course, in Las Casas' juxtaposition of the noble savage against the ruthlessly destructive Spaniard. As this became increasingly a dogma of the Enlightenment and the liberalism which followed, there evolved strong tendencies to view the Spanish invasion of America as something completely and purposefully destructive of Indian cultures which are sometimes described by enthusiasts as something quite superior to what the benighted white conqueror had to offer. In milder form, this Indianism often decries the eternal injustice of the conquest by Catholic Christianity, exemplified by depraved Spaniards. Thus in today's Mexico, Aztec leaders are national heroes and Cortés is the classical villain. Diego Rivera's muralistic contortions—Las Casas *cum* Karl Marx—are simply one of the more famous expressions of this; it runs all through the educational system and the national consciousness, with the exception of intellectual leaders whose scholarly integrity quite properly rejects such distortions.

The absurdities of this Indianism were given much public airing in Mexico's recent "Battle of the Bones." The remains of Conqueror Cortés were rediscovered in 1946, and this set in motion a determined effort to locate the bones of the last leader of Aztec resistance, Cuauhté-moc. The latter just had to be found; and they were, in a demonstrably fraudulent performance by some of Mexico's most famous Cortéshaters. It was a pitifully comic bit of hanky-panky in historical perspectives, duly reported in our country.[5]

Hispanophobic Continuity in the United States

> *Remember the Maine, to Hell with Spain!*
>
> SPANISH-AMERICAN WAR
> SLOGAN, 1898

Spanish American aspects of black-legendism, especially when allied with the story of the achievement of independence and subsequent Latin American liberalism, exercised some influence on our own thinking with regard to matters Hispanic. Along with this, we popularized among ourselves, in the nineteenth century, a significant amount of writing of the Black Legend variety.

In introducing this theme, it must be recalled that Spain had been one of our long-standing frontier enemies; Anglo-American expansion in North America had come into sharp conflict with Spanish territorial interests, notably in the Old Southwest, the Floridas, then along the Mississippi frontier, including tension over use of Spanish New Orleans as an outlet for our western commerce. And along with all this flowed that tradition of anti-Spain and Nordic superiority, which came from our European ancestry.

From the late eighteenth century into the twentieth our political and intellectual trends have generally derived from prevailing liberal ideas imported from Europe, as was generally the case in Latin America. In addition, we had started a strong revolutionary current of our own, highly subversive of monarchical legitimacy, very much a child of the Enlightenment, and with a brand of republican government that by the time of the Latin American revolutions had resulted in our developing a nationalistic and rather bumptious pride. Thus, when we took some cognizance of the separatist conflict to the south of us, we were predisposed to favor the American as against the European side. Our hemisphere cohabitants seemed to be throwing off the yoke of monarchy, as we had done. Many were also, we were convinced, trying to free themselves from a uniquely obnoxious tyranny, that of Spaniards. And, as Spanish American areas achieved freedom from that yoke and appeared more and more republican in their goals, our sympathies became increasingly one-sided. Given all the circumstances, this was natural enough. But a principal result was, of course, deeper entrenchment of anti-Spanish sentiment, even though we had little enough knowledge of actual events and conditions in Spanish America.

An even more unfortunate effect has been that the Spanish American independence movement has remained much more a heroes-and-villains affair in our literature and in our classrooms than a careful recogniton of the complexities of the process. We usually accept the patriotic Spanish American viewpoints uncritically. The thesis that the Spanish American patriots destroyed more than they constructed when they rejected Spain and tried to dehispanize their new nations can be well defended—but it would be almost worth one's life to try it in Spanish America, and our own literature reflects this. Serene histories of those revolutions, done with the utmost scholarly objectivity and human understanding, still seem a long way off, as is so true of many other aspects of Latin American and Spanish history.

In the intellectual modes that crystallized in the United States during the nineteenth century and often have extended to the present, there are several main lines in which popularization of hispanophobic biases is clearly seen. Some of our frontier clashes were still, irritatingly, with the Spanish (or Mexicans), and in the Texan-Mexican struggle and then in our war with Mexico, we transferred some of our ingrained antipathy toward Catholic Spain to her American heirs. And Spain continued ruling and fighting rebellions in nearby Cuba, leading to disagreeable incidents that kept alive the ancient antagonisms. This abrasive proximity to persons of Spanish speech, especially a darker-hued Mexican (remember those long-ago German disparagements of the smaller, darker men of Iberia?), encouraged our faith in Nordic superiority. It was a small step, really, from "Remember the Armada" to "Remember the Alamo." Highly intemperate utterances in the United States Congress and elsewhere contained abusive references to Latin America's Spanish past and advocated our takeover of those lands, at least as far as Panama and sometimes beyond.[6] And, as we shall see, at century's end a heady mixture of Darwinism, war with Spain, and faith in a kind of Nordic "manifest destiny" heightened superior race concepts in the Anglo-American mind.

Meanwhile, our influential nineteenth-century travel and historical literature confirmed the acceptance and spread most of the stereotyped portrayal of Spain and Spaniards. An increasing literature of travel through the century, although occasionally brightened by able, perceptive, and relatively sympathetic approaches to the Spanish scene and history, generally continued to portray the inquisitorial, gloomy Spain of ineptitude, bigotry, cruelty, and obscurantism. This literature has been arrayed and commented on by Stanley T. Williams, in his *The Spanish Background of American Literature* (2 vols. Yale University Press, 1955), and there is no need to review it here. Probably more important as basic influences upon our educational distortions in treating Spain and her history, were the romantic and tremendously popular United States historians—Francis Parkman, George Bancroft, William H. Prescott, John Lothrop Motley—for they fashioned, upon earlier foundations, the concepts of Spain that remain with us today. The four historians I have mentioned are simply the best known and most influential; they "dominated American historical writing for fifty years," [7] and they were guides for a number of lesser lights and a host of textbook authors.

All four of those famous historians were literary men of Romantic beliefs, much to be admired for diligence in utilizing source materials, and particularly laudable in bringing to the writing of history a literary quality that it too often lacks. However, when all this is acknowledged, it must also be remembered that these men thought and wrote as Protestant, Nordic preachers, and certainly did so whenever they juxtaposed Catholic-Protestant, Spanish-English, Spanish-Dutch, or Teutonic-Latin concepts and historical actions. This is even true of Prescott, whose main efforts were in Spanish and Spanish American history. They were all anti-Catholic; they were thoroughly imbued with an uncritical concept of Nordic superiority over the Latin; and they were, in some ways, "antisophistication" or even "antiintellectual." [8] In their moralistic naïveté, in which they emphasized the heart rather than the head, they painted awesome, literarily thrilling pictures of heroes (Nordic) and villains (Latins, especially Spaniards), and in the hypocritical patterns of Black Legend writing, they abundantly contradicted themselves in order to make their conclusions (anti-Spanish, anti-Catholic) fit their preconceived, progressive, and materialistic view of a world clearly destined for domination by the obviously superior Teutonic type.

From Motley, author of the classic *Rise of the Dutch Republic,* we get a clear picture of the deepest-dyed villainy of Philip II as contrasted with the "spotless marble" character of the Protestant heroes, especially William of Orange. To Motley, the Dutch rebellion "was nothing but an illustration of the eternal struggle between right and wrong. To him Catholicism and Absolutism were Powers of Darkness, while Protestantism was one with Liberty, Democracy, and Light. The contest between the Netherlands and Spain is to him a contest between the principles of good and evil, in which he feels compelled by the most sacred obli-

gations of morality to join, and of course to join on the right side." [9]
Motley, among his other aberrations, was completely wrong in his nu-
merical lineup of Catholics and Protestants in the Low Countries. He
could find excuses for the devious statesmanship of William, but not for
Philip; he could ridicule Spanish motives of religion and material gain,
but laud the combination of the two in the Dutch or English. In short,
he favored his heroes and damned his villains with a passion and lack
of sophistication that appealed, on a grand scale, to an uncritical audience already steeped, through previous generations, in similar prejudice.[10] No longer ago than my schooldays in the 1920s, Motley was
standard reading; I seem to recall a version called *The Boy's Motley,*
from which I (and perhaps you) imbibed some first perspectives on
Nordic heroes and Spanish villains.

Francis Parkman was unreservedly anti-Catholic and anti-Spanish;
this shows up in his writing on European travel and, worse luck, in his
famous histories. A Parkman could find praise for the "fruitful energy
and manliness" of the intolerant Puritan, but invariably, in his treatment of Catholics, he felt called upon to question the bases of their
piety. His Spanish priests and nuns rival those of the Gothic-Romantic
novelists. In his *Pioneers of France in the New World,* for example,
Parkman makes it obvious that he bases his account of the French-
Spanish clash in Florida far more on French sources than on Spanish,
and it reads like a Hollywood lineup of virtue and villainy. Virtuous
Huguenots versus Spanish devils! And, like his colleagues in romantic
historiography, Parkman gratuitously insults Spain, common sense, and
historical accuracy, with such phrases as these:

> In the middle of the sixteenth century. Spain was . . . a tyranny of
> monks and inquisitors, with their swarms of spies and informers, their
> racks, their dungeons and their fagots [crushing] all freedom of thought
> and speech; and, while the Dominican held his reign of terror and force,
> the deeper Jesuit guided the mind from infancy into those narrow depths
> of bigotry from which it was never to escape. . . . Mistress of the Indies,
> Spain swarmed with beggars. Yet, verging to decay, she had an ominous
> and appalling strength. . . . The mysterious King [Philip II], in his den
> in the Escorial, dreary and silent, and bent like a scribe over his papers,
> was the type and the champion of arbitrary power. More than the Pope
> himself, he was the head of Catholicity. In doctrine and in deed, the inex-
> orable bigotry of Madrid was ever in advance of Rome.
>
> Not so with France. She was full of life,—a discordant and struggling
> vitality. Her monks and priests, unlike those of Spain, were rarely either
> fanatics or bigots; yet not the less did they ply the rack and the fagot, and
> howl for heretic blood. Their all was at stake: their vast power, their
> bloated wealth, were wrapped up in the ancient faith. Men were burned,

and women buried alive. All was in vain. To the utmost bounds of France, the leaven of the Reform was working.

The monk, the inquisitor, and the Jesuit were lords of Spain,—sovereigns of her sovereign, for they had formed the dark and narrow mind of that tyrannical recluse. They had formed the minds of her people, quenched in blood every spark of rising heresy, and given over a noble nation to a bigotry blind and inexorable as the doom of fate. Linked with pride, ambition, avarice, every passion of a rich, strong nature, potent for good and ill, it made the Spaniard of that day a scourge as dire as ever fell on man. . . . Spain was the citadel of darkness,—a monastic cell, an inquisitorial dungeon, where no ray could pierce. . . . On the shores of Florida, the Spaniard and the Frenchman, the bigot and the Huguenot, met in the grapple of death. . . . A darker spirit urged the new crusade (the Menéndez de Avilés expedition to oust the French from Florida),—born not of hope, but of fear, slavish in its nature, the creature and the tool of despotism; for the typical Spaniard of the sixteenth century was not in strictness a fanatic, he was bigotry incarnate.[11]

These excerpts from Francis Parkman—famous in American historiography and one whose works are classic to this day—can be paralleled in Motley, Bancroft, and even, to some extent, in Prescott; to say nothing of John Fiske and many other writers of history books for use in our elementary and high schools, and even at times, in our colleges and universities. It will be obvious to any reader pretending to an educated mind, that this was not history that Parkman and the others wrote when they touched on Spain; it was simply anti-Spanish prejudice —melodramatic fiction in the Gothic-Romantic manner, making the reader shiver with the thrilling confrontation of Good and Evil and, of course, the triumph of the former. But, I repeat, *it is not history*.

Even a casual reading of these excerpts from Parkman shows clearly the contradictions. When writing of a Spain already well into its golden intellectual age, where even a Las Casas could without fear openly challenge the King's right to rule the Indies, Parkman remarks that this is a land where "all freedom of thought or speech" is "crushed." And his lack of any comparative objectivity is truly appalling; French priests, admittedly doing the same thing as Spaniards, were "unlike those of Spain, . . . rarely either fanatic or bigots." The passionate prejudice of Parkman lacks that sense of the past that would place Spain properly in its times. Instead, in the full current of the Black Legend, Spain is stigmatized with *unique* bigotry, cruelty, tyranny, and a *uniquely* treacherous and despotic king.

The tragedy is that Parkman, Prescott, Motley, Bancroft, and others not only wrote their histories in the spirit of the Black Legend but they greatly helped to enthrone this distorted view of Spain. They set most of the standards and popular patterns of American classical writing of history in vogue from the end of the nineteenth century into our own times. And their achievement was vastly facilitated by the fact that they represented their American times, pleasantly fitting prejudices already strong among their readers. They contributed greatly to the education of more than one generation of our immediate forebears; and their Nordic superiority, with its doctrinaire hispanophobia, blended perfectly into the preconceived notions of a nation that was to deliver the *coup de grâce* to a dying Spanish empire.

In our country, propaganda usage of Black Legend concepts against Spain is classically illustrated by our approach to and prosecution of the war with Spain at the end of the last century. As one of our well-known historians put it, "The belief that the Spaniards were inherently cruel to all the natives and harsh to their own people, had great effect in bringing on the Spanish-American war and the annexation of the Philippines." [12] All the skeletons in the closet of Spanish depravity were hauled out, including an 1898 New York edition of Bartolomé de las Casas, with the horrifying title: *An Historical and True Account of the Cruel Massacre and Slaughter of 20,000,000 People in the West Indies by the Spaniards.* Professor Lewis Hanke comments on this:

> The great majority of English speaking people of the world today . . . have a deep-rooted feeling that Spaniards are cruel people. This feeling must be attributed in considerable part to the accusations of Las Casas, printed at Sevilla in 1552 and subsequently spread broadcast through translations and revolting illustrations. The last English translation, or rather publication based upon Las Casas, for the translators were no more faithful to the original text than are some of our propagandists today, appeared in New York in 1898. It was designed to incite Americans against the Spaniards in Cuba. . . . This last known version in English had one subtle propaganda twist which no previous editor had thought of. Although a number of the famous and horrible illustrations were reproduced, one page in the book was left blank since, explained the editor, the illustration originally planned to go there was simply too frightful to include! [13]

Heroes and villains again! Cuban atrocities against Spaniards were overlooked in the alacrity with which politicians, Cuban propagandists, the "yellow" American press (mainly Hearst and Pulitzer), the muscle-flexing advocates of naval expansion, and even the scholars rushed to blacken Spaniards and encourage Cubans. The intemperate speeches in our Congress—so crudely insulting to Spain that serious anti-United States riots took place in that country—were paralleled by anti-Spanish demonstrations of Princeton University students and Leadville miners. The Spanish general in Cuba, Weyler, became "Wolf," or "Butcher" Weyler, a "human hyena," a "mad dog." "Weyler the brute, the devastator of haciendas, the destroyer of families, and the outrager of women. Pitiless, cold, an exterminator of men. There is nothing to prevent his carnal, animal brain from running riot with itself in inventing tortures and infamies of bloody debauchery" (Hearst's *Journal*). "The old, the young, the weak, the crippled—all are butchered without mercy" (Pulitzer's *World*).

Headline in the New York *Journal:* "THE MAINE WAS DESTROYED BY TREACHERY!" And Teddy Roosevelt blasted out that "The Maine was sunk by an act of dirty treachery on the part of the Spaniards." An unthinking, uncritical populace, all too avid for horror stories and all too burdened with a grand view of themselves as a kind of "master race," especially by comparison with that villainous, Latin-Catholic archenemy of the past three centuries, soaked it up and loved it. "Remember the *Maine,* To Hell with Spain!" Francis Drake, Thomas Scott, and William Davenant would have reveled in it. But Bartolomé de las Casas, for all that he had contributed so much, might have been a bit startled at some of the consequences; surely it might have nonplused the doughty old crusader to try to understand the Youngstown (Ohio) Chamber of Commerce's boycotting of the Spanish onion.[14]

Wondrous historical perspectives were unfolded by historians and politicians alike.

From the coming of Cortés and Pizarro to the going of Weyler, the flag of the Spaniard in the Western Hemisphere was the emblem solely of rapine and pillage. . . . Incalculable rapacity begot inconceivable brutality, and, as a result, Spain, from the first, became the last of the great European powers. . . . After Columbus and his wondrous New World, Cortés and Pizarro, and the other minor tyrants and robbers, down to Weyler, came in a kind of geometric progression, as simple matters of course.[15]

John Henry Barrows, prominent Presbyterian clergyman and president of Oberlin College, speaking at the Peace Jubilee in Chicago, on November 19, 1898, revealed himself as a man who could truly see the great perspectives of history:

Glorious results have come from this last great struggle between the Middle Ages and the Declaration of Independence, between the Inquisition and the common school, between the rack and toleration, between the Duke of Alva and George Washington, between Philip the Second and Abraham Lincoln.[16]

The applause must have been deafening; as it probably was when Senator John M. Thurston of Nebraska, on March 24, 1898, solemnly declared:

Christ died nineteen hundred years ago, and Spain is a Christian nation. She has set up more crosses in more lands, beneath more skies, and under them has butchered more people than all the other nations of the earth combined. Europe may tolerate her existence as long as the people of the Old World wish. God grant that before another Christmas morning the last vestige of Spanish tyranny and oppression will have vanished from the Western Hemisphere.[17]

Given three centuries and more of cumulative effect, a traditionalizing of Las Casas and all the other main themes of the Black Legend, it is no wonder that such utterances conned our grandparents not only to accept but actually to demand a totally unnecessary war with Spain— what we would today call a war of aggression. But when those known to be serious scholars also joined in, it took on the sound and color of that later academic lockstep that so vociferously clamored for Left-handed intervention in the Spanish Civil War.

Thus, Henry C. Lea, who spent much of his lifetime compiling a history of the Inquisition, revealed, in taking up anti-Spanish cudgels in the respected *Yale Review* (August, 1899), his own flair for contradiction and his acceptance of Lascasian views. He also saw in the story of Spain some valuable lessons for a nation newly assuming the "white man's burden," a literary gimmick popular with writers since Las Casas and Hakluyt.

In view of the responsibilities which the United States are assuming in the remnant of Spain's colonial empire, a brief review of early Spanish experiences may perhaps be not without wholesome warning.

As he writes this lesson, he says, *inter alia:*

It is to Bartolomé de las Casas that we owe most of our knowledge of the seamy side of Spanish conquest and colonization. . . . Las Casas' great influence at the Spanish courts was enhanced by his recognized disinterestedness. . . . Las Casas was not a coldly scientific historian, but an advocate and preacher, who gathered hearsay evidence from all sources and heightened the pathos of his narrative with his own warm sympathies. . . .

But, continues Lea, we must believe the Las Casas indictment in spite of his inaccuracies and his exaggerations. [Why? one may logically ask here, when, as Lea himself probably knew, there is a great abundance of Spanish source materials which, far better than Las Casas, illustrate not only some of Las Casas' generalizations but also the answers to them; in other words, come far closer than the choleric bishop to the truth of the matter.]

Lea also reveals a complete lack of knowledge and understanding of the whole Spanish colonial process when he pens this absurdity: "The Spaniards who sought the New World were largely of the vilest class, either criminals escaping from justice or punished by transportation." He certainly got his Englishmen and Spaniards mixed up when he wrote that! No historian in his right mind would thus characterize

Spanish seaborne migration, much less imply that this was a "system" for overseas empire-building.

I have purposefully stressed the anti-Spanish aberrations of our war with Spain, for they represent a climactic outburst thoroughly grounded in a strong United States predisposition to dislike, and even hate, Spain and Spaniards as a result of tradition. This hispanophobic renewal also reflects the first great peak of our aggressive Nordic superiority complex, partly inherited from the Northern and Protestant European concepts of history, and partly fattened by newly popular implications of Darwinism, combined with that prideful "manifest destiny" concept that was then, and later, so much of our makeup. This *fin-de-siècle* outburst of anti-Spanish prejudice in our country also paved the way for some twentieth-century aberrations in our foreign policies, as we shall see.

In summary, by the opening of the twentieth century our popular views concerning Spain and Spanish history had become dogmatized along the following lines which were quite acceptable to and even propagated by our intelligentsia:

1. Spaniards were uniquely cruel. This was an article of faith, based on centuries of acceptance of the Lascasian views, and now freshly confirmed by our most respected historians and by the "typical" behavior of Spaniards in Cuba.

2. Spaniards were uniquely treacherous. This was known from the days of the devious, scheming, "jesuitical" Philip II, through the late eighteenth-century "Spanish Conspiracy" on our own frontiers, the Mexican treatment of heroic Texans, and now through that definitive evidence, the destruction of the *Maine*. Conversely, of course, Englishmen and their American descendants always played fair—the cricket fields of Eton and our Romantic historians had seen to that.

3. Spaniards were uniquely bigoted. This was due, as every schoolchild knew, to their strong Catholicism and the uniquely horrifying Inquisition. It was confirmed by three centuries and more of supposed obscurantist oppression in the American colonies.

4. Divine Providence (the Nordic Protestant version, with Spanish American patriotism in a supporting role) had finally writ large the inevitable punishment of Spanish iniquities in her decay, her fall from power, and the loss of her rich empire. This was now freshly confirmed by the quick, stunning victory of Nordic arms by the people destined by Protestant Providence to bring a higher civilization to the world and to be its leader.

5. Spanish Americans, it is true, were suspiciously Spanish in their ways of life and their benighted Catholicism, but they, like us,

had cast off European tyranny. They were fellow-Americans, of a sort, and they certainly represented vast commercial possibilities for the new, aggressive industrial complex upon which we were riding to summit power. They surely could not be blamed for all the evils that had come out of their Spanish heritage. In any case, we would help them—by force, if necessary—to achieve civilization by assisting some of their own efforts to dehispanize themselves. (Perhaps this could be called the beginning of our "germicidal" approach to Latin-American affairs, helping them banish all their diseases, from Hispanism to hoof-and-mouth.)

6. The noble savage was getting a new lease on life with our growing awareness of pre-Columbian cultures, and with the increasingly popular versions of Spanish American history and nationality by Indianists. The Black Legend—Las Casas version—had already seen to our inheritance of the "noble" Indian versus "savage" Spaniard. Now this was being reinforced as a black-and-white (or rather, brown-and-white) historical perspective, even when our own treatment of the Indian was being revealed as none too savory. Naturally, however, we could not bring ourselves to believe we had ever been as devilish as the Spaniards. This renewal of Indianism was destined after the turn of the century to give great impetus to some peculiar twists in our own and in Latin American views of history, with Spaniards, as usual, getting the dirty end of the stick.

Ironically enough, our United States, ushering out the old century with a victory over decadent Spain, began to undertake the "white man's burden" that Spain had assumed so long before. We knew that special flaws of religion and basic characteristics had caused Spain to fail in this task. We, of course, would succeed. In further ironic parallel, we felt, as did sixteenth-century Spaniards, a unique sense of mission to bring humanitarian Christianity and higher civilization, to an eagerly awaiting "heathendom"—Filipinos, Puerto Ricans, and Cubans, as a trial run, and later, millions more of Asians and Latin Americans. The road to summit power is invariably paved with high moral purpose.

Various villains would try to block us, just as Protestant heretics, English and French pirates, Dutch Sea Beggars, Moslem infidels, and Jewish subversion had worked to thwart Spanish enterprises. But we started out with confidence in our causes, sure of our destiny, and naïvely unaware of the high costs and awesome responsibilities of global power. Our historians had fed us romanticized history, and we and our British forebears had, of course, always been on the good side. How could we fail?

With irony compounded and more than a little poetic justice, it was to be the descendants of Spain in America who would lead in the attempt to puncture such dreams. Their literature of Yankeephobia, bursting forth at the new century's beginning, and with such sequels as a Guatemalan Jacobo Arbenz and a Cuban Fidel Castro, would one day bring us about as much trouble as Philip II faced in the Low Countries and in England.

Part iii

Echoes of the Legend

Chapter 7

EDUCATING AMERICA, IN CHIAROSCURO

> *The English language historian who deals with Spanish civilization and culture has to think as much of how he is going to grapple with the bias of his public as he does of finding what the case is.*
>
> JOHN TATE LANNING [1]

It is my firm conviction, based on thirty years of university teaching in Hispanic and Latin American subjects, that this observation by Professor Lanning errs, if at all, on the side of understatement. I doubt that there is a foreign area taught in our schools and universities so burdened by inhibiting prejudices as is that of Hispanic culture. No teacher of French civilization, for example, has to begin his work with a lengthy apologia for the culture which he professes; everyone knows that French culture is eminently worth studying—and, of course, the French themselves are the first to admit it. No one really has to apologize for German culture; even the dullest student has heard of Beethoven and, possibly, Goethe and Schiller. And, though every good Nordic knows that Renaissance Italians poisoned each other and were generally rather immoral, we grant unquestioned greatness of culture to Rome and to much of the Italian past. And there is, of course, our easy acceptance of the splendor of our English cultural heritage.

It is only when we turn to Spain and Spaniards that difficulties ensue. Since everyone knows, automatically, that the Inquisition successfully crushed freedom of speech and thought in sixteenth- and seventeenth-century Spain, it is nearly impossible to convince students that there was a concomitant Spanish intellectual Golden Age, eminently worth studying if only for the fact that it had significant influence far beyond the Peninsula. And, since everyone knows that Spain started to decay under Charles V and Philip II (especially because they persecuted

Jews, Moslems, and Protestant heretics) and has remained backward and static ever since, what value could attach to the study of Spanish culture? And since, as everyone knows, the ruthless Spaniards savagely killed so many millions of Indians in the conquest of America (leaving only benighted Catholic Spaniards, one would suppose), why even take a second look at Latin America between Cortés and Simón Bolívar?

Jaundiced views of the Hispanic world are taught very early in our schools and they are thoroughly inculcated by the time we enter college and university. If our students know any history at all when they reach college (increasingly a moot point), it is apt to be a naïve, parochial version of United States development, in which Spain is honored by brief glimpses of Columbus, Balboa, Magellan, Cortés, Pizarro, De Soto, Coronado—interjected with Menéndez de Avilés butchering those virtuous French Huguenots in Florida. Students come out of elementary and high school with a view of their own hemisphere consisting of a strong, enlightened United States democracy, as leader, and of an Indian-killing slavocracy-dictatorship during centuries of Latin American colonialism, with Spanish guilt at the root of these evils.

It is always a shock to university students to learn that most Spaniards came to America not only to find gold but also to seek better opportunities than the Old World could offer them, in about the same way that our forebears moved across the Atlantic and across the continent. Or that they simply came as officials, churchmen, lawyers, businessmen, sundry employees or family members, adventurers, inquiring scholars, etc. Or that most of them did not come to the New World to kill or enslave Indians, or to engage in such pursuits once they arrived. It is a jolt to our high school graduates to learn that Spaniards were really human beings and well within the main streams of European civilization, despite the Pyrenees, Philip II, and the Inquisition.

It is similarly disconcerting to learn that, in the Spanish American lands of Catholicism and Inquisition, a sophisticated European culture flourished, almost from the moment of the Conquest itself. This included everything from complex municipal and regional government, vast projects for Christianization (i.e., Europeanization), and protection of even the most savage aborigines, to encouragement and successful establishment of all kinds of schools and universities, hospitals, and the production of scholars and a very respectable literature—a far more exciting and plentiful literature, by the way, than colonial English-America produced. This is to say nothing of economic and commercial activities on the grand scale. Students are invariably surprised to learn that, for all its weaknesses, the general system and aim was that of "ennoblement" *(ennoblecer)* rather than destruction; much like our later self-confident (and very self-conscious) concepts concerning help to backward nations and lifting everyone's standard of living. (Considering all the circumstances, if we are relatively as successful in such aims as Spain was between 1500 and 1800, we will have gone far toward our goals; a challenging thought, if examined with some objectivity.)

Most of this student shock is due to the extremes of naïveté and provinciality that generally characterize our teaching and writing of history for elementary and high schools, where historical perspective is lost in the inflation of our own past so that it will be consonant with our recent world-power status. This has the effect, of course, of belittling the French, Spanish, Italian, Portuguese, and even Dutch achievements. All this may be racially or politically patriotic—but it is bad history and it leads to unnerving experiences in university classrooms, where professors must begin over again, and on a necessarily elementary level adjust historical perspectives. Within this broad context, of course, is rooted our very notable condescension and ignorance with regard to all foreign cultures. Not even a Peace Corps or an Experiment in International Living can do much to close this sophistication gap, for most of the work must be done here at home.

More specifically, in relation to the Hispanic World, the sometimes disagreeable effects of having to learn almost exactly the reverse of what was taught and read prior to university experience, is due in great part to cumulative effects of the Black Legend. Our elementary and high school textbooks and supplementary reading are still based upon the spirit and the detailed errors of, at best, a slightly modified Lascasian view of Spain in America. At worst, it is out-and-out Las Casas combined with obvious Protestant biases and the Nordic superiority complex. And this despite at least one concerted effort on the part of scholars (1944) to point this out to educators and publishers.[2]

The 1944 exposure of the Black Legend and related errors in our educational reading matter was based upon recognition of the harmful effects of such distortions upon United States-Latin American relations. This was a consciously limited approach, the fruit of our then bustling Good Neighbor enthusiasm. While the exposure laudably enough recognized some of the deleterious effects of these errors in our foreign policy, it also emphasized, without intending to do so, our truncated view of Hispanic culture. That is, our overcommitment to the Latin American portion of that culture (for political and economic reasons), with a corresponding undercommitment to the totality of that civilization, which is not educationally any more sound than a history of Canada isolated from its English connections.

The 1944 American Council on Education (ACE) *Report* is a good departure point for illustrating most of what is perniciously and perennially wrong in our teaching and writing for elementary and high school students. After showing what this *Report* said concerning the Black Legend, I shall offer some specific examples from recent schoolbooks, to show the inadequacy of subsequent reform and how these books still differ from the views of authoritative scholars. Following are the comments of our scholars in 1944. First, under the heading of "Conclusions," following careful examination of the histories, biographies, etc., that our students are exposed to:

6. A more serious matter [than the larger quantity of factual errors] is the widespread perpetuation in our teaching materials, especially in history textbooks dealing with the colonial period of the Americas, of the "Black Legend" of Spanish (and, to a lesser degree, of Portuguese) colonial ineptitude, cruelty, faithlessness, greed, and bigotry. The "Black Legend" (*la leyenda negra*) is a term long used by Spanish writers to denote the ancient body of propaganda against the Iberian peoples which began [sic] in sixteenth century England and has since been a handy weapon for the rivals of Spain and Portugal in the religious, maritime, and colonial wars of those four centuries. The legend naturally took a strong hold in the anti-Catholic England of the Elizabethan period, and was thus a part of the colonial heritage of the United States. It gained an ever firmer foothold in the United States as a result of this country's series of disputes with Spain, beginning with the 1790's and culminating in the Spanish-American War of 1898. The prejudicial and inaccurate comparisons of English and Spanish colonies which still persist in our elementary school histories well illustrate the continuance of *la leyenda negra*. By a natural process of transference, many writers in the United States have, from the beginning of Latin American independence, tarred the Creole groups in Latin America—the descendants of the Spaniards and Portuguese—with the brush of the Black Legend. This prejudice has greatly diminished in the present century, but it is still too strong and pervasive. Traces of the prejudice are reported in virtually all of the studies included in this report; *the elimination of the legend and of its effect on our interpretation of Latin American life is one of our major educational and scholarly, as well as political, problems* (p. 31; italics mine).

Also under the same heading, the ACE *Report* says:

8. Because of the assumptions of the Black Legend and of cultural and racial prejudices and prejudgments there is sometimes apparent in our teaching materials a sort of Kiplingesque condescension toward Latin American peoples and states (p. 32).

In discussing United States college textbooks on United States history, the *Report* says:

As it stands now, many people in the United States have gained the impression, through the media of the radio, cinema, press, fiction, music, uncritical travel accounts, and the like, that most Latin Americans are

ignorant, lazy and incapable of governing themselves, and that their countries are rich but fallow ground awaiting cultivation by the superior and
enterprising people of the United States. Some United States history texts
. . . have contributed to these misconceptions (p. 79).

And on the subject of general history textbooks:

Certain old clichés which are characteristic of these books are not simply
isolated errors of particular historians, but, rather, form a part of what
has come to be designated *la leyenda negra* of Spain in American historiography, . . . starting in the lurid pages of Bartolomé de las Casas . . . [and]
preserved in the theme of the noble savage. . . . (p. 91).

With particular reference to high school texts, the ACE *Report* is
very clear:

The traditional story of Spanish shortcomings is characteristic of the
high school texts. . . . The causes that originally brought about this (Black
Legend) legacy of hatred and misunderstanding have long since ceased to
be operative, but the tradition of infamy still lingers in the pages of the
textbooks and in the minds of their readers. . . . In these high school
texts with regularity, among the traditionally "bad things" are found the
Spaniards. . . .
The traditional inference has impelled the authors of some of the texts
to express themselves in such startling generalization as the following: The
Spaniards "led the people of Mexico into slavery. . . . From the results of
this submission the Mexicans have never completely recovered." From denouncing Spaniards it is easy to proceed to condemning their system.
"Under the colonial system it was possible to compel free Indians to labor
for the state in the mines or upon public improvements and few Indians
survived this ordeal. In Peru . . . it is estimated that more than eight
million Indians died as the result of this vicious and enforced labor." "From
the first," says this same author, "Spain thought of her colonies as a means
of enriching her empty treasury. There was no idea of serving the colonists
or even of giving them justice." Furthermore, "This condition (oppression
and political unrest) continued for 300 years under the harsh rule from
royal governors appointed by the Spanish king."
There is also the constant refrain of tyranny in government and of intol-
erable restriction. "Since Spain itself was an absolute monarchy of the
most complete character, neither at home nor in the colonies were the
people given any share in the government." Perhaps the most devastating
condemnation of the colonial system is given by the author who says that
Spain made no attempt to encourage any form of self-government in the
colonies, and adds: "Colonialists were forbidden to trade among themselves,
to publish papers, to plant certain crops, to read liberal books or to establish schools. No wonder that Latin America after three centuries of mis-
rule was willing to battle for her freedom" (pp. 99–101).

Ending its discussion of high school texts, the ACE *Report* contains
this warning: "The usual and vicious misapprehensions concerning the

heinous character of the Spanish conquest should be diligently guarded against." And, in listing ten recommendations for improvement of Latin American subject matter in general history texts, the number one recommendation is: "Guard against the effects of *la leyenda negra*" (pp. 101, 105).

Biographies, which are so often used as supplementary reading in our schools, also came under scrutiny in the ACE *Report,* resulting in the following comments:

> In many books . . . the Black Legend . . . emphasizes that the Spanish system was highly oppressive and evil, and the source of most later Spanish-American troubles. Also, Protestant writers of the United States face an obvious difficulty in understanding or treating religious aspects of the life of a people who are predominantly Roman Catholic.
>
> For the whole four centuries, one finds misinterpretations and errors about the land system, the status of the Indian, and the status of the church. For the colonial period, besides misunderstanding of the Spanish system in general, they concern especially self-government and the level of intellectual life. The background of the independence movement and of the succeeding disorders, difficulties, and "backward" culture is rarely understood. Most of the biographers dealing with independence, and some others, apparently influenced by the Black Legend, are so ignorant about the colonial regime that they not only fail to give it its due as an *unparalleled achievement in cultural transplantation* [italics mine] but present the colonial background so peculiarly as to make the independence movement and its leaders unintelligible. The unqualified statement, "As the Spaniards had not yet been able to regulate themselves properly, they could not of course organize the Indians," is an outright lie or the statement of an ignoramus. Again one finds, "The Spaniards in America did not enjoy any rights of self-government as did our English colonial forefathers." By ignoring the *cabildo* as an embryo agency of extensive self-rule, the writer leaves one unable to account for its conspicuous and rather successful role at the outbreak of the independence movements" (pp. 146–147).

Fourteen years after this report, which was designed to help educators improve texts and teaching with regard to the more glaring errors in treating of Spain and Latin America (in effect, the Black Legend and its many ramifications), one of our well-known scholars in the field, Professor Charles Gibson, then of the State University of Iowa, again pointed to the problem in these words, under the heading "The Black Legend":

> By the term "Black Legend" (*Leyenda Negra*) is meant the accumulated tradition of propaganda and hispanophobia according to which Spanish imperialism is regarded as cruel, bigoted, exploitative, and self-righteous in

excess of the reality. The teacher confronts a serious problem in dealing with the Black Legend, for he will normally find students already predisposed toward it and in combating it he runs the danger of pronouncing an unconvincing apologia.[3]

This reiteration of the problem occurs in a small study designed specifically to help teachers of history in our schools, and it explicitly affirms the continued pervasiveness of the problem.

Such pronouncements, emanating from prestigious scholars, known for their knowledge of Latin American history, are clear enough in pointing to the Black Legend as a basic source of our widespread misinformation and misunderstandings concerning this large portion of the Hispanic world. That their warnings and suggestions have gone largely unheeded, especially in elementary and high school education, can be readily demonstrated by a look at some representative reading matter. Periodically over the past thirty years and especially since the ACE *Report* of 1944, I have examined elementary and high school reading matter as it pertains to the Hispanic countries. There has been some improvement, but the basic errors remain in almost all areas.

Whatever lessening of Black Legend interpretations and errors there has been has often derived from what are possibly more grievous causes, such as the watering down of content to very thin history and a recent tendency to vagueness, which seems designed to avoid hurting anyone's feelings. It reflects, perhaps, our increasingly mawkish approach to all foreign culture areas and general international relationships. This new religion is constantly paraded before immature students in the form of suffocating clichés of the brotherhood-of-man type. Waved aloft with true missionary fervor, it dilutes history and blurs the legitimate lines of political, religious, cultural, and racial differences, which make observation of human beings, historically and otherwise, so fascinating. According to this new faith, humanity is "one," and our writers of texts seem to be reaching toward a day when everyone on the globe will be completely happy and will understand everyone else—and high school history will be even duller than it is now.

In perusing present-day schoolbooks, a historian often gets the uncomfortable feeling that we are beginning to do away with history, for, in the new glow of supposed international understanding, all humanity is so much alike, really, that there is hardly any need to examine differences growing out of varied historical backgrounds. It seems sufficient that we are endowed with goodwill and rely upon the United Nations—and go on building factories and showing other peoples how to do likewise. For example:

Spain has only a few friends among the nations of the world. The western nations feel that Spain should have helped them win World War II. . . .

Spain must learn, as other nations have, that it is best to work closely with the United Nations. The United Nations could help Spain. . . .

The story of how Spain and Portugal lost their colonies one by one and became weak is an important story in geography and history. It is a story of two nations going to sleep to dream of their great past. While England, France, and other countries to the north were building factories and trading with one another, Spain and Portugal did not build factories.

The authors of this 1956 work, designed as a basic, seventh grade history and geography text, gave New Zealand and the Philippines full chapter treatment; Spain, millennial champion of Western civilization, does not even come close to such flattering coverage.[4]

I suppose that any Hispanist in the United States should be rather pleased with the new vagueness and thinness, for this at least brings a bit of restraint as far as critical comments on any country or people (even Spain!) are concerned. The "all humanity is one" idea might allow us, for example, to sneak across the idea that European humanity was "one" in the sixteenth and seventeenth centuries also, and that Spanish crimes of cruelty, greed, bigotry, tyranny, and treachery were fully shared by their fellow Europeans. And the new thinness (there are so many wonderful pictures, maps, and diagrams that there is less and less room for even a watered-down text) leaves, of course, diminishing space for the Black Legend. But these changes do not alter the state of affairs for Spain and Spaniards, for when they do manage to get into the story, the same old clichés are used.

Using some representative quotations from more recent schoolbooks, let us see how this operates. If you will bear in mind the errors pointed out in the ACE *Report,* and also recall the common mistakes of interpretation and fact discussed especially in my Chapter "Spain in America" the following quotations will be easily recognized for what they are—continuing echoes of the historical Black Legend.

In selecting the following examples, I have examined books in California, Utah, and Colorado. With rare exceptions, the books are issued by nationally known publishers, whose educational materials tend to conform in a great many respects. Hence, it can be considered that the following random samples from books in the three states mentioned are typical of nationwide schoolbook use.

False and misleading information concerning the Hispanic world begins as early as the fourth grade, but this is perhaps too soon to be significant. Training our children to make invidious comparisons between Nordic and Hispanic peoples and teaching them outright errors begins on a more important scale in the fifth and sixth grades. Here are some illustrative excerpts from a 1964 text of sixth-grade level.

The following sentence was starred and in red letters, for stress by the teacher: "Most Spaniards and Portuguese came to the New World to get rich. Most settlers in the English colonies came to build permanent homes and a better way of life." Marked also for teacher stress is: "Democracy, or self-government, was unheard of in the Latin American colonies." Along with the continuous reminder to emphasize the Spanish search for gold, the teacher is advised: "Discuss the beginnings of colonial life in Latin America versus English colonies in North America. Spaniards came to get rich—left women behind. English came to build homes—brought families along."

Let us look at a history of Mexico, a supplementary text for the sixth grade.[5]

In a chapter called "The High and the Humble," we find that in Mexico:

No one ever learned anything new, because in the towns and the villages only the priest was supposed to have knowledge. . . .

No one at all was supposed to ask questions about nature, or government, or anything beyond the daily life of the town. No one tried to do anything in a new way, because the people criticized any person who was different. They also criticized anyone who tried to make life better for himself. Year after slow year, life in the towns of Mexico changed scarcely at all. This suited the Spaniards very well. As long as the people did what the priests told them and paid the tribute, it was easy for the Spaniards to keep on being the bosses of the country. . . .

In other parts of the same book there are these statements: "A great part of Mexico's silver was sent to Spain as the king's share. . . . The kings got so that they depended on the silver and cared much more for it than for the people of Mexico."

This volume contains the standard invidious comparison of Spain's empire with that of England.

During those [300 years] Mexico was not a country—it was a colony. This means that it belonged to Spain in very much the same way that a ranch in California may belong to a person living in New York City or Chicago.

During part of those three hundred years, our country was made up of colonies belonging to England. There were some important ways in which these colonies were different from New Spain. The people in the English colonies had much freedom to worship as they chose and to believe whatever seemed right and true. They were allowed to have town meetings in which they decided how to run their own affairs. . . . The people elected men to help govern each of the colonies.

Because they had some freedom and because they had a hand in running their affairs, the people of our country learned the things they needed to know when the time came to make the United States out of the thirteen colonies. . . . They already had experience in governing themselves, and so they knew how to manage when freedom was won.

The people of Mexico had no such luck. The Spaniards would not let them get any experience in governing themselves. . . . Men who dreamed of being free kept their dreams to themselves, for fear of being terribly punished. . . . Mexicans got no experience in acting like free men and women so long as Spain ruled them. For three hundred years these separate groups [Peninsulars, Creoles, mestizos, Indians] of people lived side by side without ever coming to understand one another or to trust one another.

From a text used for geography and history in the intermediate grades one finds that in Spanish America:

The viceroys and their assistants carried out the laws made by the king and his council. They had to protect and increase the wealth of their viceroyalties. But they did not pay much attention to what the people thought. . . . The mestizos and Indians had no chance to improve their lot.

The authors point out that the former thirteen colonies of England had plenty of problems in starting a new nation,

But they had many wise, educated men to plan a new government and to help make it work. The Spanish settlers had no experience in governing. For more than three hundred years the colonists in Spanish America had been told what to do by the Spanish king.

In another text for intermediate grades the tenor is similar. The Armada defeat is described as "a great naval battle in which England defeated Spain and destroyed her power on the seas." Under the heading "The Struggle for Independence," the authors tell us that "Spain kept its colonies in America for three hundred years and ruled them with an iron hand. . . . [The colonies] had no opportunity to develop the natural resources of their land for their own benefit."

In the Guidebook portion of this text, this advice is given to the teacher:

During the discussion help pupils understand that *the people living on land claimed by England had more freedom than the Spanish colonists and had enjoyed some self-government even before they came to the New World, which the Spanish had never experienced.*

Because English colonists had learned to govern themselves, they were able to become independent much sooner than the Spanish colonists who lived under strict Spanish rule. . . . The English built a self-sustaining, even rich, agricultural economy, while the Spanish used their energy to seek gold and precious treasures.

Well, this could go on almost forever, for, as I say, our elementary texts are quite standardized through the country and the same clichés and stereotypes, half-truths, outright errors, and offensive Anglo-Hispano comparisons are ubiquitous. In short, starting at about ages 9–12, our children receive a highly erroneous picture of the three centuries of Spanish achievement, especially as related to the Americas. As all teachers know, basic impressions formed at elementary and junior high levels are very hard to change in subsequent years.

I wish I could report that our high school texts and other reading material have made the proper corrections. But, in the main, they reiterate what has gone before. Let us look at a representative case, a world history used as a basic text in the ninth and tenth grades, and watch the Nordic superiority complex expand with pride for our high school students.

This chapter told how a great migration of Europeans began moving to new colonies about the end of the 15th century. Part of this stream, from Northern Europe, began moving early in the 17th century. These people set up homes in what became the United States, Canada, Australia, New Zealand, and South Africa. They established democratic governments. Political liberty developed even faster in these places than in the mother countries. Hard work, vast natural resources, and the use of smart business methods helped the new nations (especially the United States) to become wealthy and powerful.

The earliest stream went out from southern Europe, mostly from Spain and Portugal. The people of this stream opened a vast stretch of land. They brought with them many outworn customs that were to block progress. But they also brought their language, religion, and culture. . . . Spain gave the Latin-American countries little chance for self-government. Nor did she encourage the education of most of the people. . . . As a result, Latin America made much less progress than the United States.

There is worse to come.

Portugal had a large and greedy neighbor—Spain. The Spaniards decided to unite the whole Iberian Peninsula and take over Portugal. This gave the Dutch—another seafaring nation—an opportunity to seize [greedily?] many of the Portuguese trading posts. When the Portuguese finally threw off the Spanish rule, most of the widespread Portuguese trading empire was gone.

By contrast with "greedy" Spain and general Iberian inefficiency, the Dutch are then described:

The Dutch, who were taking over much of the Eastern trade, were fine sailors. . . . The Dutch had more ships, more efficient methods, and soon had most of the Indies trade. They were thrifty and hard working, and later built up the world's finest system of colonial plantations in the East Indies.[6]

These phrases are also typical.

The Spanish in the Americas were not much interested in farming. . . .
Spain was lucky not to lose the American colonies when Spanish sea
power was lost [the unwary reader is earlier informed that this sea power
was lost by defeat of the Spanish Armada, when "England's long mastery
over the oceans of the world" began]. . . . Another weakness of Spain was
the fact that it was cut off from the rest of Europe by the rugged Pyrenees
Mountains. This isolation shut off new ideas. Years of religious wars with
the Moors had also contributed to making the Spaniards a backward people
who were unwilling to learn new ways.

In a high school text used nationwide—a typical world history for
this level—Spain gets the usual treatment, as these samples show.

Under Charles V, and later under his son Philip, Spain owned rich colonies in the New World and ruled most of the countries of Western Europe.
But she governed poorly. Instead of helping her colonies and territories and
winning their loyalty, she overtaxed the people and took their gold for
herself. Soon parts of the Spanish Empire were agitating for independence.
By the destruction of the Spanish Armada, England wrested from Spain
her rule of the sea. From that time Spain began to sink into the background,
while England ruled the waves and became a leading world power.

And under the heading "The Glory of Spain and Portugal Came to an
End," there are these statements:

The eclipse of Spain lasted for three centuries. During that time she lost
all her rich colonies and played an ever smaller and less important part in
world affairs.

Given among the causes of Iberian decline are: "There was no religious
liberty," and "The Church and State in each country had combined to
gain wealth and to destroy economic and religious liberties."

Treatment of Spain and Portugal in more recent times contains the
same hackneyed disparagement. "The reasons for their slow development are not hard to find. Both countries lack a middle class. (It is that
class, you will recall, that has made England and France prosperous
democratic nations.) Most of the population of Spain and Portugal is
uneducated and does not understand change; the upper class does not
want change."

In addition to the textbooks, let us recall what the 1944 ACE *Report*
had to say about such other educative fare as biographies (standard
supplementary reading), radio, cinema, press, fiction, uncritical travel
accounts, etc. Herewith a sampling from the opening pages of a classic
so often found on our high school reading lists—Charles Kingsley's
famous *Westward Ho!*

It was the men of Devon, the Drakes and Hawkins, Gilberts and Raleighs, Grenviles and Oxenhams, and a host more of "forgotten worthies," whom we shall learn one day to honour as they deserve, to whom [England] owes her commerce, her colonies, her very existence. For had they not first crippled, by their West Indies raids, the ill-gotten resources of the Spaniard, and then crushed his last huge efforts in Britain's Salamis, the glorious fight of 1588, what had we been by now, but a Popish appanage of a world-tyranny as cruel as heathen Rome itself, and far more devilish?

I tell you, those Spaniards are rank cowards, as all bullies are. They pray to a woman, the idolatrous rascals! and no wonder they fight like women.

In another category of materials, a 1959 *Hammond's American History Atlas,* obviously designed for student use, page A-6 contains a graphic contrast of Spain, France, and England under the title "Early Economic Bases for Colonies." For France, "furs, fishing, and feudal agriculture" are pictured. For England, "fishing, commercial and subsistence agriculture." For Spain, "mining, cattle raising, slavocracy" (this last illustration shows a Spaniard in morion and breastplate, whip in hand, managing slaves who look as if they were toiling on an Egyptian pyramid). Agriculture, the greatest single base of Spanish Empire in America, is not mentioned. Unfair? Yes. Misleading? Yes. But quite typical.

Television, that noisy reflector and disseminator of our national prejudices, has come into use since the ACE *Report* and now contributes its share to our youngsters' education. When Lee J. Cobb is presented to us as Cervantes along with scenes from the *Quijote,* we must have an obbligato of sinister Inquisition sound effects, completely irrelevant. I could hardly believe this when I saw and heard it, even though I had pessimistically predicted some such Black Legend injection before the show came on.

Perhaps, too, our students of recent years picked up a bit of their extracurricular education in *The Saturday Evening Post.* In such case, they could have confirmed and strengthened their schoolbook view of Spanish cruelties with this little gem on the ultimate in Spanish depravity: "In the direction of man's cruelty to man, the Spanish conquistadors practiced viral warfare long before anybody had heard of bacteriological warfare. Finding the Indians of Mexico highly susceptible to smallpox, the Spanish colonizers deliberately infected them with the disease, virtually exterminating many Indian communities." [7] There is, incidentally, such a case recorded in North American history, but the heinous deed was perpetrated by Englishmen. An enlightened Spanish government sponsored very early use of vaccination against smallpox in the Americas, precisely because the disease was so dangerous to the Indian population. Tarring Spaniards with purposeful viral warfare is about on a par with the sneer (attributed to H. L. Mencken) that "all the Spaniards have contributed to the world is hemophilia."

Fortunately, our college and university textbooks are somewhat better and improving, albeit all too slowly. They have sundry weaknesses, of course, but they are usually written by men and women who have at least done some below-the-surface peering into the dependable sources of Spanish and Latin American history. Although usually an improvement, they are not free from simplistic generalizations and remnants of political, religious, or "racial" prejudice. Thus, a well-known text on Latin American politics and government presents to our future experts in the field such statements as these:

In some respects . . . the Aztec civilization was actually more advanced than that of Europe. It could boast of learned architects and astronomers. It was a land of artists and poets. But in military matters its people were no match for the invaders. . . .

The Spaniards were not at all concerned with the preservation of the Aztec civilization. They were interested solely in gold. . . . Primarily these precious metals enriched the Spanish crown. During the centuries of Spanish control they were never used for the benefit of the people of Mexico.

In the Bibliography, especially Section III, I have listed a number of scholarly works that can serve as guides for the confused and as helpful reading for those who aspire to write textbooks or other material about Spain and Spanish America. These works do much to correct the errors I have been pointing out. With this, and with what has gone before, I trust that I have made the point about the unfair and unhistorical treatment so often accorded Spain, Spaniards, and Latin Americans in our educational system.

Chapter 8

BEDEVILMENT IN FOREIGN POLICY

Over recent months [1961] Latin-American affairs have drawn more attention from the U.S. press and public than at any time in our century. When it is suddenly increased, such attention can add to the inherited burden of misunderstanding; it can deepen the stereotypes and aggravate the clichés. But the people of the Americas can't afford the luxury of clichés and stereotypes any longer.

ADLAI STEVENSON [1]

Today's Spain, of course, does not generally spark in us the automatic antagonisms of earlier days. Present-day Spain is experiencing growing tourism and the mellowing of Civil War harshness, and in a world with so many other problems, it mainly excites hostility among fundamentalist anti-Catholics, Communists, and the diehard anti-Franco chorus. The Black Legend dogmas are, however, generally frozen into our schoolbooks and educational structure, where they constitute a perennial disparagement of Hispanic culture, both past and present. This severely inhibits fair judgment of Spanish matters all the way from the Spanish American War to the Gibraltar question. Although latter-day anti-Francoism, regularly stimulated by Herblock cartoons, is primarily aimed at keeping alive the antifascism of the 'Thirties and World War II, it also finds fertile ground in the broader suspicions and hostilities that echo the Black Legend in our schoolbooks.

In the case of Latin America, our perpetuation of Black Legend aberrations creates for us a complex of obstacles—a "luxury of clichés and stereotypes" tied to the perennial Nordic myth—which damages, almost every step of the way, our relationships with that vast area. In short, our continuing misconceptions, distortions, and ignorance concerning the total Hispanic world constitute an unnecessary and even dangerous educational burden, which adversely affects the making and functioning of our foreign policies.

To indicate some of the costs of this let us return, briefly, to the Spanish American War period. Hispanists are well acquainted with the Spanish "Generation of '98," meaning thereby the large group who, finding themselves in the decline so embarrassingly confirmed in their war with us began an appraisal of themselves and their culture. This new Spanish generation critically evaluated their political, educational, social, and philosophical systems to determine what had gone wrong, and it was often done with a "let the chips fall where they may" abandon. This same war also stimulated a United States "Generation of '98," which was strongly characterized by a new aggressiveness in foreign relations, a determination to expand our role on the world stage and live up to the grand destiny that seemed to be in store for us. The very ease with which we defeated the traditional Spanish villain encouraged further flexing of our muscles and shot new vitamins into that satisfying superiority complex of the Anglo-Saxon "race." This was, of course, before we really discovered all the Mexicans, Jews, Italians, Asiatics, and Negroes among us.

Just prior to the Spanish American War, our leadership had shown some hankering for such a role, when, in the curious twistings of the famous Venezuela Boundary Controversy, we managed, with more belligerency than historical accuracy, to force the British to knuckle under to our own aggressive interpretation of the Monroe Doctrine. Secretary of State Richard Olney's note to the British government, in 1895, said flatly and unblushingly that "Today the United States is practically sovereign on this continent [read hemisphere], and its fiat is law upon the subjects to which it confines its interposition." [2] The Irish among us were delighted, and the Venezuelans, whose side we had favored, were momentarily jubilant; but some Latin Americans saw the handwriting on the wall.

Memories of our aggrandizement at the expense of Mexico were still fresh, and our filibusters in Central America could also be recalled with distaste. Then, quickly on the heels of the Olney ultimatum, our war with Spain resulted in our domination over Cuba and acquisition of Puerto Rico and the Philippines. This gave Latin Americans additional grounds for fear and distrust. For all their nationalistic antipathies toward Spain, Latin Americans found themselves temporarily sympathizing with their former mother country's role as underdog against the now cockier-than-ever "Colossus of the North." As if this were not enough, Theodore Roosevelt soon (1903), "took" Panama (his own way of expressing it), one of the most shameless and unnecessary aggressions our country has ever committed. "Remember Panama" then became a perennially useful slogan in Latin America, akin to our own "Remember Pearl Harbor," or "Remember the Alamo," recurrently livened by later episodes of our interventions in the Caribbean area.[3]

The Roosevelt vigor in the case of Panama illustrated several things about us. The abusive, intemperate language with which Roosevelt referred to the Colombians ("bandits of Bogotá") and his callous disregard for Latin Americans by comparison with his solicitude for the financial welfare of the French company that had tried to construct a canal in Panama personified the supreme contempt that the Nordics had for the inferior Spanish-speaking Latin. The Panama episode and its long aftermath also illustrate some of the hypocrisy for which we are often criticized abroad. We glossed over our aggressions in order to make clear our great contribution to the world in the form of the Panama Canal, and this "end justifies the means" tenor remained in our schoolbooks. The lessons were not lost on Latin Americans.

It was not long before the President further buttressed our obvious superiority over the peoples of Ibero-America. In establishing our basis for interventions in Latin America, Roosevelt, in his 1904 message to Congress, made this statement:

Chronic wrongdoing [Latin American] . . . may in America, as elsewhere, ultimately require intervention by some civilized nation, and in the Western Hemisphere the adherence of the United States to the Monroe Doctrine may force the United States, however reluctantly, in flagrant cases of such wrongdoing or impotence, to the exercise of an international police power.[4]

This presidential wording was, of course, highly contemptuous of Spanish American culture. His attitude toward Hispanic "inferiority," shared by most of his countrymen, was destined to have long-range and disastrous effects, ringing down to our own day. Roosevelt's utterances, and the subsequent United States interventions in the Caribbean, Mexico, and Central America, which grew out of concepts so unfortunately phrased, can at least be partly accounted for in our entrenchment of the Black Legend in our traditions and educational system. Theodore Roosevelt was an acknowledged devotee of history and quondam practitioner of the art. He certainly knew his Parkman, Motley, Bancroft, Fiske, etc., those influential echoes of Las Casas and the whole baggage of anti-Spanish prejudice. Our illustrious President, in short, was educated in a day preceding any significant or influential scholarly revision of the deep-rooted clichés of the Black Legend.

Thoroughly Nordic in his heritage, he reflected and stimulated a hispanophobia that was passionately increased in the charged atmosphere surrounding the Spanish American War and that encouraged our "Generation of '98" toward imperialistic actions.

The Rooseveltian concept of our superior civilization policing an inferior one gave rise to two developments that would strongly affect our foreign policies. One was a practice of direct and indirect intervention in the affairs of Caribbean Latin America, a form of imperialism that found some rationalization in the Monroe Doctrine and in the argument that sea power was necessary to defend the approaches to the Panama Canal. This interventionist action reached its high point under Woodrow Wilson and endured into the 1930s; and a recent Dominican Republic intrusion shows that we are not free of it yet. While we must credit ourselves with a sizable popular antagonism toward such imperialism, the "Roosevelt Corollary" of the Monroe Doctrine generally fitted the strategic needs and desires of our country during most of the period it was in effect.

The second growth was not so noticeable at first but it was destined to have devastating effects long after official renunciation of the Roosevelt Corollary in the early 'thirties. In the heyday of Theodore Roosevelt, we had no such pervasive complex about our image abroad as we seem to have today; or, at least, we were not quite so sensitive to adverse foreign attitudes about us. Thus, before we realized it, an extensive Latin American literature of Yankeephobia had come into being, a new kind of Black Legend aimed directly at us. We did not replace Spain in the Latin American demonology—we were added to her. Well before World War I, the United States had become, in the minds of many, or even most, Latin American intellectuals, a greedy, money-grubbing, territory-grabbing, morally and spiritually insensitive industrial giant that constituted a far greater threat to them than any other on the horizon.

Well before 1930 this opinion of us, increasingly in vogue and constantly embellished, became thoroughly entrenched in the Latin American mind. To the severe indictment of our economic and religious imperialism was added our Marine Corps landings. This antagonistic view of us was cheerfully encouraged in European diplomatic and intellectual circles, where there had always been a strong dislike of our Monroe Doctrine and of our bumptious ways. Paris, that Mecca of Latin American intellectuals, contributed much to the formation of the anti-Yankee picture, thus strengthening the French cultural role in Latin America.

The rapid rise and spread of Yankeephobia was a superb demonstration of the immense power wielded by the formulators of literary fashion in molding political tastes in Latin America. And in passing, I must observe that even now, this power is not well enough understood or appreciated in our official circles, where narrow political and economic considerations too often—sometimes exclusively—form the basis of our policies.

Paralleling the Roosevelt Corollary and Yankeephobia's growth was the attempt, largely by us, to develop a Pan-Americanism that would range Latin America and the United States together in a kind of hemispheric union, partly to offset European threats and partly to encourage closer economic ties. Down to the 1930s, Pan-Americanism moved along by fits and starts and with some relatively minor accomplishments. It was increasingly handicapped by Latin American Yankeephobia or apathy, our own interventionist actions and policies, and the lack of strong popular interest. In the background, France had long since displaced Spain as Latin America's intellectual patron, smoothly making the most of her general cultural preeminence and of Spanish American hispanophobia. This, along with other European efforts, undercut the Pan-American idea. And underneath ran the deep current of fundamental differences in the Hispano- and Anglo-American ways of life, constantly kept visible by Latin America's literati and by our own hispanophobic characteristics. The latter were too often manifest in the condescension that was shown all the way from our educational processes to our diplomatic circles. After all, weren't those Americans to the south direct descendants of the people who had so cruelly and benightedly conquered the New World and for centuries exploited it? They certainly looked and talked like Spaniards—and, by and large, they attended the same church.

Starting about the turn of the century, however, a thin silver lining began to appear. A few United States scholars, along with others in Europe and Latin America, began to reassess the Black Legend on the basis of more thorough and objective approaches to the sources of Spanish and Spanish American history. There had been in our country, from the days of Irving, Bryant, Longfellow, Prescott, and others, some lively literary interest in Spain and Spanish-America.[5] This was now bolstered by additional intellectual activity. Although scholars were not entirely free from the deep prejudices of the past, they were at least showing more concern for finding the facts than for mere repetition of the traditional distortions and misconceptions.

To a considerable extent, unfortunately, this new scholarly attention often originated in and consequently abetted a too narrow interest in only the American phases of Hispanic culture. It reflected the new Pan-Americanism, growing archeological and anthropological interest in the American Indian, and, in general, an attachment to purely hemispheric matters. This is illustrated, for example, in the title and subject matter of *The Hispanic American Historical Review,* founded in 1918. Although the intent of some of the founders and others connected with its growth was broader, the *HAHR* became almost exclusively concerned with Latin America or, at most, those Iberian backgrounds very directly related to the hemisphere. The considerable increase of other scholarly publications, also geared to an American interest, tended to split the Hispanic culture area along lines already strong in Spanish America's tendency to dehispanize itself.

This hemispheric self-consciousness makes Hispanic America far less intelligible to us than should be the case. We lack understanding and appreciation of the Iberian elements that constitute so very much of Latin American civilization. We also fail to see or comprehend the significance of the very large and continuing Iberian presence in the American countries: immigration, trade, trans-Atlantic family ties, sports, and literary, political, and scholarly interrelationships, etc.

There is also a somewhat uglier side to this dichotomizing of the Hispanic World, of which we, as a global power, should be aware. It tends to perpetuate our alignment, in concepts and in individual or collective action, with the dehispanization or hispanophobic prejudices still strong in Latin America. Our educational edifice, as we have seen, encourages us to think in this vein. Translated into foreign policy and practice, this makes us generally sympathetic to Indianism and against the Spanishness we see to the south of us. To put it in starker terms, we are, thus, easily conned into believing that Latin America consists solely of a small, white aristocracy (the bad guys) lording it over a vast Indian peasantry (the good people). This is what I call the "myth of the no middle class." Let us take this example from Drew Pearson, who was forever touting himself as an authority on Latin America: ". . . it is not Castro who causes the real trouble for the United States in Latin America, but poverty and the wide gap between the wealthy aristocracy at the top, and the landless, illiterate Indian peons at the bottom. In Latin America, there is no middle class." [6]

This brand of Las Casas-*cum*-Marx, strong in our university classrooms, naturally predisposes us to the cause of so-called social revolution—peasants versus aristocrats—without any thought about that vast middle class that is also Latin America and that has been there for centuries. Today, the Latin American middle class contains many millions—Indians, mestizos, whites, Negroes, mulattoes. They are, for example, the ones you see, male and female, issuing from government buildings when the day's work is done; but tourist and missionary photographers do not bother to show you this, for it is far less picturesque than their scenes of Indian marketplaces or slums. This is the class from which come intellectuals and professionals—military leaders, poets, journalists, historians, physicians, businessmen, essayists, government bureaucrats high and low, politicians, demagogues, etc. And, incidentally, these are also the ones who make up a large percentage of our present ex-Cuban population.

All too many of our own intelligentsia, especially those best tuned in on the nuances of class conflict, prefer to believe the white aristocrat versus Indian underdog concept of Latin American life. We can see the disastrous effects of this in the tragically naïve support given in our country to Castro's rise in Cuba. We have only to recall Herbert L. Matthew's (*New York Times*) heroic and very successful efforts in propagandizing Castro and his cause (summed up in *Time Magazine,* October 6, 1961, p. 3). Or the friendly reception given Fidel Castro by Harvard University students, which somehow reminded me of the anti-Spanish student demonstration at Princeton, back in 'ninety-eight—perhaps because, in both cases, Cuba was involved.[7]

The decade of the 1930s is usually considered to have been a period when basic changes in our approaches to Latin America were made. It is quite true that we tried, governmentally and privately, to wipe away some of the stigmas attached to our earlier high-handedness in Latin American affairs and, to some extent, we did—temporarily. Some in this country leaped so far backward in this that it was positively embarrassing.[8] The pre-World War II period of the so-called Good Neighbor Policy was strongly marked by long overdue attention to some of the causes of Latin American Yankeephobia, urged on by our sudden awareness that we needed Latin America on our side in the aligning of forces that was taking place. With a vigor and passionate intensity that often startled Latin Americans, we began to woo them.

There was a vast amount of naïveté in all this, and waves of artificially stimulated sentimentality. But it is also true that by this time there was an extensive and discernible genuine interest in and affection for Latin America in our own public. Some of this undoubtedly came from a sense of fairness and a desire to make amends for our past behavior; some of it from a realization of the needs of the hemisphere in preparing itself against outside threats. Some of it certainly grew out of the enlarged place that Latin American studies held in our university curricula, begetting more and more interest in the culture of that area. Increasing numbers of scholars were dedicating themselves to the study and teaching of Latin American subject matter. As an example, the previously mentioned *Hispanic American Historical Review* and the scholars associated with it deserve much credit for this development.

The troubles of the Depression decade and the shining new liberalism that we shared with many Latin Americans, plus a growing vision of danger from across the Atlantic, made international relations relatively cozy in the hemisphere during the later 'thirties. True, there were a few flies in the goodwill ointment: a war hangover in the Gran Chaco; some tough-looking dictators and sundry coups and revolts; and Mexico's rough expulsion of foreign oil interests. But the new rapprochement tended to suffuse us with a benevolent glow, as we happily discovered that our suddenly acquired friends to the south had had universities long before the landing on Plymouth Rock; that not all of them had native or national dress like the Mexicans or Guatemalans; that they did not all eat chili and tamales. We even made the important basic discovery that not all of them spoke Spanish; and that they had poets, novelists, painters, and all the other purveyors of cultural manifestations that civilized people are supposed to have. Such discoveries, the millions of words of goodwill, and even some deepening of interest in the now bustling Inter-American system made Teddy Roosevelt look a bit uncouth.

All this helped us bear the demise of the League of Nations, and made us feel less alone in a world increasingly shaken by the thundering nationalisms of Hitler, Hirohito, and Mussolini. It seemed very worthwhile, this love-the-Latin intoxication, for it did help to unite the hemisphere against outside dangers; it did improve our educational perspectives of a vital foreign area; and it did nourish to slightly better health a worthy regional organization of American nations. All this, I repeat, did many good things, though our allies and enemies in Europe did not like it, though some cynics knew it would not last, and many a Latin American seemed to squirm uncomfortably in the embrace of this vigorous love affair. They had so enjoyed writing and reading and talking Yankeephobia that they were reluctant to take the cure, even for the short time necessary to visit the United States at our invitation and expense.

Beneath the surface, however, there were troubles brewing. For one thing the cynics were right; it did not last. Because so much of our interest in Latin America was based on self-interest, once we were in the war hemispheric good neighborism went quickly out the window, except for what was considered absolutely essential for the war effort. The Peruvian-Ecuadorian fight was swept under the carpet in 1942 to our eternal discredit and the disadvantage of Ecuador. We continued to cooperate in matters concerning the military and supply; to root Nazis out of Latin America with a vigor that sometimes astonished and displeased our neighbors; and to pursue certain propaganda activities, etc. We had urged the new inter-Americanism mainly because we knew we were going to *need* Latin America. Then, once the need was gone, Latin America began to recede from our view, even before full victory was in sight. We turned from the hemisphere and began to aim our energies—intellectual, financial, and political—at the rest of the world. Then we stumbled into the Cold War.

A decade later, despite plainly visible warnings, which our government did not heed, Latin America exploded right behind us. It would have exploded in our faces had we not been so busily looking the other way. Although we had so often patted ourselves on the back for our Good Neighborliness, the underlying flabbiness of this policy was clearly visible between 1945 and 1950; but even the famous "bogotazo" of 1948 did not awaken our leadership.[9]

In connection with our central theme, there are certain aspects of our Good Neighbor Policy worth noting. For example, the ubiquitous and seductive thread of Indianism ran through the tapestry of fervent rapprochement. The Indianist version of Latin American historical development reached truly vertiginous heights: our press and intellectual leadership sang the glories of the latter-day Mexican Revolution and its historically twisted versions in the murals of Diego Rivera; and Mexico's "new deal" president, "Indian" Lázaro Cárdenas, got rave notices for his radical Six-Year Plan. [Cárdenas, incidentally, was more recently given the red-carpet treatment in Communist China.] It was Indian Cuauhtémoc throwing off the shackles of slavery that Spanish Cortés had put on him; this was propagandistically shoved down the throats of Mexico's populace and schoolchildren, and it was peddled by Communist writers, as well as others, to a gullible Yankeeland. Along the way, leftist hero Cárdenas and his Mexico gained further plaudits by loudly refusing to recognize Franco Spain.

There was a titillating Marxian flavor to this period, and hispanophobic Indianism blended smoothly into it, and vice versa. This is the period, you will recall, when it was fashionable to flirt and even bed with Communism in avant-garde and academic circles, here and abroad. Latin America's and our own Indianist sympathies were made to order for this: there was the proper anti-Spanish twist; the necessary underdog-versus-aristocrat clarity; a convenient parallelism with the New Deal's "common man" concepts; and it was a delightful cocktail-hour cause in which no one, except Latin America's Spanish blood and heritage, could be hurt. The Indians of the Andes received flattering attention from good Marxists in this period, possibly originating that crude, class-conscious limerick:

> The kings of Peru were the Incas,
> Who were known far and wide as great drincas:
> They worshipped the sun
> And had lots of fun;
> But the peasants all thought they were stincas.

There is a clear line of continuity from the popular Indianism of the 'thirties, with its historical anti-Spain ingredients, to the intellectual underpinnings of the enthusiasm for that underdog "antidictator," Fidel Castro—and Communism certainly has had no difficulty following (or creating?) that line.

The ease and rapidity with which our attention was diverted from the Latin American portion of the Hispanic world during and immediately after the war, demonstrated the artificiality of our earlier Good Neighbor enthusiasm. In any case, it was never the resounding success that our own propaganda and sentimentality led us to believe. This is amply shown by its immediate aftermath—a period of United States official and public apathy, which encouraged the growth of a Latin American Yankeephobia even more pronounced and dangerous than in the past.

Another significant echoing of the Black Legend can be seen in United States relations with Spain since the mid-thirties. In this, a strong blend of traditional anti-Spanish prejudices and propagandistic fervors generated potentially dangerous pressures in our foreign policies.

Contrary to what has been pumped into us from the Left side of our intellectual leadership for more than three decades, the Spanish Civil War of 1936–1939 was not simply a heroes-and-villains, Fascist-versus-Democracy episode. When that war broke out, we generally were little better informed about Spain than our parents or grandparents had been in 1898. Our schoolbooks were still propagating the stereotypes of Spain, Spaniards, and their history. True, we were beginning to learn a bit more about Latin America, but much in the Lascasian vein, which further encouraged, as already noted, basic anti-Spanish views. Even more unfortunate, the conflicting political, social, and religious partisanships and complexities in Spain itself were not well understood even by those who should have known them (e.g., many of our Hispanists and Latin Americanists). How, then, could we be expected to form sound judgments of a conflict such as the Spanish Civil War? We could not—and we did not—as propagandists for both sides well knew. News and opinions about the Spanish tragedy reached us through well-oiled machines of propaganda.

Our people were not much interested in the Spanish Civil War at first. But there were plenty of consecrated zealots who saw to it that we were quickly enlightened. Many Catholics tended, at least in the early stages, toward some sympathy for the Nationalist, or Franco, side of the picture; and some Church publications encouraged this. But the greater part of the propaganda to hit us favored the Loyalist, or Republican side. Catholics in this country were generally inclined to talk about "their" side with reserve, since they themselves were still a distrusted minority and they did not want to be labeled with that odious "fascist" epithet that was so rapidly gaining currency.

The pro-Loyalist propaganda, on the other hand, was supremely confident, plentiful, and strident; there were good reasons for the confidence. They were upholding the anti-clerical side—always a popular theme in our country, especially when Catholicism is involved. Also, we were already conditioned, from a variety of other angles, to accept the view that the Loyalist was simply the anti-fascist side, and this received seemingly irrefutable confirmation when the Nationalists received military aid from Italy and Germany. Any republican side, of course, would always appeal to us more than an alignment of military, Fascist, and Catholic forces, regardless of other important circumstances. Then, too, Soviet Russian Communism and Socialism generally were enjoying considerable popularity amongst our intelligentsia—and Communism and Socialism supported the Loyalist side in Spain. By contrast, the Nationalists represented the traditional kind of Spain, which we had always been taught to view with jaundiced eye.

It did not matter to us—we hardly considered the possibility—that, as in virtually all civil wars there were at least two respectable sides involved; otherwise there could hardly have been a war of such proportions. Nor that many Spaniards fought wholeheartedly and passionately on both sides. What really mattered was that the propaganda victory in the United States and throughout the West generally was won, hands down, by the anti-Franco side.

But then the unforgivable happened; the Nationalist side won. Worse yet, the Franco government stayed on and on, walking dangerously but very astutely on a tightrope between the contending forces of World War II. The Nationalist victory and Franco's continuation in power can never be forgiven by those who, with passionate, ideological commitment, worked so hard for the opposite result.

Despite the bitterness that so many felt over the Nationalist victory,

Franklin Roosevelt's administration maintained diplomatic relations with Franco through the war, apparently for the very good reason that it served our interests. But this bit of good sense was soon followed by one of those incredibly juvenile performances of which we are sometimes capable. With pressures from some of our quondam allies plus some loud hurrahs at home, we agreed to join in a collective withdrawal of ambassadors from Madrid as a reprisal against the Franco government for earlier relationships with the Axis; in short, guilt by association. This wrist-slapping was akin to our almost simultaneous attempt to label Argentina's Perón a Nazi and tell the Argentines, through our ambassador, that they should not vote for him. Both actions were, in that very apt Spanish term, *contraproducente;* they strengthened both Franco and Perón—perfectly predictable outcomes. Finally, during 1950–1951, we reversed our stand *vis-à-vis* Franco, and Cold War considerations led us into strategic military ties with Spain.[10]

It is true that many who have continued their antagonism toward Franco-dominated Spain are influenced by a sincere hostility against whatever appears to have a fascist or nazi coloration. This can be both respected and understood because of the emotions aroused during the recent global conflict, but it does militate against fair appraisals of Spanish history and culture in a broader sense. The Franco period has represented, to a large extent, the ascendancy of those conservative, traditional, or nationalistic forces whose beliefs seem uncongenial to our own prevailing political and religious thought. These forces, however, are a major part of the Hispanic way of life, deeply rooted in all classes, and it is this aspect of Spain that we understand least and tend most to dislike. Somehow this side of Spain makes us recall, even if only subconsciously, epithets out of the past such as: "bigotry," "obscurantism," "intolerance," "cruelty," "Inquisition," etc. Thus in many small but cumulative ways, the continued sniping at post-Civil War Spain, so prevalent in our university classrooms, works against understanding the more conservative side of the Spanish character. For us, Spanish conservatism is too much associated with that long record of religious, diplomatic, military, and "racial" abrasiveness that nourished the Black Legend.

In the year in, year out planning and action of United States foreign policy relating to Spain, Portugal, and Latin America, our roster of personnel always contains an abundance of officials and their wives who are unsympathetic to the cultural environment in which they are supposed to be effective. Relatively few of our representatives in those areas take the trouble to learn the languages well; and fewer still study sufficiently to comprehend the history and literature that are so requisite to understanding the countries. If they do take some time to study the histories of those countries, they are hardly prepared to discriminate between the Black Legend versions because of the distortions presented in their early schooling and the writings of sound and conscientious scholars. The words of a Spanish journalist, long observing us in Washington, perceptively illustrate some consequences of this weakness:

One of the problems of United States ambassadors in Hispanic America is that they do not understand the southern continent. They go there with the idea that the Colossus of the North will impose a political trajectory to the South. If Washington would send men familiar with and specialized in the political and economic conflicts of that continent, such conflicts would be avoided, but it is not this way. Washington sends either political activists or businessmen or political favorites who do not know anything about the political realities of Hispanic America. It does not occur [to the United States government] to send ambassadors with objective and professional sense of their mission or even with a moderately satisfactory knowledge of the Spanish language. . . .

I have said many times that the importance of the American continent [read hemisphere, or Latin America], as a political factor, is such that the United States needs an executive department (*secretariado de Gobierno*) exclusively occupied with the affairs of Iberoamérica, and such a department should be in the hands of men who are wholly dedicated and possess great cultural and technical knowledge of the problems to the south of the Río Grande. . . . The truth is that the United States has ignored South America until now, has confused it with an inferior zone of colonization without understanding that it is a great continent in crisis in a world which needs something more than the "American Fruit Company" or the financial protection of Washington.

The Americans are now at a dramatic crossroads. Either something intelligent and constructive is to be done, or a whole continent will be left to the mercy of the explosion of many and tragic Castrisms.[11]

What this Spanish observer has said about our relations with Latin America is, essentially, also applicable to our behavior *vis-à-vis* his own country and Portugal. In Spain, our personnel are often pleased by the way of life, the courtesy and sobriety of Spaniards, and the many delights experienced while touring the Peninsula. But they seldom look beneath the surface, historically, or even realize that their deeply imbedded prejudices come from their essentially primitive schooling about Hispanic cultures. And there is always in Spain, Portugal, or Latin America, the abrasive effects of the deeply rooted Nordic superiority complex.

Some of this feeling of superiority may have to do with the arrogance of power [like, perhaps, the behavior of some Spaniards in sixteenth-century Italy?]. Or it may reflect our well-known distaste for "racial" mixture. Or it may stem from our abiding faith in industrial might and technological proficiency as criteria for evaluating civilization and progress. Whatever the case, it too often finds expression in that well-known "American colony exclusivism," which has caused us so much ill will abroad. In Iberia and Latin America, particularly, the fact that there is a need for remedying this is truly shameful, for here we are dealing with peoples and cultures long in our own hemisphere, their history intertwined with ours, their people living among us and elsewhere in proximity. And we share centuries of the cultural stream of Western civilization, however much black-legendism tends, at times, to obscure this.

In relation to the Hispanic world, the answer to all this is not to be found in a rolling up of sleeves and living-with-the-natives kind of thing. The answer lies in a far, far more complete and sophisticated education of our governmental, business, and academic personnel before sending them into Hispanic areas or, for that matter, before selecting them to be top-echelon planners of policy or teachers in our classrooms. We cannot afford, for example, such luxuries as the appointment of Richard Goodwin as a presidential adviser on Latin America, when the appointee has never set foot in Latin America, and has none of the necessary knowledge—not even of the languages.[12]

If we are to be successful in our relationships with the Hispanic countries, it is imperative that we quickly and fully eliminate the simplicities and naïveté which have grown out of our long conditioning in Black Legend kind of thinking. The people of the Hispanic areas are highly sophisticated in human relationships, with their more than millennial cultural experience and notable achievement. It is quite possible that a triangular alliance of Iberia, Latin America, and the United States might yet come to be an essential bastion of their and our well-being and security. In this, I cross the ancient Line of Demarcation to add a bit to the thoughtful and warning words of the well-known Mexican intellectual, Daniel Cosío Villegas: "I have the firmest conviction that the worst evils that can befall the United States will be engendered in Latin America and that without Latin America the United States will not have even the minimum that it needs for its own happiness." [13]

Chapter 9

PERSPECTIVES AND PRESCRIPTION

> *The elimination of the [black] legend and of its effect on our interpretation of Latin American life is one of our major educational and scholarly, as well as political problems.*
>
> ACE *Report* [1]

> *Before dealing with the concrete problem of Spanish cultural history, the American scholar must first dispose of myths that surround it.*
>
> JOHN TATE LANNING [2]

If only in pursuit of excellence, it would be worth the efforts of our scholars to embark upon extensive revision of our educational processes pertaining to the Hispanic world. As the above quotations and my earlier chapters indicate, there is much to be done, despite some slight improvement in recent years. Faulty education is always worth correcting, of course; but, in this case, there are some additional benefits which might accrue.

The anti-Spanish propagandas that were utilized so effectively in stimulating attacks upon that country and in building up the nations that succeeded Spain at the European summit, contributed much to the weakening and decline of that country and empire. Those same propagandas, and the deep prejudices they produced or augmented, have also cost Spaniards generations of anguish in terms of the defamation and disparagement which continue to this day. Thus, the high costs of hegemony in the Old World and the New are still being paid, long after the Spanish Golden Age came to an end. For us of the United States, facing the possibility of having less time than the Spanish had at the summit, lessons out of the Spanish experience should be of profit —to study, ponder, and inculcate in our society and intellectual leadership. If nothing else, such lessons should heighten our capacities for discernment and for evaluating inimical propagandas—along with their promoters, their aims, their consequences. The people of a great power need such wisdom.

It has long been popular to look back to the decline and fall of Rome for our homilies on the pitfalls of great power. Our intellectual and political leadership might do much better to study the rise, achievements, mistakes, and decline of Spain and the Spanish Empire. The Spanish experience was much closer to our times, and Spain's was the first global empire. Its problems of swollen and bumbling bureaucracy, of inflation and of bankruptcy, of trying to maintain Christendom's unity while simultaneously protecting Europe against a hard-hammering Eurasian threat, its trials and errors and accomplishments in carrying civilization to lesser cultures and to primitive peoples, its attempts to reconcile high idealism with life's practicalities, its ways of racial and cultural integration, the sufferings from internal divisiveness, the periods of magnificent courage, fortitude, and unity of purpose—all these things, and many more, could be profitably studied by the people and leaders of a summit power with similar problems. And the triumphs and failures of the Portuguese Empire and global straddle, reaching to our own day, might similarly serve to enlighten us—perhaps even generate a bit of understanding and sympathy for our NATO ally.

As a contribution to the increased sophistication of our people, a few historical comparisons with the Hispanic world might be profitably weighed. For example, our own period of summit power has so far extended only about as long as little Portugal's heyday of major power status. And our own decline, which may already have begun, seems likely to set in before we equal Spain's long record at the top. And a bit of humility in perspective in our schools might become us, great power though we be. We could do without those homiletic textbooks that make invidious and usually erroneous comparisons of our colonial period with that of Spanish America. Even a recognition that as late as the opening of the past century we were but a small portion of this hemisphere by comparison with the Iberian colossus to the south and west of us, would encourage some merited and greater respect for the other cultures sharing our American world. We do not need to salve our egos by blowing up our colonial past while belittling Ibero-America. Let us be satisfied with whatever praise we might wish to lavish on our phenomenal rise to power in the past century or so.

It is a bit sobering, too, to reflect upon such matters as the depth in time and experience of a Hispanic civilization that was flourishing in the days of Rome, while so much of our North European ancestry was still in comparative savagery or barbarism; or the cultural riches of an Iberia of the Middle Ages—Christian, Moslem, and Jewish. These are too often skimped in our general histories, which only reluctantly touch anything south of the Pyrenees. Also sobering is the thought of a Spanish Golden Age of empire and intellectuality lasting nearly two centuries and reaching the heights along almost every line of cultural endeavor. A golden age, incidentally, of the kind that comes to few peoples and which our own country may never see. And, by the way, a golden literary and artistic age that flourished during the heyday of the Spanish Inquisition, a historical fact which demands much more careful scrutiny and understanding than it has so far received, especially in our own country.

Also, there is what we might call a selfish need for educational reform *vis-à-vis* the Hispanic World. We are already witnessing a shrinkage of our global hegemony, and a lessening of our credibility as paladin of the West against a Eurasian threat that now extends energetically into Africa and the Americas. There is noticeable maneuvering in Europe and elsewhere to placate and live with the consequences of Soviet and Red Chinese imperial and ideological expansion, and this stems from a steadily decreasing faith in United States courage, power, and promises. And in Latin America we have failed miserably, especially since World War II, to establish any fundamental rapprochement—mutual respect and recognition of mutual defense interests—that would not crumble in the face of Communist muscle-flexing. Latin Americans know too well our arrogance, our ignorance, and our condescension with regard to them, and the constant stream of their Yankeephobia keeps them eternally aware of our incompetence and the insufficiency of our interest in that part of the hemisphere. Germany, Italy, France, and England are convinced that we will not risk our own survival to defend them against a Soviet onslaught. And Latin Americans, with *machismo* (manliness) and wit as traits they greatly admire and respect, have seen how badly we measure up against the astuteness of Castro and blatant displays of Soviet power in this hemisphere.

In any future short of thermonuclear holocaust, we might well have to face the prospect of being reduced to some version of a hemispheric "fortress America," with outer perimeters, perhaps, at such places as the Pyrenees and the Philippines. With such a possibility, we are assuredly behind schedule in forging firm bonds of mutual respect between the two major cultures of the Western world. In weighing this, we might optimistically refresh our historical memories a bit: the word "guerrilla" is of Spanish origin. It was the fighting fortitude of Spaniards that punched the first holes in the Napoleonic military machine. It was Spanish soldiery that dominated the European military picture for more than a century after 1500. It was an almost incredible Spanish-Portuguese courage, hardihood, and faith in God and themselves that opened the Atlantic, American, Pacific, and Far Eastern worlds to European view and expansion. Moreover, it was a Spanish chieftain who, in David-versus-Goliath style, faced down the Hitlerian might at the Pyrenees and thus greatly eased the Allied Nations' 1942–1943 triumphs in North Africa.[3]

The AC *Report* of 1944 was a clear recognition by our scholars that, as a basic step in bridging the chasms between Latin America and ourselves, we had best eliminate our educational errors concerning those countries. We were then still in the Good Neighbor glow and still feeling the need for allies in a world at war. As we have seen, this call for educational improvement was too much unheeded in subsequent decades. It seems now even more imperative that that task be seriously and quickly undertaken, and that it be broadened to achieve excellence in our general and specific knowledge of all the areas of Iberian languages and culture. We not only need a great increase of highly expert personnel for every portion of that vast area, but we also need an intellectual and political leadership truly knowledgeable in those cultures so that the languages, peoples, institutions, and mores of the Hispanic world will no longer be treated in our country as second, third, or fourth class—or virtually ignored. Our long habit of North Atlantic provincialism, that New York-London-Paris axis that barely acknowledges the existence or respectability of Hispanic culture, is a luxury we can no longer afford, especially in our intelligentsia and statecraft.

By cleaning out of our educational systems the echoes of the Black Legend—perhaps as part of our antipollution crusade—which are so often accompanied by offensive comparisons of our own virtues with Hispanic vices or backwardness, we might take some too long delayed strides in the direction of improving conditions for our very large population that speaks, or formerly spoke, Spanish. If our schoolbooks, our teachers, and our other media can be freed from the Black Legend and its derivatives and the Hispanic world accorded its proper place and respect in our society, those of Hispanic background can be properly encouraged to hold their heads higher, to be proud of the great past from which they come, and perhaps have some real fun twitting their "Anglo" fellow-students about the relative merits of a Daniel Boone and a Francisco de Urdiñola, or of a Sor Juana Inés de la Cruz and an Anne Bradstreet, or of Spanish triumphs at Lepanto and Garigliano counterbalancing an Armada defeat—the possibilities are endless, of course. I am firmly of the belief that much of the Anglo's depreciative ("greaser") concept of the Mexican comes right out of the Black Legend inculcation in us of concepts of Nordic superiority over those uniquely cruel and benighted Spaniards and their American progeny. Let me repeat my juxtaposition of "Remember the Armada" and "Remember the Alamo."

I do not advocate forming an antidefamation league to revise our education in Hispanic matters (although the idea is a tempting one, to be sure), nor do I suggest that we expurgate from our classical literature all snide and erroneous references to Spain, Spaniards, and Latin Americans. And it is certainly not necessary or desirable to try to create a "white legend" about Spanish deeds and misdeeds, as some of our more timid professors seem to fear,[4] although this, too, is a bit tempting in view of the long life and pervasiveness of the Black Legend and its echoes. But I do urge that our acknowledged experts and scholars in all matters Hispanic should conduct a much more thorough assessment than heretofore of our errors or, perhaps worse yet, the partial truths, in our education about Hispanic peoples and countries. All that is required, and all that should be demanded, is accuracy of facts, elimination of invidiously erroneous comparisons, and sophisticated historical perspectives. If only as a matter of self-interest, our Hispanists and Latinamericanists should demand that this be done, beginning in our elementary schooling, to the end that teaching and learning at university levels and beyond be based upon foundations that would ease their own burdens.

Our inherited and continuing educational depreciation of the Hispanic World is basic to the fact that our government has not yet been willing to apply that mixture of hard work and high intelligence demanded by our engagement with those countries. Our continuing failure to put forth heroic efforts in the indicated educational reform enormously handicaps our production of sufficient and truly expert personnel for such purposes. Let me illustrate some of this with the words of one of our leading authorities on Latin America, Professor Harry Bernstein:

Look around at the United States, with its millions of Spanish-derived people in New York, Florida, the Southwest, examine the Pacific, or glance throughout the Western Hemisphere, acknowledge the importance of Spain and Portugal to critical North and Central Africa, the Philippines in Southeast Asia—then look at your colleges and universities. See how the Spanish language is handcuffed to literature, unable to break out as the invaluable tool for history, economics, anthropology and social studies, which it certainly is. Do go a bit further and see how Spanish, clinging to its literary self-esteem, transfers its own segregation along to isolate Portuguese. If Spanish has the half-world of literature in which to flourish, Portuguese has still less. A basic language for the contemporary novel, modern art, the study of Brazil today, as well as the history of Luso-Brazilian empire in America, Asia, and Africa, the Portuguese language in American colleges and universities exists in a never-never land; never offered and never studied.

We [who teach in the field] . . . are a lost generation. Not lost in action; lost by inaction. Not lost because of its soul, but because it has lost a generation in its growth. A generation of scholars and teachers in and for the Latin American field is missing. This chapter is missing from the long record of Inter-American cultural history. It never had a chance to grow; the colleges and universities treated it like an orphan. Since 1943, and indeed earlier, Latin America as a field of study has withered on the vine in at least four universities, that I know of, east of Chicago. These places boast of libraries and teaching traditions in the field, but their instructional departments have squeezed the subject. It does not exist, produces no teachers or scholars, gives no serious information to graduates.[5]

Although these statements were made in 1961, they are still essentially true.

Out of the Black Legend kind of error and misconception comes our intellectually suffocating missionary complex with regard, particularly, to Latin America. With self-righteous flourishes and phraseology, we seem determined to fit Latin America to our own pattern, that is, to our brand of democracy and material achievement—and our religious practices, too, if some could have their way. This complex is firmly rooted in the past, with religious and "racial" characteristics inherited from our north European traditions and ancestry. Some of our modern zealots, in their anxiety to reform Latin America—and they do not overlook Spain and Portugal—are not less silly than our seventeenth-century Cotton Mather's dream of Puritan conquest of that area.[6]

A couple of random samples show how this kind of irritating condescension can be unfortunately phrased or timed. Thus, Eric Sevareid, in a documentary on Brazil, presented by CBS in November 1961, indicated that there was hope for that country because "God and, under her new policies, the U.S. government, helps those who help themselves."[7] Or take the case of our famous evangelist, Billy Graham, who, in January 1962, went crusading into Venezuela and Colombia, right on the heels of President Kennedy's goodwill trek through that area; a badly timed and blatant exhibition of missionary arrogance. And remember, as Latin Americans do, what Teddy Roosevelt said about that lack of civilization to the south of us.

Our intelligentsia are still so thoroughly in the habit of what I have called "North American provincialism" that they find little interest or time for any serious examination of our Hispanic relationships, and this inhibits sound appraisal of our views of Hispanic areas. Thus, such a long-standing opinion-maker as Walter Lippman was writing, at the end of 1960: "In our short visit to Brazil I often found myself having to explain why I had never been to South America before and why it was that I had come now." [8] His trip obviously grew out of the panic which hit us relative to the Cuban situation and Latin American hostility and anxieties so vociferously expressed during the unfortunate Nixon tour. It seemed rather late for such a seasoned pundit to be on his first visit to South America. An indication, surely, of where that continent had hitherto been in his scale of values.

As we have seen in our schoolbooks, Spain and Hispanic values do not receive the respectful treatment accorded England, the Netherlands, France, and other north European cultures, and this perpetuates such provincialism. Here is another example of the consequences: John Crosby, the columnist, writing about the opening of Federico García Lorca's play, *The House of Bernarda Alba,* in New York.

. . . The eternal jailhood which is the normal state of Spanish women from birth until death. . . . Passion in Spain is nurtured on deprivation and that fans the flames to a degree almost inconceivable to the rest of us. . . . And there you have all the elements of Spain—today, yesterday, and always—death, poverty, heat, pride, cruelty and passion. . . . Since Spain is almost as foreign to our nature and to our culture as the Far East —the rest of Europe seems as understandable as New England next to Spain—the play has a fascination and exotic allure. . . .[9]

Spain, you see, is hardly a part of "our culture"—about as remote as the Far East. I do not know of any other way to account for this mixture of cultural snobbery and ignorance than to blame it on our general depreciation of Hispanic values and unwillingness to make the effort to understand them. Similar samples of this brand of north-of-the-Pyrenees parochialism could be adduced *ad infinitum;* but, again, there is no need to drink the whole barrel of wine.

Educational reform in the United States, leading to sound, scholarly elimination of the popular myths and prejudices which so badly distort our views of Spain, Portugal, and Latin America is, *ipso facto,* a major order of business. Unfortunately, the corrective scholarship of piecemeal research and the ivory tower academic conference, though necessary and valuable, are too often of the navel-contemplation species. The results trickle down much too slowly into the textbook and teaching areas below the college level. Our scholars should have made massive efforts to speed this trickling, much as scholars in other fields (sciences and mathematics come to mind) have applied themselves to remedial measures—at least partly under the pressure of national interest (especially since "Sputnik"), but also, presumably, in pursuit of excellence. It behooves Hispanists and Latin American specialists to go and do likewise—quickly.

I can think of no more effective propaganda abroad than the news that we are, at long last and seriously, doing this. Instead of propagandistic spread of our self-praise or efforts to make them more like us with a flood of dollars, this should have been the essence of our vaunted "good neighborism," as it should be the foundation of our future course. Along this path, we might not only pull some of the teeth of a dangerous Yankeephobia now become global, but also take some satisfaction in destroying the kind of intellectual parochialism that comports so ill with summit power status. And even without such selfish considerations, the languages and literatures and histories of those peoples are well worth knowing when viewed without the grotesque caricatures, the jaded clichés, and the outright errors that have clouded our vision up to now.

Just prior to World War II, as we have seen, we came close to realizing the importance of acquiring a second idiom, that of the vast Hispanic culture area to the south of us. But antagonistic and distracting political and cultural interests led us away from this into a contortionistic global straddle in which we abandoned interest in the Hispanic nations and rushed to put our thumbs and dollars into dikes everywhere. Our intellectual and political leadership persuaded us that England, France, Germany, and Italy (to mention only some of the major ones) really needed all the money and attention that we lavished upon them. We came to think that the opinions of a Nehru were more worthy of our respect than were the warning opinions of our hemispheric cohabitants (or the rights of Portugal in Goa); that Yugoslavia's Tito (former fighter for Communism in the Spanish Civil War), Chinese agrarian reformers, and a Communist Poland should be placated and wooed; but that Spain should be ostracized and Latin America virtually ignored. Also, we believed that it was more intellectually (and socially) respectable to have euphoric faith in the United Nations than it was to strengthen the Organization of the American States. In short, we looked so far beyond the inner defenses of our future well-being and our possibly penultimate security bastion that we forgot those defenses were there. And they began to crumble for want of intelligent and sympathetic attention.

The neglect of such inner defenses as Latin America and highly strategic Spain and Portugal was a grand and wholly irresponsible aberration. But it was so easy to turn away from them because we had not been taught to respect or understand them. It should be our everlasting shame that military pressure rather than intellectual sophistication brought about our rapprochement with Spain in the 1950s. In the case of Latin America, it required the abusing of our Vice President and the demonstration of violent hostility toward a past formulator (Nelson Rockefeller) of our Latin American policies that caused us to even partially remember that the area is also on our planet and an integral part of Western civilization.

Destruction of the Black Legend and its long chain of echoes and consequences—that historical "tree of hate" whose fruit poisons the English-speaking world and robs it of the capacity to approach the Hispanic world with fairness, with sympathy, and without prejudices—must be the first great step in bridging the chasm that now separates the two largest culture areas of the West. This could also be a significant advance toward readjusting, with some degree of humility, those faulty perspectives that in the earlier years of this century led us into the illusion that we, as instruments of a Divine Providence, were destined to save humanity by making it over in our own image.

The voice of the Spanish people over the millennium could tell us what happens to those who hold global sway and who fail to heed the lessons of propaganda which can harden into history.

Notes

Whenever a work has been given full entry in the Bibliography, the author's name only is given in the Notes, except where a shortened title is added to avoid confusion among several works by the same author.

Chapter 1
Introducing the Hispanophobic Fallacy

1. Throughout this work, I use the terms "Hispanic world," "Hispanic Civilization," and similar phrases, to designate the total of those areas where Spanish and Portuguese speech predominate; i.e., mainly Latin America, Spain, and Portugal.

Portugal, by virtue of a centuries-old English alliance and some of her own anti-Spanish attitudes and actions (plus, in some ways, a less aggressive Catholicism and certainly a smaller role than Spain in European and world affairs), has generally escaped the denigrating attacks suffered by Spain. However, the Portuguese are sometimes damaged indirectly by anti-Spanish attitudes since they are, after all, closely related to Spaniards by blood, history, religion, language, and customs. Thus, they share with Spaniards that general belittlement of Iberian languages and cultures so noticeable in our own and European intellectual circles. Throughout the following pages, then, some Portuguese involvement is usually to be understood.

2. Quoted by John Tate Lanning in "A Reconsideration of Spanish Colonial Culture," *The Americas,* I (October, 1944): 167.

3. See in the bibliography, p. 194, a summary of the movie, *The Spanish Main,* which contains most of the standard clichés. See also Chapter 7 for similar concepts in our educational materials.

4. ". . . Son muy avaros, . . . y . . . son . . . son aptos . . . para robar. . . . No son dados a las letras. . . . Son en sus demostraciones y en el aspecto exterior muy religiosos, pero no de hecho." From *Viaje a España de Francesco Guicciardini, embajador de Florencia ante el Rey Católico,* tr. and ed. José María Alonso Gamo (Valencia, 1952), p. 57.

5. Julián Juderías, *La leyenda negra: Estudios acerca del concepto de España en el extranjero,* 13th ed. (Madrid: Editora National, 1954), p. 161. This work was first published in book form in 1914.

6. "Del concepto que hoy se forma de España," in *Obras completas,* XXXVII, p. 289 (quoted in Juderías, p. 27).

7. Juderías, p. 158.

8. See especially Chapter 3, pp. 50–57, for some comment on the origins of Jewish hispanophobia; and Chapters 4, p. 66, and 5, pp. 102–105, for some refer-

ence to Jewish action against Spain. I owe this parallelism to Carlos Dávila's perceptive article, "The Black Legend," *Américas*, I (August, 1949): 12–15.

9. Juderías, pp. 25–26.

10. See John Francis Bannon, *The Spanish Conquistadores: Men or Devils?*

11. Samuel Flagg Bemis, *A Diplomatic History of the United States*, p. 541 (1942 edition). Also his *Latin American Policy of the United States*, p. 12. See my Chapter 2 for a synthesis of scholarly views showing the errors in these statements.

12. The allusion is to John Walton Caughey, *Gold is the Cornerstone*, Berkeley: University of California Press, 1948. See also my "The Forty-Niners of Sixteenth-Century Mexico," *The Pacific Historical Review*, XIX (August, 1950): 235–249, for some comparative parallelism of this type. My "Peacemaking on North America's First Frontier," *The Americas*, XVI (January, 1960): 221–250, also contains parallelistic observations aimed at making some adjustment of the historical perspective in these matters.

13. The reference is to the offer that Franco made to Winston Churchill to mediate to offset the obviously dangerous consequences of "unconditional surrender" and the Morgenthau Plan (under the byline of John M. Hightower and titled "Churchill Spurns, Exposes Franco's Anti-Red Plan," Santa Barbara *News-Press*, April 9, 1945). Under the byline of Richard Mowrer, there is, incidentally, a provocative echo in the *Christian Science Monitor* of November 10, 1961: "As Arriba [Spanish newspaper] put it three years ago: 'We know that today's world is returning to our trenches, that it is speaking our language, that it is denouncing the enemy [Communism] that we fought yesterday.'

"Generalísimo Francisco Franco recently castigated the tendency abroad to identify authoritarian Spain with Nazi Germany and Fascist Italy 'without taking into account our own characteristics. In the same way,' he said, 'we could tar as Communist the countries of the West which allied themselves with the Soviets in the last conflict and contributed greatly to their power.' "

Chapter 2
Spain in America:
The Real and the Unreal

1. The ruthless fury, the greed for gain
    Were crimes of the time and not of Spain.

Quoted in Charles L. G. Anderson, *Life and Letters of Vasco Núñez de Balboa* (New York: Revell, 1941), p. 4.

2. Two of the principal documentary collections, the Archivo General de Indias (Sevilla) and the Archivo General de la Nación (Mexico) are so massive that they are still largely unexploited. There are other important collections in Spain and numerous, similarly unexploited, local and national collections in Spanish America.

3. This theme is discussed in various works, including: Parks, *Richard Hakluyt*, p. 89; Cawley, *Voyagers*, pp. 304, 380, 381, 388, and his *Unpathed Waters*, p. 220, pp. 252–253. The quotation here given I can vouch for, though I have lost the title and author's name.

4. Hyland, *A Century of Persecution*, p. ix.

5. Leonard, *Books of the Brave*, p. 8.

6. Toynbee, *Study of History*, quoted in Leonard, *Books of the Brave*, p. 10.

7. Hanke, *Spanish Struggle for Justice*, p. 175. Constantino Bayle, *España en*

Indias, Chapter 6 (titled "Quién despobló a América?") and in other parts of this volume injects many sensible comments on this whole subject of Indian diminution.

8. Leonard, *Books of the Brave,* pp. 4, 12, 3.

9. University of California *Bulletin,* V, No. 28 (February 25, 1957): 134–135.

10. Vera Brown Holmes, *A History of the Americas From Discovery to Nationhood* (New York: Ronald Press, 1952), p. 190: "The great majority [of Spaniards] had come to the New World as adventurers and seekers after quick wealth; they were not true colonists in the sense of their being immigrants fleeing an overcrowded homeland or oppressive political conditions in Europe to seek new permanent homes in America."

11. For some indication of the various types going to the New World from Spain, see *Catálogo de pasajeros a Indias durante los siglos XVI, XVII y XVIII,* edited by Cristóbal Bermúdez Plata, 2nd ed., Sevilla, 1940, 1942, 1946. Along this line, and possibly of special help and availability for those interested in correcting broad perspectives in our educational process, I suggest Professor Herbert E. Bolton's essay, "Cultural Cooperation with Latin America," *The Journal of the National Education Association* (January, 1942): 1–4.

12. Just a few of the better known: Doña Mencia de Sanabria and her two daughters, taking some six years to travel from Spain to Paraguay (via Brazil, then overland) to govern there in the name of her son (mid-sixteenth century); the famous mistress of Pedro de Valdivia in the conquest and settlement of Chile. There was a very vigorous and high-handed woman governor of the island of Margarita, in the 1570s; her entertaining story waits, in the Archivo General de las Indias, to be written. There were numerous Spanish women living on the farthest northern frontiers of Mexico in the sixteenth century (see Vito Alessio Robles, *Francisco de Urdiñola y el norte de la Nueva España* Mexico, 1931; also my "Peacemaking on North America's First Frontier," *The Americas,* XVI [January, 1960], 221–250). Notice also, William Lytle Schurz, *This New World,* especially pp. 282–299.

13. Bayle, *España en Indias,* p. 83.

14. Other than the classic Mexican conquest, the diplomacy of Vasco Núñez de Balboa in the Isthmus and of Domingo Martínez de Irala in the Plata area illustrates this basic characteristic of Spanish conquest in America. It might be added that Spaniards, in expanding their American frontiers, proved adept at winning Indian allies and quickly incorporating them into their forces for diplomatic and military service (see, for example, my *Soldiers, Indians and Silver,* Chapter 9).

15. Again, the stories of Cortés, Núñez de Balboa, and Martínez de Irala are illustrative. See Silvio Zavala, *New Viewpoints,* pp. 69–70; in this work and some of his other writings, Zavala, in showing the pretensions of the conquerors and their followers, perforce reveals the essentially middle- or lower-class origins of these invaders of America.

16. ". . . Regulations governing [conquests] and those who waged just war in Mexico, Peru, and even on the periphery of the empire in New Mexico, Chile, and the Philippines never escaped the scrutiny of those who insisted that the Christianization of the Indians and their welfare were the principal aims of the Conquest" (Hanke, *Struggle for Justice,* p. 174). See also, Bayle, *España en Indias,* especially Chapters 1–4.

17. Simpson, *Many Mexicos,* beginning of Chapter 6, titled "Don Antonio de Mendoza."

18. *Colonial Elites: Rome, Spain and the Americas* (The Whidden Lectures). London: Oxford University Press, 1958, p. 42.

19. For example, when the Spanish king introduced the sales tax in Mexico

Notes

in the 1570s, it was at a much lower rate than in the mother country (my "Portrait of an American Viceroy: Martín Enríquez, 1568–1583," *The Americas*, XIV, 11). Arnoldsson, in his *La leyenda negra* (pp. 40–41) indicates that Spain taxed her own kingdom of Castile in heavier fashion, for empire upkeep, than she did her dominions in Italy. "Less than a quarter of the king's annual revenues [mid-1590s] came from remittances of American silver; the rest was borrowed, or was paid for by taxes raised primarily by Castile" (Elliott, *Imperial Spain*, p. 279).

20. See above p. 18 and also note 9.

21. The monumental *Recopilación de leyes de los reynos de las Indias*, the great collection of Spain's legislation for the Americas, is readily available in most college and university libraries, and can be purchased without great difficulty. This one work, even if only lightly perused, will illustrate the point. But, in addition, there are many other collections of viceregal correspondence, royal edicts, and ordinances (local and imperial) which bear out this assertion; plus some good monographic studies now available in English. For anyone interested in pursuing investigation along this line, the nearest university library catalog should be utilized. I have also included in my Bibliography, Section III, some of the more easily available English language authorities in these matters.

22. Just to take the one example of the Dutch: "Holland has but very recently decided to institute higher education. Three centuries after the founding of Batavia (1619) there was still nothing of this nature in the Indies" (Georges H. Bousquet, *A French View of the Netherlands Indies,* London: Oxford University Press, 1940, p. 95). Amry Vandenbosch, *The Dutch East Indies: Its Government, Problems and Politics* (Berkeley: University of California Press, 1944) and Bernard H. M. Vlekke, *The Story of the Dutch East Indies* (Cambridge: Harvard University Press, 1946) generally bear out the same impression, that there was practically nothing at all of the university type even in recent times and that the Dutch record was even weak at the secondary level.

23. Lanning, "A Reconsideration . . . ," *The Americas*, I, 166–178.

24. Meyer, pp. 163–164, and Janssen, XVI, especially Chapters 5, 7, and 8.

25. For some readings that confirm and elaborate the points indicated, see Bibliography, Sections I and III. See also Chapter 3, pp. 53–54, concerning particularly the establishment of the Inquisition in relation to the problem of crypto-Jews. See Chapters 4, pp. 43–44, and 5, pp. 95, concerning anti-Inquisition propaganda.

26. An example, Cecil Roth, *Marranos*, p. 84.

27. The effort of Henry C. Lea, the only sizable treatment in English with any claim to scholarly respectability, is now outdated and badly marred by factual error and prejudice. See Bibliography, Section I, and the Richard Greenleaf work cited in Section III.

28. Hanke and Giménez, pp. xii–xiii.

29. From Lewis Hanke, *Struggle for Justice*, pp. 175, 177, 178. See also Hanke, "Conquest and the Cross," *American Heritage*, XIV, 2 (February, 1963): 4–19, 107–111.

30. Quoted by Lanning in "A Reconsideration"; Spanish version in Juderías, p. 273.

31. For some account of the purposes and history of the printing of this work, see especially: Hanke, *Bartolomé de las Casas: Bookman, Scholar and Propagandist* (Philadelphia: University of Pennsylvania Press, 1952), pp. 42 *et seq.;* Hanke and Giménez Fernández, *Bartolomé de las Casas, 1474–1566* (an annotated bibliographical study), pp. 139 *et seq.*

32. Lanning, "A Reconsideration," p. 166.

33. Mathematically, and obviously, as Indian women produced mestizo chil-

dren, relative Indian numbers declined, for a mestizo was no longer a full-blooded Indian. This is a significant circumstance that too many writers fail to take into account in carelessly recording their (or Las Casas') guesses on Indian diminution. And, time and again, Indians happily slaughtered each other in Spanish-Indian versus Indian alignments; often doing so despite Spanish efforts to prevent it. Indians also died, on a grand scale, from various epidemics. Las Casas probably never knew or experienced any of the great epidemics that decimated the Indians (Hanke and Giménez, p. 151, based on George Kubler, "Population Movements in Mexico, 1520–1620," *The Hispanic American Historical Review*, XXII [1942]: 606–643).

34. Bayle, *España en Indias*, especially Chapter 6, discourses quite reasonably on this general theme of Indian diminution. See also, Diffie, 178–179.

35. For example, Marcel Brion, *Bartolomé de las Casas (Father of the Indians)*, an example of some of the worst features of modern Black Legend writing, based on Las Casas plus seemingly strong hispanophobic prejudice; or Ralph Korngold, *Citizen Toussaint* (for full citations, see Bibliography).

36. Quoted in Hanke and Giménez, p. xvii.

37. Carbia, in Part Three, "La reacción contra la leyenda," pp. 197–238, gives a resumé of the best known literature attacking Las Casas and the Black Legend generally. One of the most recent critical attacks on Las Casas is that of Ramón Menendez Pidal, the eminent Spanish scholar, in his *El Padre Las Casas: Su doble personalidad* (Madrid: Espasa-Calpe, 1963). For an answer to this, see Hanke, "More Heat and Some Light. . . ."

Chapter 3
Roots of Hispanophobia

1. Quoted in Arnoldsson, p. 59.

2. Sverker Arnoldsson, *La leyenda negra: Estudios sobre sus orígenes* (Acta Universitatis Gothoburgensis; Göteborgs Universitets Årsskrift, LXVI, No. 3, 1960): 7. For the Italian and German phases of early anti-Spanish expression, I rely upon Arnoldsson's book, unless otherwise indicated. I have reviewed this work in *The Hispanic American Historical Review*, XLI, 563–564, and, at greater length, in *Historisk Tidskrift* (Stockholm, 1962), pp. 183–186.

3. Gonzalo Jiménez de Quesada, *El Antijovio*, 1567, edited by Rafael Torres Quintero (Bogotá, 1952). Quoted in Arnoldsson, p. 10.

4. Arnoldsson, pp. 22–23. Quotations from this work are my translations.

5. Arnoldsson, pp. 26–34.

6. Arnoldsson, pp. 41–45.

7. Arnoldsson, pp. 58–59.

8. Arnoldsson, p. 99.

9. Approximately: "Attack the Spanish pigs and dogs as if they were frogs, and teach them well what it means to challenge Germans" (a German song of the Schmalkaldic War period, quoted in Arnoldsson, p. 207).

10. Arnoldsson, pp. 115–117.

11. Arnoldsson, pp. 120–123.

12. Arnoldsson, pp. 128–133. The most notable and influential of the anti-Inquisition publications was that of one who called himself Reginaldus Gonsalius Montanus, publishing under the title *Sanctae Inquisitionis Hispanicae artes . . .* (first edition; Heidelberg, 1567). This work was enormously popular for its ring of authenticity in describing minute details of Inquisition tortures and other pro-

cedures. In rapid succession, it was published in German again, then in French, and two each in Dutch and English. It became a veritable bible of anti-Spanish propaganda for another two centuries and more, down to the time of Llorente's famous work.

The work of Montaño (or Montes?), though abounding in errors and exaggerations, placed emphasis upon the theme of Jewish-Moslem heretical tendencies in the Spanish people and upon the Inquisition's pursuit of heretics and Protestants in many parts of Europe, thus reinforcing fears of Spanish universal domination. For an account of this work and its significance, see Marcelino Menéndez Pelayo, *Historia de los heterodoxos españoles,* IV, 152–157.

Among others, Sombart, especially pp. 14 and 187, indicates the Jewish concentration at Frankfurt.

13. Arnoldsson, p. 133. See also some of the quotations from Dutch pamphlets in my Chapter 4.

14. The official Israeli statement, as reported in our press, was approximately these words: "Spain itself did not persecute Jews, but it consorted with nations [i.e., Germany and Italy] which did." There is irony in some later Jewish recognition of Spain's role in aiding Jews to escape from Axis persecution. Thus, "Label A. Katz, president of the Jewish International B'nai B'rith Society, yesterday thanked chief of state Gen. Francisco Franco for Spain's granting asylum to Jews during World War II. At present there are 5,000 Jews in Spain." (Santa Barbara *News-Press* [February 14, 1963]: A-2.) *Newsweek,* March 2, 1970, carried an interesting account of the research of Rabbi Chaim Lipschitz, of Brooklyn's Torah Vodrath and Mesivta Rabbinical Seminary, on Franco's saving Jews from Axis persecution.

15. There is a sizable literature on this, but I shall mention only a few works that are easily available. Cecil Roth, *The History of the Marranos* (there is a paperback edition of 1959, published by Meridian Books and The Jewish Publication Society of America); José Amador de los Ríos, *Historia de los judíos de España y Portugal* (the Buenos Aires 1943 edition); Américo Castro, *The Structure of Spanish History* (Princeton University Press, 1954) gives much on Jewish influences in Spain, especially of a literary nature; Salvador de Madariaga, "Spain and the Jews" (in his *Essays with a Purpose,* London, 1954)—an intriguing little essay, of penetrating insight, which is a good beginning for the bedeviled in these matters.

16. William Thomas Walsh, in *Isabella of Spain,* gives an extensive summary of Jewish prosperity and power in late fifteenth-century Spain; see also, Amador de los Ríos.

17. Cecil Roth, *History of the Marranos,* pp. 27, 30, 31.

18. Newman, *Jewish Influences,* p. 392.

19. Pope Adrian VI, for example, spoke of the whole Spanish nation as "the Jews" (Walsh, *Philip II,* p. 90). ". . . The power, the wealth, the freedom, and the prestige the Jews achieved in Christian Spain between the tenth and fifteenth centuries are without parallel in the history of Israel. . . . More than once the Spanish monarchs were admonished by the pope for their pro-Jewish policy. . . . The tradition of the Spanish kings, whether of Aragon-Catalonia or of Castile, was definitely pro-Jewish" (Madariaga, "Spain and the Jews," *Essays with a Purpose,* pp. 139–141).

20. Neuman, *The Jews in Spain,* especially Part II, Chapter 2; Walsh, *Philip II,* pp. 89–90, and his *Isabella,* pp. 274–275.

21. Let us recall that Jews were still excluded from England, and when they were allowed to return, in small numbers (sixteenth and seventeenth centuries), this immigration was unofficial (Hyamson, *Sephardim of England,* especially pp.

2–13). Dubnow's *History of the Jews in Russia and Poland* recounts some Jewish tribulations that make the Spanish story seem quite mild. And the full story of Jewish persecutions in France, on which there is a sizable literature, makes interesting reading for anyone trying to make a fair judgment of Spanish official action.

22. Jerome Münzer, following his travels in Spain during 1494–1495, wrote that "the Jews and the Marranos were formerly the masters (*amos*) of Spain, because they held the principal posts and exploited the Christians," but now God, through the Catholic Kings, had cured this evil. "Repeatedly, he records the service that King Ferdinand rendered Christianity by defeating the infidels, demolishing the Jewish ghetto of Granada . . . and harshly castigating renegade Christians . . ." (quoted in Arnoldsson, p. 113).

Notice also this perceptive comment: "As long as the victims of the Inquisition were Catholics of Jewish descent who had been proved to be hypocritical members, boring from within during a crucial war for independence against Mohammedans, there never was much outcry against the institution in England or Germany. But it was a great piece of good fortune for the international foes of Spain when they could represent some of their propagandists in the Peninsula as martyrs to Lutheranism" (Walsh, *Philip II*, p. 237).

23. Notice an eighteenth-century Rousseau, in his *Contrat Social:* "There is a profession of purely civic faith the articles whereof it is for the Sovereign to determine. He can force no one to believe in them, but can exile all those who do not. And should any one, after publicly acknowledging these dogmas, behave as if he did not believe in them, let him be punished by death; he has committed the worst of crimes: he has lied before the laws." (Quoted by Madariaga, in his "Spain and the Jews," *Essays*, p. 153.)

In today's United States, be it remembered, perjury (on entry to the country) is grounds for deportation; and advocating the overthrow of our government by force can be punished by imprisonment. The execution of Julius and Ethel Rosenberg on June 19, 1953, is a reminder that treason is punishable by death in our country, in about the same way that religious dissidence or, rather, traitorous fraud, could be so punished in sixteenth-century Spain, England, France, and everywhere else in Europe.

24. Madariaga, "Spain and the Jews," *Essays*, pp. 148–152.

25. In 1474, for example, there were only 12,000 families of Jews in Castile (Merriman, II, 91). "The total number of exiles, of the dead, and of those who submitted to baptism to escape expulsion was probably rather less than more than 200,000" (*Ibid.*, II, 93; based on Lea, I, 142). See also, Olagüe, I, Chapter 4.

26. For an example of some of the best in modern scholarship concerning the decline of Spain in measurable terms rather than unproved generalizations, see Earl J. Hamilton, "The Decline of Spain," *Economic History Review*, VIII (1937–1938): 168–179. See also the four volumes of Olagüe's *Decadencia*.

27. Santa Barbara *News-Press*, November 7, 1961: A-2.

28. "The Spanish Jews, in spite of the Inquisition, were an important factor in the spread of printing in that country." (MacMurtrie, *The Book*, p. 194.)

29. Newman, *Jewish Influences*, especially Books III and IV. See also Chapter 4 of this book.

30. For example: Roth, *Marranos*, pp. 233–234, 285–286. The works of Hyamson, Graetz, Wolf, and other Jewish historians provide many instances of this. Madariaga's *Fall of the Spanish Empire*, pp. 245–254, is an easily available summary of Jewish international action against Spain. Walsh, *Philip II*, also contains a great deal of comment on this. See also Chapter 5, pp. 102–105, of this book.

Chapter 4
The Paper Wars

1. P.A.M. Geurts, *De Nederlandse Opstand in de Pamfletten, 1566–1584* (Nijmegen-Utrecht, 1956). This excellent doctoral thesis provides much of the basis for my comments on this phase of Dutch propaganda in fighting Spanish rule.

2. For some of the most recent and reliable judgments on Dutch-Spanish conflict see: Pieter Geyl, *The Revolt of the Netherlands (1555–1609)*, and his *The Netherlands in the Seventeenth Century (Part One, 1609–1648)*.

3. The first sentence is from Geurts' summary in English, p. 299; the remainder is on p. 35.

4. The Dutch version is:

> Voor Godt wil ick belijden
> End zijner grooter Macht,
> Dat ick tot gheenen tijden
> Den Coninck heb veracht:
> Dan dat ick Godt den Heere,
> Der Hoochster Majesteyt,
> Heb moeten obediëren
> In der gherechticheyt.

(Theodoor Weevers, *Poetry of the Netherlands*, p. 195.) See also Geurts, p. 158.

5. Geurts, pp. 49, 134. For example, the pamphlet *Pandorae sive veniae Hispanicae Belgicis Exvlibus* (Number 222 in Willem Pieter Cornelis Knuttel, *Catalogus van de Pamfletten-verzameling berustende in de Koninklijke Bibliotheek*, 9 vols, The Hague, 1889). Hereafter, references to this basic catalog will be shortened to "Knuttel," plus pamphlet number.

6. Notice Levin, *History as Romantic Art*, p. 255, with reference to Motley's stress on Dutch fear of the Spanish Inquisition.

7. Geurts, pp. 175–178.

8. See above, p. 48, based on Arnoldsson. As Arnoldsson points out, Orange's German origins and continuing connections, plus other German-Dutch relationships undoubtedly account for such borrowing of anti-Spanish themes and phraseology.

9. Geurts, p. 161.

10. There is much literature on this; for a recent, balanced resumé, see Lynch, *Spain under the Hapsburgs*, I, pp. 175–180. See also Geurts, pp. 164–167, "Don Carlos in the Pamphlets"; and Walsh, *Philip II*, especially Chapters 21 and 22.

11. Geurts, pp. 174–175.

12. Geurts, p. 183.

13. An illustrative Dutch admission is described in Bayle, *España en Indias:* "[Padre Petters, speaking in the Congreso Misional, Barcelona, in 1931, said] I am Dutch, that is to say I am a victim of national antipathy toward Spain; antipathies so deeply rooted that they are virtually taken in with mother's milk and fermented by an absurd system of education and historical instruction in our schools." This quotation is taken from Petters' "Vindicación de España en Filipinas," Archivo Agustiniano, July, 1931.

14. Roth, *Marranos*, p. 90. For a recent American textbook "double standard" treatment of Dutch-Spanish actions *vis-à-vis* Portugal, see Chapter 7, p. 141.

15. Koninklijke Bibliotheek (The Hague), Pamphlet 1449. (Hereafter KB, followed by pamphlet number.)

16. KB, 1078.

17. KB, 1199.

18. KB, 1230.

19. KB, 1300.

20. KB, 1345.

21. Walsh, *Philip II*, pp. 412, 464; Isidore Harris, "A Dutch Burial-Ground and its English Connections," Jewish Historical Society of England, *Transactions*, VII, 113. Dutch, English, and French flirting with Moslems to encourage attacks on Spain seems a bit like recent tendencies in certain circles to see more danger in cultivating relations with a very Western and Christian Spain than in building bridges to a Communist Russia.

22. KB, 1424.

23. KB, 1581.

24. See Note 13, above. One Dutch Professor, J.W.A. van Soest, long gathered materials illustrating Black Legend manifestations in his own country, and he has published articles in Dutch and Spanish on the theme. But he admits, in conversation, that it is still impossible to convince his countrymen of the distortions of the Legend (personal conversations, The Hague, 1961).

25. Geyl, *Revolt*, p. 265. See Arnoldsson, pp. 138–140, for some comment on Marnix's library holdings as they reflected Black Legend influences.

26. Geyl, pp. 268, 270, 271.

27. Walsh, *Philip II*, especially pp. 404–416, pulls these threads together in convenient form.

28. Geyl, *Revolt*, p. 291.

29. Weevers, *Poetry*, pp. 108–109, 95–96.

30. *Ibid.*, pp. 194–195.

31. Adrianum Valerium, *Neder-landtsche Gedenck-clanck . . .* , Haerlem, 1626.

32. Lindabury, *Patriotism in the Elizabethan Drama*, p. 59.

33. Hughes, *Reformation in England*, III, pp. 401–402.

34. Cawley, *Voyagers*, p. 278.

35. The introduction bears this title: "To the Reader. Spanish cruelties and tyrannies, perpetrated in the West Indies, commonly termed The newe found worlde. Briefly described in the Castilian language, by the Bishop Fryer Bartholomew de las Casas or Casaus, a Spaniarde of the order of Saint Dominick, faithfully translated by James Aliggrodo, to serve as a President and warning, to the XII, Provinces of the lowe Countries." This is followed by an epigraph: "Happie is hee whome other mens harmes doe make to beware."

36. W. G. R. Taylor, *Writings of the Two Richard Hakluyts*, II, p. 246, note 2.

37. See especially, Parks, *Richard Hakluyt*.

38. See Bibliography, Section II, under Antoine Arnauld and Robert Ashley, for full citation of these pamphlets.

39. Scott, *The Belgicke Pismire* (see Bibliography, Section II).

40. For a list of some of Scott's major publications against Spain, see Bibliography, Section II.

41. Schelling, *Foreign Influences in Elizabethan Plays*, pp. 124–126.

42. *Ibid.*, pp. 113–115.

43. Cawley, *Unpathed Waters*, p. 134.

44. *Ibid.*, especially pp. 220, 224, 253; and his *Voyages, passim.*

45. Cawley, *Voyages*, p. 304.

46. *Ibid.*, pp. 125–126.

47. *Ibid.*, p. 364.

48. Under the title: *Kurtze Erklaerung der Fuernembsten Thaten so durch die Spanier beschehen in etlichen Orten der neuwen West so in Folgenden Kup-*

fferstuecken schoenzierlich vnd kuenstlich derselben bey jeder Historien jetzt ins Teutsch dar gegeben werden.

49. Parks, *Hakluyt,* especially pp. 161–163. For reproductions of the De Bry engravings, see pp. 81–90. Lewis Hanke's "Conquest and Cross" reproduces watercolors that evidently served as a basis for the De Bry engravings and were originally intended, apparently, to accompany a 1583 French edition of the *Brief Relation.*

Chapter 5
The Arrogance of Enlightenment

1. For a convenient resumé of the Antonio Pérez story in English, see Lynch, *Spain under the Habsburgs,* pp. 304–306, 340–343.

2. Some of the best scholarly efforts in evaluation of Philip II are listed and appraised in Tomo XIX, Volumen I of the large *Historia de España* (directed by Ramón Menéndez Pidal); the "Prólogo," pp. ix-xliv (by Cayetano Alcázar Molina). This "Prólogo" and the following "Preámbulo" also summarize the main lines of controversy regarding Philip and his times.

3. For successive foreign editions of Las Casas, see the work of Lewis Hanke and Giménez Fernández. The González Montaño work saw the following repetitions, partial or complete and in various languages, following the first edition in Heidelberg, in 1567: Heidelberg, 1569, 1603, 1611; Hamburg, 1611; London, 1568, 1569, and 1625; a French translation of 1568; a Dutch translation done in London, 1569, and in Amsterdam the same year (the latter reprinted in 1620). In addition, this work was very frequently the basis for all kinds of summaries, extracts, engravings, popular stories, novels, etc.

4. Charles E. Passage, "Introduction," in Schiller, *Don Carlos, Infante of Spain,* p. xiv. On pp. xvi-xxii, there is a brief resumé of the growth of the literary Don Carlos from Saint-Réal to Schiller to Verdi.

5. *Ibid.,* p. xvii.

6. *Ibid.,* p. xviii. The *Don Carlos* was first presented in the theater at Mannheim, in 1787.

7. Juderías, pp. 229–233. Schiller's *Don Carlos* was presented in New York as early as 1799.

8. See Carbia, especially Chapter 4, pp. 97–124.

9. See especially Carbia, pp. 97–124.

10. For some examples of Jewish literary activities and other anti-Spanish action and writing see: Bueno de Mesquita, "The Historical Associations of the Ancient Burial-Ground of the Sephardic Jews," JHSE, *Transactions,* X, 225–254; David W. Davies, *The World of the Elseviers, 1580–1712* (The Hague: Nijhoff, 1954): 129–130; Henry V. Besso, *Dramatic Literature of the Sephardic Jews of Amsterdam in the XVIIth and XVIIIth Centuries;* Roth, *Marranos,* especially Chapter 8, but also *passim;* Hyamson, *Sephardim of England,* pp. 12–13; Israel Solomons, "David Nieto and some of his Contemporaries," JHSE, *Transactions,* XII, 1–102; Lucien Wolf, *Essays in Jewish History,* especially Essay II, "Cromwell's Jewish Intelligencers," pp. 93–114.

11. Editor's Introduction, p. xvi, *Thomas Gage's Travels in the New World;* edited by J. Eric S. Thompson (Norman, Okla., University of Oklahoma Press, 1959).

12. Hanke and Gimenéz, pp. 139–156.

13. Carbia, pp. 115–118. It was this brand of defamation, coming from an

Italian author that provoked Constantino Bayle's *España en Indias,* which I have used extensively.

14. Carbia, pp. 119–121. For full citation of Marmontel's work, see Bibliography, Section II.

15. On Davenant's *Cruelty,* see Cawley, *Voyagers,* p. 291, 298, 304, pp. 344–345; and his *Unpathed Waters,* pp. 249–253. On Las Casas and our war with Spain, see my Chapter 6, p. 122.

16. See Hanke and Giménez, pp. 141–142, on the popularity and wide distribution of the Las Casas tracts in our early private and public libraries. Notice also the comments in Williams, *Spanish Background of American Literature,* especially pp. 3, 17, 23, 36, 37, pp. 41–43.

17. Hyamson, *Sephardim of England,* gives a full account of this story and, *passim,* mentions various Jewish actions directed against Spain.

18. Bloom, *Economic Activities of the Jews of Amsterdam,* especially pp. 45–46, pp. 61, 88, 130.

19. *Ibid.,* p. xv, pp. 8–9.

20. *Ibid.,* pp. 20–21, based on A. C. Kruseman, "Aanteekeningen betreffende den Boekhandel van Noord Nederland in de 17e en 18e Eeuw," *BGNB,* VI (1893): 98 ff.

21. *Ibid.,* 45, based on M. M. Kleerkooper and W. P. van Stockum, *De Boekhandel te Amsterdam, voornamelijk in de 17e eeuw* (The Hague, 1914–1916).

22. Newman, *Jewish Influences,* pp. 392–393, 629.

23. Davies, *Elseviers,* pp. 129–130.

24. Bloom, pp. 75–81, and Besso, *passim.*

25. See especially the works of Hyamson, Roth, Lucien Wolf, and Bueno de Mesquita, listed in Bibliography, Section I.

26. Steinberg, *Five Hundred Years,* pp. 180–181.

27. Madariaga, *Rise of the Spanish American Empire,* p. 173.

28. *Time,* European Overseas Edition (February 3, 1961): 32.

29. Juderías, p. 238.

30. *The Spirit of the Laws* (Thomas Nugent translation, New York: Hafner, 1949), Book VIII, 18, pp. 121–122.

31. *Ibid.,* Book X, 4, p. 137.

32. For full citation, see Bibliography, Section II. Raynal and his work are bitterly discussed in both Juderías, pp. 239–240, and Carbia, pp. 151–155.

33. Summers, *The Gothic Quest,* p. 196.

34. *Ibid.,* pp. 154–155.

35. *Ibid.,* pp. 191, 193.

36. *Ibid.,* pp. 190, 193.

37. *From Paris to Cadiz,* tr. and ed. by A. E. Murch, London, 1958, pp. 72–76.

38. *A Romantic in Spain* [*Un Voyage en Espagne*], tr. and Introduction by Catherine Alison Phillips, New York, Knopf, pp. 107, 109, 113.

39. Lewis Hanke, "Dos palabras on Antonio de Ulloa and the *Noticias Secretas,*" *The Hispanic American Historical Review,* XVI, pp. 479–514. This article is very useful as a small guide to the literature concerning the use of Las Casas, especially in the eighteenth century, by the French and others; and as commentary on this phase of the *leyenda negra* as background for the Spanish American independence struggle.

40. Juderías, especially in Book IV, discourses on this interesting theme. Juderías sternly takes to task those of his countrymen who, due to apathy or to uncritical acquiescence in foreign views of Spain, bear much blame for the Legend's success and perpetuation.

Chapter 6
Of Matricide and American Dogmas

1. "Progress is dehispanizing one's self." 1864. Quoted in Carbia, p. 177.

2. *Ibid.,* especially pp. 156–173, treats this theme and cites examples; in subsequent pages, he illustrates some of the postwar utilization of the Black Legend in Spanish America.

3. Such as a Spanish-Mexican clash at Vera Cruz in 1829; Spanish participation in the early phase of the invasion of Mexico, 1861; the so-called War of Revindication, 1865–1867, a minor clash along the coasts of Peru and Chile; circumstances connected with the brief return of the Dominican Republic to Spanish rule, 1861–1865; the off-and-on festering of the Cuban situation; individual country diplomatic imbroglios with Spain. There was also some continuing antagonism toward Spanish citizens who remained in the new American nations.

4. Carbia, pp. 179–194, devotes a chapter to the theme of Liberal utilization of the Black Legend, with many illustrative examples.

5. For an amusing resumé of the story, see the 1967 edition of Lesley Simpson, *Many Mexicos,* pp. 22–24.

6. Some quotations and bibliographical references are to be found in the easily available Bailey, *A Diplomatic History of the American People,* especially the chapters concerning war with Mexico and the United States *vis-à-vis* Cuba.

7. Levin, *History as Romantic Art,* p. 3.

8. *Ibid.,* pp. 35–36. Unless otherwise indicated, I am using this author and my own reading for generalized comments concerning these historians.

9. Pieter Geyl, *Revolt of the Netherlands* (New York: Barnes and Noble, 1958), p. 15. Notice also Wheaton, "Motley and the Dutch Historians," *The New England Quarterly,* XXXV (September, 1962): 318–336.

10. Geyl, *Revolt,* p. 16; and Levin, *op. cit.,* pp. 40, 42, and *passim.*

11. Francis Parkman, *Provinces of France in the New World: French and English in North America. Part I* (Boston, Little-Brown, 1914; earlier copyrights in 1865, 1885, 1897). Prefatory Note and pp. 20–21, 96–97, 102.

12. Albert Bushnell Hart, *The Monroe Doctrine, an Interpretation* (Boston, 1917), p. 21 (quoted in Hanke, *Bartolomé de las Casas, Scholar and Propagandist,* p. 59).

13. Hanke, *op. cit.,* pp. 58–59, and his "Conquest and Cross," in *American Heritage.*

14. Bailey, *Diplomatic History* (various editions; see the chapter titled "The Coming of the War with Spain, 1895–1898"). See also Millis, *The Martial Spirit,* and Wisan, *The Cuban Crisis as Reflected in the New York Press (1895–1898).*

15. Henry Watterson, *History of the Spanish-American War: Embracing a Complete View of our Relations with Spain* (San Francisco: Bronson & Co., 1898).

16. *Patriotic Eloquence Relating to the Spanish American War and Its Issues,* compiled by Robert I. Fulton and Thomas C. Trueblood (New York: Scribner's, 1903), p. 14.

17. *Ibid.,* p. 307.

Chapter 7
Educating America, in Chiaroscuro

1. "The Church and the Enlightenment in the Universities," John Tate Lanning, *The Americas,* XV, No. 4 (April, 1959): 333–349.

2. *Latin America in School and College Teaching Materials: Report of the*

Committee on the Study of Teaching Materials on Inter-American Subjects (American Council of Education, Washington, D.C. 1944). Hereafter cited as ACE *Report*.

3. Charles Gibson, "The Colonial Period in Latin American History," *Service Center for Teachers of History: A Service for the American Historical Association*, Washington, D.C., 1958.

4. This and the following quotations come from schoolbooks in use during the period 1956–1970. Since the authors of these books were undoubtedly sincere and certainly not to be accused of purposeful distortion, I do not cite names, titles, or publishers. Instead, I follow the ACE *Report* method of using representative samplings to convey the flavor of such texts, in things Hispanic, for purposes of comparison with scholarly judgments and to illustrate the fact that the ACE *Report*'s warnings have largely gone unheeded.

5. James Mitchell Clarke, *The People of Mexico: A History for Children.* Quotations from pp. 164–166, 171, 185–187.

6. The great Dutch historian, Geyl, has this to say about Dutch overseas colonization interests: "Unfortunately the theory of colonization, such as Usselincx developed it in masterly pamphlets, never appealed to the rulers of the North Netherlands state, and the Amsterdamers who made use of his services certainly were more interested in privateering raids at the expense of the Spanish colonies than in the founding of settlements of their own race." In commenting on the Dutch plan for a West Indies Company, he calls it "a project directed against Spain's own colonial territory in America. . . ." (p. 254 of his *Revolt*). This is all very different, of course, from the Spanish theories and practices of overseas effort which were, from the start, firmly founded upon colonization and cultural transplantation.

Incidentally, during residence in The Netherlands (1961), I examined some high school texts designed for use there as well as in the Caribbean territories. I found that, although they are very similar to ours in the hispanophobic bias, they seem, on the basis of this sampling, to be more sophisticated in such matters as recognizing the complexities of Spanish overseas efforts and in judgment of the European aspects of Spanish action. That is, despite the deep entrenchment of hispanophobia growing out of their conflicts with Spain and pamphleteering against her, their texts for high schools seem more mature than ours—less of the simplistic kind of naïveté. The two texts from which I took notes and quotations are: *Leerboek der Geschiedenis,* by Dr. J. J. Westendorp Boerma (Zwolle: Tjeenk Willink, 1958), for use in The Netherlands; and *Geschiedenis van Amerika I,* by Drs. C. Ch. Goslinga, A. C. H. J. van Noort, and H. E. SjahShie (Groningen: J. B. Wolters, 1961), for use in the Caribbean possessions.

7. Greer Williams, "Hunting the Invisible Killers," *The Saturday Evening Post* (September 26, 1959), p. 56.

Chapter 8
Bedevilment in Foreign Policy

1. From his Foreword to William Benton's *The Voice of Latin America,* New York, 1961.

2. Thomas A. Bailey, *A Diplomatic History of the American People* (3rd ed.; New York: Crofts, 1947), p. 482.

3. *Ibid.,* pp. 533–547, for a lively discussion and resumé of the Panama episode (including bibliographical references, p. 547 and pp. 890–891).

4. *Ibid.,* p. 558.

Notes

5. See especially Williams, *Spanish Background of American Literature,* where considerable attention is given to this.

6. Drew Pearson's column in the Santa Barbara *News-Press,* January 5, 1963.

7. Unfortunately, student judgment in such matters is often bedeviled by professorial behavior. For example, this quotation from the public performance of a Stanford economics professor at the end of 1960: "Fidel Castro is one of the great men of this century. I wish more countries had more Castros. I consider him one of the most brilliant men I have ever met. . . . An election [in Cuba] could give [the anti-Castro] group an opportunity to take form and become organized." This professor thought that eventually an election would be necessary, but that if it were now held it would "merely help the counterrevolutionists." (Quoted by Bob Considine in a column in the San Francisco *Examiner,* December 5, 1960.) Even if this is a misquotation (always a possibility, of course), it did represent the thinking of a very vocal segment of our academic world, as I verified by personal conversations. The doctrinaire Leftists in our academic world were generally quick to sympathize with Fidel Castro, but wiser heads, including most of those genuinely conversant with Latin American affairs, were not usually so rash.

8. Professor John Tate Lanning penned a delightfully sarcastic commentary on this in his "Reconsideration," pp. 168–170.

9. "Bogotazo" is a word now commonly used in Latin America to designate the destructive upheaval that occurred in Bogotá during the Ninth International Conference of the American States (April, 1948). Much of the center of the city was gutted by Molotov cocktails and other weapons, and some hundreds lost their lives. The immediate cause of this *tumulto* was the assassination of Jorge Eliécer Gaitán, popular demagogue of the Left wing of the Liberal Party.

The *bogotazo,* if only because of its sensational qualities, should have awakened our government and our public to the strong stirrings of Latin American discontent and resentment against us which were reflected in the Conference itself. But this fundamental was swept under the carpet by our delegation, in one of the sorriest of our performances in inter-American conferences; but few—except Latin Americans, of course—seemed to care. This was one of the earliest and clearest examples of that foot-dragging process that carried on through the Eisenhower administration and got its rude awakening during the Nixon travels of 1958 and the subsequent crescendo of the Cuban crisis.

10. At the moment when Secretary of State Acheson and President Truman were so outspokenly rejecting rapprochement with Franco Spain, there was, in our country, a campaign—complete with posters in store windows—to encourage us to attend church as an antidote to Communism. Quite obviously, Spaniards were attending the wrong church. Mr. Acheson, publicly and distastefully (for a Secretary of State, at least), criticized Spain for not having a habeas corpus law, and Mr. Truman swore, also publicly, that he would never be a party to the return of our ambassador to Madrid. Both reversed their stands before the year was out.

11. José María Massip, Washington correspondent for Madrid's *ABC,* in *Diario de Barcelona,* August 18, 1962.

12. Recalling the Massip comments, note this 1961 vignette in the *Saturday Evening Post:*

Hanging on his White House telephone, Richard Goodwin, 29-year-old adviser on Latin American affairs, examines an Ecuadorian magazine as his call goes through [accompanying picture shows him looking at said magazine]. A ring from Goodwin sets things moving. As President Kennedy's assistant special counsel, he helps frame such major programs as the Alliance for Progress. He has also worked on conflict-of-interest policy and on civil-rights. A *summa cum laude* graduate of Harvard Law School, Goodwin clerked for Supreme Court Justice Felix Frankfurter, later was an investigator for the House subcommittee which broke open the TV-quiz scandals. He joined the campaign staff of fellow Bostonian John Kennedy early, wound up with a White House desk. Goodwin is married and lives in Arlington, Virginia. Some columnists and commentators harp on his inexperience—despite his specialty, Goodwin cannot speak Spanish (he is study-ing it now) and when appointed had never set foot in Latin America. Goodwin's boss, accustomed to attack from the pundits, views the criticism of his young aide as a good omen. "Why," says the President, "I wasn't getting belted like that until I was thirty-six."

13. Donald M. Dozer, *Are We Good Neighbors? Three Decades of Inter-American Relations, 1930–1960* (Gainesville: University of Florida Press, 1961), p. 188.

Chapter 9
Perspectives and Prescription

1. *Latin America in School and College Teaching Materials* . . . , p. 31 (for full citation see Bibliography, Section I).

2. "The Church and the Enlightenment in the Universities," *The Americas,* XV (April, 1959): 333.

3. Spanish fortitude, which is certainly more pleasant to know as ally than as enemy, has interesting facets, illustrated by this anecdote. In 1962, during an interview I had at El Pardo with Chief of State Franco, we discussed, *inter alia,* the Black Legend defamation of Spain and Spaniards. The Generalísimo, like most of his patriotic countrymen, is sensitively aware of the damage the Legend has done to his people, and he immediately pointed to the unfairness of damning the Spanish conquistadores for their iniquities when it is their almost superhuman courage and fortitude that should be recognized and praised. He then broadened this to express a great pride in the general hardihood of his people. "They can put up with almost anything," he said, "and the best proof of it is that they have put up with me for twenty-five years."

4. See, for example, Benjamin Keen, "The Black Legend Revisited: Assump-tions and Realities," *The Hispanic American Historical Review,* XLIX (November, 1969): 703–719. Then read Lewis Hanke's "A Modest Proposal . . . ," *HAHR,* Vol. 51 (February, 1971), an excellent scholarly answer to Professor Keen.

5. From a speech titled "Cold War in the Curriculum," delivered before the Eighth Annual Conference on International Education of the Metropolitan Com-mittee on International Education, New York, March 4, 1961. Availability and permission to quote kindly granted by Professor Bernstein through the good offices of my colleague, Professor Donald M. Dozer.

6. Williams, *Spanish Background of American Literature*, p. 17.

7. Quoted in the Santa Barbara *News-Press,* November 3, 1961.

8. Quoted in the Santa Barbara *News-Press,* December 2, 1960.

9. From a column in the Paris *Herald-Tribune,* June 14, 1960.

Bibliography

Explanatory Note

The following lists are by no means exhaustive. They are samplings of the kinds of evidence relatively easily available to the English-language reader in the United States. This is especially true of Section II, "Black Legend Manifestations," for it is obviously not feasible to try to cite all works which contain disparaging, false, or misleading comment of Black Legend type—the very size of such a task is the best evidence of the pervasiveness of such expressions in our national life. And Section III, "Scholarly Revision of the Black Legend," is also but a taste, for much of this corrective work has been done in foreign languages. The bibliographies contained in many of the works cited in Sections I and III can lead the interested reader to additional materials.

Section I consists mainly of those works that I have found most helpful in assembling ideas or evidence for telling the broad story of the Black Legend and its effects in our country. This list necessarily contains some materials in foreign languages, but I have tried to limit such references to works specifically cited in text or notes or to those which serve as samples of a class of materials (such as the Knuttel catalog of Dutch pamphlets). German, French, Italian, and other ramifications of the Black Legend are many, but a comprehensive list of all such materials would be unnecessarily long and not of use to the general reader. The Arnoldsson work can serve as a guide especially to the German and Italian; and the very basic Sánchez Alonso bibliographies can be helpful in most every line.

There is inevitably some overlapping of these lists, for works in Section III are often of use in the general story of the Black Legend and vice versa (for example, the writings of Professor John Tate Lanning). But I have made separate entities of Sections II and III in the hope that they will be useful especially to teachers or publishers as guides to "do's and don't's," so to speak, in correction of Black Legend fallacies. Thus, by comparing the sounder judgments contained in Section

III with the common brand of error in Section II, one can evaluate for himself the great disparities which are the essence of the hispanophobic fallacy.

Section I
General Bibliography

Amador de los Ríos, José. *Historia social, política y religiosa de los judíos de España y Portugal.* 3 vols. Madrid, 1875–1876.

Arnoldsson, Sverker. *La Conquista Española de América, según el juicio de la posteridad: Vestigios de la leyenda negra.* Madrid, 1960.

———. *La leyenda negra: Estudios sobre sus orígenes.* Göteborg, 1960 (Acta Universitatis Gothoburgensis, Göteborgs Universitets Årsskrift, vol. LXVI, no. 3, 1960).

Bailey, Thomas A. *A Diplomatic History of the American People.* New York: Crofts, 1940.

Bayle, Constantino. *España en Indias: Nuevos ataques y nuevas defensas.* Vitoria, Spain, 1934.

Bernstein, Harry. "Cold War in the Curriculum." Speech read before the Eighth Annual Conference on International Education of the Metropolitan Committee on International Education, New York, March 4, 1961. Mimeographed copy made available to me by Professor Donald M. Dozer and utilized with the permission of the author.

———. *Making an Inter-American Mind.* Gainesville: University of Florida Press, 1961.

Bertrand, Louis. *El enemigo de Felipe II: Antonio Pérez, secretario del rey.* Madrid, 1943.

Besso, Henry V. *Dramatic Literature of the Sephardic Jews of Amsterdam in the Seventeenth and Eighteenth Centuries.* New York: Hispanic Institute in the United States, Sección de estudios sefardíes, 1947 (Reprinted from the *Bulletin Hispanique*, XXXIX–XLI).

Bloom, Herbert I. *The Economic Activities of the Jews of Amsterdam in the Seventeenth and Eighteenth Centuries.* Williamsport, Pa.: The Bayard Press, 1937.

British Museum. *Catalogue of Early English Books to 1640.*

Bullen, Arthur H., ed. *A Collection of Old English Plays.* New York, 1964.

Carbia, Rómulo D. *Historia de la leyenda negra hispanoamericana.* Madrid: Publicaciones del Consejo de la Hispanidad, 1944. Carbia was "Doctor en Historia Americana y Profesor Titular en las Universidades de Buenos Aires y La Plata." Passionately dedicated to exposure of the fallacies of the Black Legend, this work is very useful as a comprehensive summary of the history and effects of the Legend and a reference to pertinent bibliography.

Cawley, Robert. *The Voyagers and Elizabethan Drama.* Boston and London: Oxford University Press, 1938.

———. *Unpathed Waters: Studies in the Influence of the Voyagers on Elizabethan Literature.* Princeton, N.J.: Princeton University Press, 1940.

Davies, David W. *The World of the Elseviers, 1580–1712.* The Hague: Nijhoff, 1954.

Dávila, Carlos. "The Black Legend," *Américas* (Pan American Union), I (August 1949): 12–15.

————. *We of the Americas*. New York: Ziff-Davis, 1949.

Dozer, Donald M. *Are We Good Neighbors? Three Decades of Inter-American Relations, 1930–1960.* Gainesville: University of Florida Press, 1961.

Elliott, John H. *Imperial Spain, 1469–1716.* London: Edward Arnold, 1963.

Geurts, P. A. M. *De Nederlandse Opstand in de Pamfletten, 1566–1584.* Nijmegen-Utrecht, 1956.

Geyl, Pieter. *The Revolt of the Netherlands (1555–1609).* New York, 1958.

————. *The Netherlands in the Seventeenth Century. Part One, 1609–1648.* London, 1961.

Gibson, Charles, ed. *The Black Legend: Anti-Spanish Attitudes in the Old World and the New.* New York: Knopf, 1971. An anthology of nineteen selections illustrating the Black Legend kind of writing, plus three (including Julián Juderías and Ramón Menéndez Pidal) "revisionist interpretations." Some of the most famous authors presented are William of Orange (*Apologia*), Oliver Cromwell, Las Casas, Montaigne, Davenant, Montesquieu, Voltaire. The editor offers helpful commentary for each selection and a 25-page Introduction explaining the significance of the Black Legend, then describes its main tenets and contrasts them with what he terms "White Legend" views of Spain and Spaniards.

Gibson, Charles, and Benjamin Keen. "Trends of United States Studies in Latin American History," *American Historical Review,* 62 (1957): 855–877.

Graetz, Heinrich H. *History of the Jews,* 6 vols. Philadelphia: The Jewish Publication Society of America, 1891–1898. Although the author is passionately hispanophobic, his Volumes IV and V are very useful as a guide to the great variety of Jewish activity both inside and outside the Spanish Empire during the most important period of Black Legend formation. His work is also helpful in comparing the Jewish-Spanish relationship with the fate and activities of Jews elsewhere.

Hakluyt, Richard. *The Original Writings and Correspondence of the Two Richard Hakluyts.* Second Series, vols. 76 and 77. London: Hakluyt Society, 1935. Introduction and notes by Eva Germaine R. Taylor.

Hanke, Lewis. *Bartolomé de las Casas: An Interpretation of His Life and Writings.* The Hague: Nijhoff, 1951.

————. *Bartolomé de las Casas, Bookman, Scholar and Propagandist.* Philadelphia: University of Pennsylvania Press, 1952.

————. *Bartolomé de las Casas, Historian: An Essay in Spanish Historiography.* Gainesville: University of Florida Press, 1952.

————. "Conquest and the Cross," *American Heritage,* XIV (February, 1963): 4–19, 107–111.

————. "Dos palabras on Antonio de Ulloa and the *Noticias Secretas,*" *The Hispanic American Historical Review,* XVI (November, 1936): 479–514.

————, and Manuel Giménez F. *Bartolomé de las Casas, 1474–1566: Bibliografía crítica y cuerpo de materiales para el estudio de su vida, escritos, actuación y polémicas que suscitaron durante cuatro siglos.* Santiago de Chile: Fondo Histórico y Bibliográfico José Toribio Medina, 1954. As the title indicates, this is a basic work for any examination of the Black Legend. It is particularly useful as a guide to the many editions of the Las Casas works which served as propaganda against Spain and also in the many notes which illustrate the pros and cons of the Las Casas version of Spain in America. Comment on the wide availability of the Las Casas writings in early private and public libraries in our own country and on some of the echoes of Las Casas in the United States illustrates the importance of Back Legend influence in our national life.

————. "A Modest Proposal for a Moratorium on Grand Generalizations: Some

Bibliography

Thoughts on the Black Legend," *The Hispanic American Historical Review*, 51 (February, 1971): 112–127.

———. "More Heat and Some Light on the Spanish Struggle for Justice in the Conquest of America," *The Hispanic American Historical Review*, XLIV (August, 1964): 293–340.

Harris, Isidore. "A Dutch Burial-Ground and its English Connections," Jewish Historical Society of England, *Transactions*, VII (1911–1914).

Hayes, Carlton J. *Wartime Mission in Spain: 1942–1945.* New York, 1946.

———. *The United States and Spain: An Interpretation.* New York, 1951. These two books contain revealing commentaries on the strength and dangers of anti-Spanish propaganda in our country as related to our foreign policies. As clearly implied in these volumes, and as indicated in my preceding text, such propagandas aimed at Franco Spain depend partly upon deep roots of hispanophobic type for their effectiveness. The second work above cited also contains helpful generalizations concerning our relations with Spain in a historical sense, related to Black Legend attitudes in our country.

Historia de España (under the direction of Ramón Menéndez Pidal). Madrid, Espasa-Calpe, 1935–. Tomo XIX, 2 vols., under title of "España en tiempo de Felipe II" (1958) of this continuing publication is the work most pertinent, so far available, to the Black Legend theme.

Hughes, Philip. *The Reformation in England.* London, 1950, and New York, 1951.

Hyamson, Albert M. *The Sephardim of England: A History of the Spanish and Portuguese Community, 1492–1951.* London, 1951.

Hyland, St. George Kieran. *A Century of Persecution under Tudor and Stuart Sovereigns from Contemporary Records.* New York, 1920.

Janssen, Johannes. *History of the German People after the Close of the Middle Ages.* Tr. by A. M. Christie. 17 vols. New York: AMS Press, 1966. (Vols. 1–14 bear the title . . . *at the Close of the Middle Ages.*)

Juderías, Julián. *La leyenda negra: Estudios acerca del concepto de España en el extranjero.* Madrid: Editora Nacional, 1954. 13th edition.

Keen, Benjamin. "The Black Legend Revisited: Assumptions and Realities," *The Hispanic American Historical Review*, XLIX (November, 1969): 703–719.

Knuttel, Willem P. *Catalogus van de Pamfletten-verzameling berustende in de Koninklijke Bibliotheek.* 9 vols. The Hague, 1889. This is the most useful of several catalogs of this type. In addition, card catalogs and other references in the Koninklijke Bibliotheek and the University of Amsterdam Library were utilized.

Latin America in School and College Teaching Materials. Report of the Committee on the Study of Teaching Materials on Inter-American Subjects. Washington, D.C.: American Council on Education, 1944.

Levin, David. *History as Romantic Art: Bancroft, Prescott, Motley, and Parkman.* Palo Alto, California: Stanford University Press, 1959.

Lindabury, Richard V. *A Study of Patriotism in the Elizabethan Drama.* Princeton Studies in English, no. 5. Princeton University Press, 1931.

Longhurst, John. "The Black Legend and Recent Latin American Historiography," *New Mexico Quarterly*, XX (1950), 502–511.

Lynch, John. *Spain under the Habsburgs,* 2 vols. Oxford, 1964, 1970.

Madariaga, Salvador de. *Essays with a Purpose.* London, 1954. See also this author's works cited in Section III.

Margolis, Max L., and Alexander Marx. *A History of the Jewish People.* Philadelphia: The Jewish Publication Society of America, 1927.

Marriott, John. *English History in English Fiction.* New York, 1941.

Mateo, Mario. *La leyenda negra contra España: Una campaña de calumnias que dura cuatro siglos.* Mexico, 1949.

McMurtrie, Douglas C. *The Book: The Story of Printing and Bookmaking.* New York, 1938.

Menéndez Pelayo, Marcelino. *Historia de los heterodoxos españoles.* 8 vols. New edition, with notes. First edition, 1880–1882. Madrid: Consejo Superior de Investigaciones Científicas, 1946–1948.

Mesquita, Bueno de. "The Historical Associations of the Ancient Burial-Ground of the Sephardic Jews." Jewish Historical Society of England, *Transactions,* X (1921–1923): 225–254.

Meyer, Arnold O. *England and the Catholic Church under Queen Elizabeth.* New York: Barnes and Noble, 1967.

Millis, Walter. *The Martial Spirit: A Study of Our War with Spain.* Boston, 1931.

Neuman, Abraham A. *The Jews in Spain: Their Social, Political and Cultural Life during the Middle Ages.* First issued in 1942. Philadelphia: The Jewish Publication Society of America (The Morris Loeb Series), 1948.

Newman, Louis I. *Jewish Influence on Christian Reform Movements.* New York: Columbia University Press (Columbia University Oriental Studies, XXIII), 1925.

Parks, George B. *Richard Hakluyt and the English Voyages.* Special Publication no. 10. New York: American Geographical Society, 1928.

Roth, Cecil. *A History of the Marranos.* Second revised edition. First edition, 1932; first revised edition, 1941. Philadelphia: The Jewish Publication Society of America, 1959.

Sánchez Alonso, Benito. *Fuentes de la historia española e hispanoamericana: Ensayo de bibliografía sistemática de impresos y manuscritos que ilustran la historia política de España y sus antiguas provincias de ultramar.* Third edition. First edition, 1919. Madrid: Consejo Superior de Investigaciones Científicas, Instituto "Miguel de Cervantes," 1952.

Schelling, Felix E. *Foreign Influences in Elizabethan Plays.* New York and London, 1923.

Solomon, Israel. "David Nieto and Some of His Contemporaries." Jewish Historical Society of England, *Transactions,* XII (1928–1931): 1–102.

Sombart, Werner. *The Jews and Modern Capitalism.* Glencoe, Illinois: The Free Press, 1951. Translated by M. Epstein.

Summers, Montague. *The Gothic Quest: A History of the Gothic Novel.* London, 1938.

Syme, Ronald. *Colonial Elites: Rome, Spain and the Americas.* The Whidden Lectures, London: Oxford University Press, 1958.

Ugalde, Louis. "Las Casas and the Black Legend," *The Boston Public Library Quarterly,* V (April, 1953): 97–106.

Walsh, William T. *Isabella of Spain.* London, 1931.

———. *Philip II.* New York, 1937. These two works are useful in providing penetrating insights into fifteenth- and sixteenth-century circumstances which are difficult for the present-day reader to understand or sympathize with. The author wrote from a strongly Catholic point of view, and possibly with too much emphasis upon Jewish conspiracy against the Roman Church; but, perhaps for these reasons, he presents a good portrayal of the temper of those times. The Jewish historian, Cecil Roth, in characterizing Walsh's *Isabella,* says: "This work is important, psychologically if not historically, as a twentieth-century restatement of the standards and prejudices of the fifteenth." This remark was hardly intended as a compliment, but it certainly describes some of what historians should be doing in making the past comprehensible to the present. Walsh's lesser known *Characters of the Inquisition* gives an added comparative fillip which can be helpful in putting the Spanish Inquisition into larger historical perspective.

Wedgewood, Cicely V. *William the Silent, William of Nassau, Prince of Orange, 1533–1584*. New Haven: Yale University Press, 1944.

Weevers, Theodoor. *Poetry of the Netherlands in its European Context, 1170–1930*. University of London, Athlone Press, 1960.

Williams, Stanley T. *The Spanish Background of American Literature*. 2 vols. New Haven: Yale University Press, 1955.

Williamson, René de Visme. *Culture and Policy: The United States and the Hispanic World*. Knoxville: University of Tennessee Press, 1949.

Wisan, Joseph E. *The Cuban Crisis as Reflected in the New York Press (1895–1898)*. New York: Columbia University Press, 1934.

Wiznitzer, Arnold. *Jews in Colonial Brazil*. New York: Columbia University Press, 1960.

Wolf, Lucien. *Essays in Jewish History*. London: Jewish Historical Society of England, 1934. Especially Essay II, "Cromwell's Jewish Intelligencers," pp. 93–114.

———. "Jews in Elizabethan England," Jewish Historical Society of England, *Transactions*, XI (1924–1927): 1–91.

Worman, Ernest J. *Alien Members of the Book-Trade during the Tudor Period*. London, 1906. Printed for the Bibliographical Society of London by Blades East and Blades.

Section II
Black Legend Manifestations
[Primarily illustrative examples or works cited in the text]

Baron, Alexander. *The Golden Princess*. Bantam edition, 1957. First printed in 1955. A novel of the conquest of Mexico, liberally sprinkled with clichés about Spanish cruelty, greed for gold, unique treachery ("If chivalry was the face of life in this second Spain [Cuba], treachery was its mainspring"), haughtiness, lack of good sportsmanship (Anglo variety, of course), special concentration on sexual lust, and "they could recognize no other means of life but war."

Borrow, George. *The Bible in Spain: Or, the Journeys, Adventures and Imprisonments of an Englishman, in an Attempt to Circulate the Scriptures in the Peninsula*. London: MacDonald Illustrated Classics. First edition in 1843. A very entertaining and, in some ways, useful description of life in Spain; but it reflects Black Legend echoes in the English fashion.

Brion, Marcel. *Bartolomé de las Casas (Father of the Indians)*. New York, 1929.

Cadoux, Cecil J. *Philip of Spain and the Netherlands: An Essay on Moral Judgments in History*. London, 1947. An example of bitter Protestant anti-Catholicism and attack on all efforts at correction of standard views concerning Philip II, the Inquisition, etc. Similar to the Motley brand of "black legendism."

Casas, Bartolomé de las. *Brevíssima relación de la destruyción de las Indias*. Sevilla, 1552. For the many translations and subsequent editions of this work (and the other tracts he published in the same year), see Hanke and Giménez Fernández (cited in Section I, above).

Clagett, John. *Cradle of the Sun*. New York: Popular Library, 1959. The hero and his companion, respectively blonde and red-haired Spaniards, spend their adventurous lives fighting against the Spanish Church and Spanish cruelty. The picture of the hero on the book jacket shows him with blonde, wavy hair (à la Nelson Eddy) defending, blade in hand, a Mayan princess (à la Elizabeth Taylor) against the obviously evil onslaught of three Spanish soldiers. The whole tenor of this novel is strongly hispanophobic and bitterly anti-Catholic. It opens with a horrifying vision of the Inquisition being used for personal vengeance against the hero and his family, reminiscent of the opening of Samuel Shellabarger's earlier bestseller, *Captain from Castile.* The jacket blurb tells you all you really need to know: "His family struck down by the Inquisition, the woman he loved snatched from his arms, hot-blooded Juan de Moncada set out on a savage mission of revenge. In the New World he was taken captive by the Mayas—with their strange rites of human sacrifice. How he became the lover of a native princess and led her people against the brutal Conquistadors makes a taut tale of swashbuckling adventure and primitive passion." There is, incidentally, historical basis for such a tale of a Spanish captive among the Mayas, a story which deserves far better treatment than Mr. Clagett gives it.

Collier, John. *The Indians of the Americas.* New York, 1947. Strongly hispanophobic, in the "Indianist" and Lascasian tenor with such statements as: "No perspective one can get on the [Spanish] Conquest can make it appear as anything other than bitterly sad and desperately ignoble. . . . The murders and desolations [of Spaniards in the Indies] exceeded those of the most pitiless tyrants of earlier history; nor have they been surpassed since."

Cooper, Clayton S. *Understanding Spain.* New York, 1928. Fairly typical of continuing romantic literature which usually manages to make Spain look very backward by comparison with Nordic "progress" but paradoxically lauds Spain as a place of rest for "modern" men of other countries to "get away from it all." Typical condescension and faulty history: Spain will "get ahead" if she can accomplish such things as the emancipation of her women; Ferdinand and Isabella, "with their Inquisition and their fanaticism, culminating in the reigns of Charles I and Philip II, sounded the death-knell of this country and her world power. The expulsion of the Jews and the persecution of the Moors, together with seven centuries of religious warfare, brought that religious hardening of heart, than which, naught on earth is more cruel or more disintegrating to a large and noble progress."

Froude, James Anthony. *Short Studies on Great Subjects.* 4 vols. New York: Scribner's, 1888. In "England's Forgotten Worthies," pp. 358–405 of Volume I, this famous historian presents some typical British disparagement of Spain, such as the classical juxtaposition of innocent American Indians against Spanish cruelty, and such lines as: "Gold hunting and lust were the two passions for which the Spaniards cared"—by comparison, and especially in war with the Spaniards, "the conduct and character of the English sailors . . . present us all through that age with such a picture of gallantry, disinterestedness, and high heroic energy, as has never been overmatched. . . ."

Gage, Thomas. *Thomas Gage's Travels in the New World.* Edited with introduction by J. Eric S. Thompson. First printed in London, 1648. University of Oklahoma Press, 1958.

Glatstein, Jacob. "The Way it is in Bogotá: No Bed of Roses," *Commentary,* VI (July, 1948): 74–76. A terribly bitter expression of Jewish condescension toward Spanish-Americans, typified in the comment "Colombia—may it sink into the abyss." The author expresses horror at the idea of marrying what he calls "Spanish-Indian-Negroid" girls and considers it a stroke of luck for Colombian parents whose daughters are negotiated for by a Jew.

Guicciardini, Francesco. *Viaje a España de Francesco Guicciardini, embajador de Florencia ante el Rey Católico.* Translated and edited by José María Alonso Gamo. Valencia, 1952.

Bibliography

Haggard, H. Rider. *Montezuma's Daughter*. London, 1893. A novel by a writer quite popular in our recent past. Some of the opening paragraphs and phrases, strongly anti-Spanish (and, of course, pro-English), sound like excerpts from Kingsley's *Westward Ho!*—or from Richard Hakluyt and Francis Bacon.

Hays, Hoffman R. *The Takers of the City*. New York, 1946. A novel, centered around Bartolomé de las Casas' brief experience in Chiapas, Mexico, as bishop. Black Legend in interpretation, with the ever-virtuous Las Casas made to fit into recent, mawkish championship of "the common man," racial equality, the new "liberalism," etc.

Hibbert, Eleanor Alice (Burford) [Plaidy, Jean]. *The Rise of the Spanish Inquisition* (London, 1969), *The Growth of the Spanish Inquisition* (London, 1960), *The End of the Spanish Inquisition* (London, 1961). This work is strongly hispanophobic, relying heavily upon such earlier biased accounts as those of Limborch, Llorente, Lea, and Sabatini's *Torquemada*. The author is quite laudatory of Llorente and uses Rafael Sabatini to establish Llorente's integrity (on p. 120 of Vol. I: "Llorente was clearly a man of great integrity, and Rafael Sabatini, who quotes him frequently in his *Torquemada and the Spanish Inquisition*, writes that he is an historian of 'unimpugned honesty and authority.' ").

Kingsley, Charles. *Westward Ho!* London: Everyman's Library no. 20, and New York: Dutton, 1906. There are other editions; the work was first printed in 1855. A minor classic of English literature, especially for younger readers; a kind of prototype of British patriotism and other virtues versus Spanish iniquities so common in English-language history and fiction, especially when dealing with the Elizabethan "Sea-Dog" period, as this work does. A long-standing item on our high school reading lists.

Lea, Henry C. "The Indian Policy of Spain," *Yale Review* (August, 1899): 119–155. One of our intellectuals, famous for his works on the Spanish Inquisition, shows how the Black Legend could be made to fit our unnecessary war against Spain and the superseding of Spain, by us, in Cuba. A kind of forerunner of more recent intelligentsia who have often included some reference to the iniquities of Spain's colonial rule among their apologies for the Castro regime.

Llorente, Juan A. *History of the Inquisition of Spain*. Philadelphia, 1826. An English version of the famous work often utilized as anti-Inquisition propaganda since the early nineteenth century. Llorente was an *afrancesado* renegade and his work is replete with errors and faulty historical interpretations, but, like las Casas in an earlier day, he was a Spaniard who held official posts and put into his writing the kind of circumstantial condemnation that proved hypnotically fascinating for those desirous of believing the worst of Spain and Spaniards. In this, Llorente also resembles the earlier Antonio Pérez.

Marmontel, Jean F. *Les Incas, ou la destruction de l'empire du Pérou. . . .* 2 vols. Paris, 1778. There are many subsequent editions of this very hispanophobic, Lascasian work which was so influential in the period of Spanish-American independence struggle and achievement. Among others, there is an English version of two volumes published in Dublin, in 1797. Marmontel was a best seller, apparently, even in the following century.

Mason, F. Van Wyck. *Golden Admiral*. New York, 1953. In this and his earlier *Cutlass Empire*, the author, who made such a fine reputation as a writer of historical novels concerned with our Revolutionary War, exhibits some of that lofty English-New England Black Legend view of Spain and Spaniards so typical of our writers and so influential among us. This volume is historical fiction, centered on Francis Drake's exploits, and it almost outdoes Hakluyt, Thomas Scott, Davenant, and Kingsley. The jacket blurb and the text ring with such phrases as: "this wretched, forsworn King in the Escorial"; "if the

Queen's Majesty grants me permission to harry this Royal Judas *in his homeland* I'll beat Philip to the very ground." Drake becomes a Negro champion (the Cimaroons "worship" him), which is a bit startling when considered along with his beginnings in the Negro slave trade.

Mason typifies those writers among us who justly earn reputations in fields not related to things Hispanic, then turn out "potboilers" which *do* relate to Spain and Spaniards and, in doing so, repeat Black Legend clichés and show no sympathy for, or understanding of, Hispanic phenomena. Their wide reputations and influence thus perpetuate anti-Spanish prejudices, much like the famous Frenchmen of the Enlightenment and their followers.

Motley, John Lothrop. *The Rise of the Dutch Republic: A History.* Various editions, such as New York: Crowell, 1901, and New York: Dutton [Everyman's Library], 1909.

This work, along with his *History of the United Netherlands: From the Death of William the Silent to the Twelve Years' Truce, 1609,* is classic hispanophobic treatment which has been of considerable influence in our country. Motley is commented on in my Chapter 6.

O'Hara, Donn. *The Fair and the Bold.* New York: "A Graphic Giant," 1957. An historical novel of the period of the Dutch fight against Spain in the latter sixteenth century; Dutch virtues versus "incalculably cruel" Spain, in the Motley tradition. ". . . the wise leadership of the prince of Orange, as contrasted with the almost unbelievable stupidity of the sundry governors-general, most of whom were bastards while all of them were beefwits." The author indicates that being a prisoner in the Tower of London was more pleasant than a visit to the Gothic gloom of a Spanish mansion; this is the tenor of contrast of virtuous Nordics and villainous Spaniards.

Pamphlet Materials.

Major university libraries in this country, or those libraries which specialize in English literature or history (such as the Henry E. Huntington Library, San Marino, California), are apt to contain collections of English pamphlet material which will readily illustrate propaganda action against Spain, through the sixteenth, seventeenth, and eighteenth centuries, when those countries were so often at war. There are many collections of English literature of the Tudor-Stuart periods which can be referred to to illustrate the reflections of the anti-Spanish prejudice. As indicated in my text, the Dutch and English libraries contain quantities of anti-Spanish propaganda pamphlets, and there are various guides and catalogs which can be found in major United States libraries.

Raynal, Guillaume T. *Histoire philosophique et politique des etablissements dans les deux Indes.* Amsterdam, 1770. Many subsequent editions, mainly in French but also in English and German.

Rowse, A. L. *The Expansion of Elizabethan England,* New York, 1955, and *The Elizabethans and America,* New York, 1969; and other writings and speeches. This fine English historian is an echo of Hakluyt, Bacon, Scott, and Davenant when it comes to the juxtaposition of England and Spain. He is, in this aspect of his writing, an example of the Anglo-Saxon superiority complex which does so much to keep alive the anti-Spanish legend among English-language readers.

Salter, Cedric. *Introducing Spain.* New York, 1956. Presented to the reader as "An Englishman who has lived in Spain for many years and who knows it as few English or Americans do," the author is a fine example of the type that goaded Julián Juderías into writing on the Black Legend. For example: the traditional "gloomy" Philip II, described as "particularly attracted to Saints who died in demonstratively painful ways, and San Lorenzo, having been grilled (like a rump steak), was an obvious favorite"; and Spanish "lack of imagination" is demonstrated by the facts that they are not nervously apprehensive before entering the dentist's office, as Anglo-Saxons are, and they have so little ghost literature; Spanish courage is "fanatical" because they held up under Moorish impact; etc.

Schiller, Johann C. *Don Carlos, Infant von Spanien,* 1787, and many subsequent editions and versions (commented on in my Chapter 4), and his *History of the Revolt of the Netherlands,* London: H. G. Bohn, 1847, containing typical Enlightenment misjudgments of Philip II.

Scott, Thomas. Author of a large number of tracts, published in both England and the Low Countries, illustrating the strong mixture of hispanophobia and anti-Catholicism in the early seventeenth century. Examples can be found in most any English pamphlet collection which embraces the seventeenth century. Here are a few illustrative titles: *Vox Coeli, Or Newes from Heaven. Of a consultation there held by the high and mighty Princes, King Hen. 8. King Edw. 6 . . . wherein Spaines ambition and treacheries . . . are unmasked . . .* (Utrecht?, 1624); *Certaine reasons and arguments of policie, why the king of England should hereafter give over all further treatie, and enter into warre with the Spaniard* (n.p., 1624); *Sir Walter Rawleighs Ghost, Or Englands Forewarner. Discovering a secret consultation, newly holden in Court of Spaine. Together with his tormenting of Count de Gondomar . . .* (Utrecht, 1626); *The Spaniards Perpetuall designes to an universall Monarchie* (London?, 1624). There are many others, for Scott was probably England's most prolific pamphleteer against Spain.

The Spanish Main. An RKO picture (Frank Borzage Production). Screen play by George Worthing Yates and Herman J. Mankiewicz. Original story by Aeneas MacKenzie. [First shown in the middle 1940s, it has since appeared with some frequency on the TV late shows.] A classic example of the Black Legend in cinema form; it contains practically all the clichés and stereotypes. Tall, handsome, "blonde" Paul Henreid, as captain of a peaceful Dutch pilgrim ship, falls into the clutches of a gross, cruel, lazy Spanish viceroy of New Granada, in the person of Walter Slezak, complete with the standard black pointed beard. Henreid and his men escape, turn pirate, scourge the Caribbean, and capture red-haired Maureen O'Hara, daughter of the Mexican viceroy and Slezak's intended bride. You can guess the rest. Nordic superior energy and sportsmanship are contrasted with Spanish laziness, treachery, and cruelty; Dutch achievement—as makers of Brabant lace—is contrasted with "a [Spanish] bride schooled in cruelty and uselessness"; Spain's Slezak's main business seems to be signing orders for hangings; an English woman pirate is very surprised that well-born Spanish ladies are loyal to their men ("I didn't know your kind cared as much about their men as we do"). And plenty more of the same.

Ward, G. H. *The Truth about Spain.* London and New York, 1911. Another example of a formerly wellknown book that is strongly anti-Catholic in tenor (the author seems entirely too concerned about digging up religious scandal) and very expressive of the Nordic superiority complex.

War-Time Echoes: Patriotic Poems, Heroic and Pathetic, Humorous and Dialectic, of the Spanish-American War. Selected and arranged by James Henry Brownlee. Akron, New York, Chicago: The Werner Company, 1898.

Watterson, Henry. *History of the Spanish-American War, Embracing a Complete Review of Our Relations with Spain.* San Francisco: Bronson & Co., 1898. This item, and the one immediately above, will give you some idea of how your immediate forebears learned about Spain in the heat of war; a modern version of Elizabethans versus Philip II.

Williams, William C. *In the American Grain*. New York: New Directions, 1956. One of our more famous literary figures occasionally touches Spanish "tigers" versus "noble savages" and reiterates the standard greed and gold theme, in his chapter, or essay, "The Destruction of Tenochtitlán," and the following ones on Ponce de León and Hernando de Soto. This is a random sample of how the myths live on among our influential literati and are perpetuated by them.

Wright, Richard. *Pagan Spain*. New York, 1957. The wellknown American Negro writer goes to Spain to confirm his prejudices—and does so. In the vein of so many of our extreme Left, this is a mixture of Communist propaganda against the Spain of Franco and the traditional "enlightened" hispanophobia of Western World intellectuals; an echoing of "black-legendism" in extreme form.

Section III
Revision of the Black Legend

[Not comprehensive; limited to English language. In whole or in part, the following works revise the Legend's common distortions, or provide corrective insights, or indicate the complexity of things Hispanic by contrast with the Legend's simplistic concepts]

Bannon, John Francis. *The Spanish Conquistadores: Men or Devils?* New York: Holt, Rinehart and Winston, "Source Problems in World Civilization," 1960.

Bertrand, Louis, and Sir Charles Petrie. *The History of Spain*. London, 1934.

Bolton, Herbert E. "Cultural Cooperation with Latin America," *The Journal of the National Education Association* (January, 1940): 1–4. The many writings of this great historian constitute a monumental rejection of the simplistic errors of Black Legend type.

Bourne, Edward Gaylord. *Spain in America, 1450–1580*. New York: Barnes and Noble, "University Paperbacks," 1962. First published in 1904.

Brenan, Gerald. *The Literature of the Spanish People: From Roman Times to the Present*. New York: Meridian Books, 1957. First edition, 1951.

Castro, Américo. *The Structure of Spanish History*. Princeton, New Jersey: Princeton University Press, 1954.

———. "The Meaning of Spanish Civilization," Inaugural Lecture. Princeton, New Jersey: Princeton University Press, 1940.

Chamberlain, Robert S. *The Conquest and Colonization of Yucatan, 1517–1550*. Washington, D.C.: Carnegie Institution, 1948. A fine example of thorough scholarship illustrating the complexities of Spanish conquest.

Chase, Gilbert. *The Music of Spain*. Second revised edition. First published, 1941. New York: Dover, 1959.

Chevalier, François. *Land and Society in Colonial Mexico: The Great Hacienda*. Berkeley: University of California Press, 1963.

Díaz del Castillo, Bernal. *The True History of the Conquest of Mexico*. Various editions now available.

Diffie, Bailey W. *Latin-American Civilization: Colonial Period*. Harrisburg, Pa., 1945, and New York, 1967.

Bibliography

Elliott, John H. *The Revolt of the Catalans, a Study in the Decline of Spain, 1598-1640*. Cambridge, England: University Press, 1963.

Freyre, Gilberto. *The Masters and the Slaves: A Study in the Development of Brazilian Civilization*. New York, 1956 (second English edition). Translated by Samuel Putnam from the work originally titled *Casa grande e senzala*. An excellent illustration of the sheer complexity of Iberian action in the New World and the resulting amalgamation of races and cultures.

Gibson, Charles. *The Aztecs under Spanish Rule: A History of the Indians of the Valley of Mexico, 1519–1810*. Stanford, Calif.: Stanford University Press, 1964.

————. *The Colonial Period in Latin American History*. Washington, D.C., 1958 (Service Center for Teachers of History, a service of the American Historical Association).

————. *Spain in America*. New York: Harper and Row, 1966.

————. *Tlaxcala in the Sixteenth Century*. New Haven: Yale University Press, 1952. A scholarly study which, like his *Aztecs*, above, reveals some of the many complications in Spanish-Indian relationships.

Greenleaf, Richard E. *The Mexican Inquisition of the Sixteenth Century*. Albuquerque: University of New Mexico Press, 1969.

Hamilton, Earl J. *American Treasure and the Price Revolution in Spain, 1501–1650*. Cambridge: Harvard University Press, 1934. This and other studies by the same author clearly indicate the enormous complexities of Spanish imperial operation, by comparison with the commonly held view of a simple, treasure-seeking scheme for the benefit of the mother country alone. The Clarence Haring work, noted below, helps to round out the picture of imperial complexity.

Handbook of Latin American Studies. Cambridge: Harvard University Press, and Gainesville: University of Florida Press, 1936–. A very useful guide to the continuing output of scholarly monographs, interpretive works, and periodical literature.

Hanke, Lewis. *The First Social Experiments in America: A Study in the Development of Spanish Indian Policy in the Sixteenth Century*. Cambridge, 1935.

————. *The Spanish Struggle for Justice in the Conquest of America*. Philadelpha: University of Pennsylvania Press, 1949.

Haring, Clarence H. *The Spanish Empire in America*. New York: Oxford University Press, 1947.

Hispanic American Historical Review, The. Baltimore, Md., and Durham, N. C., 1918–. A quarterly review. Although the quality of the articles is very uneven, there are many excellent ones; and the whole publication is a very valuable bibliographical aid.

Humboldt, Alexander von. *Political Essay on the Kingdom of New Spain*. 4 vols. London, 1811. A now classical view of the texture of Spanish-American empire near the end of the colonial period and a scholarly reminder that a great deal happened between Cortés and the achievement of Mexican independence. Also a valuable antidote for such "enlightenment" best sellers as Raynal and the constantly revisited Las Casas.

Hume, Martin A. *Spanish Influence on English Literature*. London, 1905. A relatively little known work, but with some value as a reminder that the Western World owes more than we usually realize to Spanish literary achievements. Our famous literary figures of a century or so ago knew this, but too many of our latter-day literati seem to have forgotten it.

Iglesia, Ramón. *Columbus, Cortés, and Other Essays*. Berkeley: University of California Press, 1969. Translated and edited by Lesley Byrd Simpson.

Kubler, George, and Martin Soria. *Art and Architecture in Spain and Portugal and their American Dominions, 1500 to 1800*. Baltimore: Penguin Books, 1959.

————. *Mexican Architecture of the Sixteenth Century*. New Haven: Yale University Press, 1948. A first-class example of a growing literature (though growing too slowly) of scholarly appraisal of the sheer richness of Spanish cultural extension overseas.

Lanning, John Tate. *Academic Culture in the Spanish Colonies*. New York: Oxford University Press, 1940.

————. *The Eighteenth-Century Enlightenment in the University of San Carlos de Guatemala*. Ithaca: Cornell University Press, 1956.

————. *The University in the Kingdom of Guatemala*. Ithaca: Cornell University Press, 1955.

————. "A Reconsideration of Spanish Colonial Culture," *The Americas*, I (October, 1944): 166–178. This particular article, especially when its theme is rounded out by reading of the other excellent scholarly writings of this author, is a wittily enlightening rejection of that part of the Black Legend which constantly stigmatizes Spain in America as a unique and suffocating obscurantism.

Leonard, Irving A. *Books of the Brave: Being an Account of Books and of Men in the Spanish Conquest and Settlement of the Sixteenth-Century New World*. Cambridge: Harvard University Press, 1949.

————. *Don Carlos de Sigüenza y Góngora, a Mexican Savant of the Seventeenth Century*. Berkeley: University of California Press, 1929. These two works, as in the case of Professor Lanning, represent the results of sound scholarship in the direction of modifying or rejecting the time-hallowed denigration of Spain's cultural presence in the Americas.

Lockhart, James. *Spanish Peru, 1532–1560: A Colonial Society*. Madison: University of Wisconsin, 1968. An excellent description of the many varieties of humankind establishing themselves in the Americas, such as I have indicated in my Chapter 2.

López de Gómara, Francisco. *Cortés: The Life of the Conqueror by His Secretary*. Translated and edited by Lesley Byrd Simpson. Berkeley: University of California Press, 1964.

Madariaga, Salvador de. *Hernán Cortés, Conqueror of Mexico*. New York: Macmillan, 1941.

————. *The Rise of the Spanish American Empire*. New York, 1947 and 1965.

————. *The Fall of the Spanish American Empire*. London, 1947. New York, 1963.

————. *Bolívar*. New York, 1956. These four works, by one of Spain's outstanding intellectuals, are witty, very readable, often provocative, and certainly valuable aids to the non-Spaniard in stimulating challenge of the orthodoxies of our thinking with regard to Spain in its relationship to Spanish America. Time and again, the author offers enticing invitations to reject the simplicity of our preconceived notions in favor of the richer fare of humanistic complexity. If used with moderate caution, Madariaga's writing is not only intellectually and philosophically rewarding but far more readable and entertaining than most English-language historical fare.

Menéndez Pidal, Ramón. *The Spaniards in their History*. Translated with a Prefatory Essay on the author's work by Walter Starkie. London, 1950.

Merriman, Roger B. *The Rise of the Spanish Empire in the Old World and the New*. Four vols. New York, 1918–1934. Although this work does not carry the story beyond Philip II, it is the most comprehensive of the scholarly treatments of Spain in English. Some of the material has been modified by later studies, but careful objectivity and comprehensiveness generally characterize the total work.

Padden, Robert C. *The Hummingbird and the Hawk: Conquest and Sovereignty*

Bibliography

in the Valley of Mexico, 1503–1541. Columbus: Ohio State University Press, 1968, and Harper Torchbooks, 1970. A scholarly and very readable interpretation which rejects the "indigenista" distortions of the conquest of Mexico by the Spaniards and their Indian allies; a reappraisal that has long been needed.

Petrie, Sir Charles. *Philip II of Spain*. New York and London, 1963.

Phelan, John L. *The Kingdom of Quito in the Seventeenth Century: Bureaucratic Politics in the Spanish Empire*. Madison: University of Wisconsin Press, 1967. A good illustration of the complexities of Spanish Empire, as indicated in my Chapter 2.

Powell, Philip W. *Soldiers, Indians and Silver: The Northward Advance of New Spain, 1550–1600*. Berkeley: University of California Press, 1952 (reprinted in 1969). An illustration of the commonly ignored fact that the conquest of Mexico by Spain was far more than just the story of Cortés; and that Spanish captains and other secular officials as well as friars could plan and carry out enlightened, humane policies on far frontiers.

Putnam, Samuel. *Marvelous Journey: Four Centuries of Brazilian Literature*. New York, 1948. One of the more readable antidotes to the error of our ways in largely ignoring Portuguese language and literature, which is a kind of side-effect of our Black Legend disparagement of Iberian achievements.

Recopilación de leyes de los reynos de las Indias. Four volumes. Various editions. Madrid, 1681. Regrettably, we do not yet have this great work available in English. I cite it here, however, as the most notable example of a mass of official materials available to Hispanic scholars for assessment of Spain's historical actions.

Schurz, William L. *This New World: The Civilization of Latin America*. New York, 1954. Not nearly so comprehensive as the title suggests, but a very readable eye-opener for the initiate written by a scholar and man-about-the-Hispanic-world who unabashedly enjoyed the flavor of Hispanic life, historical and otherwise.

Simpson, Lesley B. *The Encomienda in New Spain: The Beginning of Spanish Mexico*. Berkeley: University of California Press, 1950.

———. *Many Mexicos*. New York: Putnam's, 1941. Various subsequent revised editions, including University of California Press, paperback. A witty, sophisticated interpretation of Spanish action in America, along with the sequel known as the "national period." Uneven in coverage, but with many penetrating insights.

Ten Centuries of Spanish Poetry: An Anthology in English Verse with Original Texts: From the XIth Century to the Generation of 1898. New York, 1955. Edited by Eleanor L. Turnbull, with introductions by Pedro Salinas.

Thomas, Hugh. *The Spanish Civil War*. New York, 1961. A diligent effort toward enlightenment on a subject that generally bedevils Western opinions with regard to modern Spain. Though not the definitive factual or interpretive clarification, it helps clear away some of the propagandistic fog.

Whitaker, Arthur P., ed. *Latin America and the Enlightenment*. New York, 1942. Great Seal Books, Division of Cornell University Press, 1961.

Zavala, Silvio. *The Defense of Human Rights in Latin America (Sixteenth to Eighteenth Centuries)*. Paris, 1964 [UNESCO].

———. *New Viewpoints on the Spanish Colonization of America*. Philadelphia: University of Pennsylvania Press, 1943. New York, 1968.

———. *The Political Philosophy of the Conquest of America*. Mexico, 1953.

Acknowledgments

> *Once a canonized idea is made untouchable, though men are still free to oppose or denounce it the effect is that of hurling a frail body against a log jam; then the writer is faced with the choice of being either popular or useful—he can't be both.*
> CARLOS DÁVILA,
> *We of the Americas*

It will be readily apparent to professional colleagues and others versed in Hispanic subjects that I have, at times, relied heavily upon the studies and writings of Julián Juderías (Spain), Rómulo Carbia (Argentina), Sverker Arnoldsson (Sweden), Lewis Hanke (United States), and some of the ideas, in writing and personal conversation, of Carlos Dávila (Chile). All these men have made perceptive and sometimes extensive and provocative forays into the origins, history, and consequences of the hispanophobic fallacies. The work of Constantino Bayle (Spain) and of Salvador de Madariaga (internationally famous Spanish statesman, essayist, philosopher, historian) will be quite noticeable in some parts of my text. In fact, my only claim to originality is in the ways I have put together the ideas of others for an audience of my own countrymen and in some of the interpretations I have put on the Black Legend's effects among my own people. My work, then, is interpretation especially aimed beyond academic halls and is not intended as a thorough probing or coverage of the usual monographic sort. This should leave abundant room for: 1) disagreement with my interpretations; 2) more thorough studies in English on specific aspects of the Legend and its consequences; and, possibly, 3) adaptations of the works of such men as Juderías, Carbia, Bayle, and Arnoldsson for the English-language reader.

In preparing this work, I have had help and encouragement from many persons and a variety of institutions. I am particularly indebted to the following:

Acknowledgments

Professor John Tate Lanning, Duke University, for critical reading of the manuscript in its earlier stages, help and encouragement in many other ways, and for much good advice which, perhaps unfortunately, I did not always follow. Count Magnus Mörner, former Director of the Ibero-American Institute of Stockholm, for courteously speeding my acquaintance with the work of the late Professor Sverker Arnoldsson (University of Gotëborg) and helping with arrangements for utilizing the Arnoldsson notes. Mrs. Sverker Arnoldsson, for generously making available to me some of her late husband's notes and for kindly hospitality in Gotëborg. Professor Emeritus J.W.A. van Soest, The Hague, for valuable ideas and stimulating conversations along the lines of our mutual interest in the origins and continuation of the Black Legend, especially in The Netherlands. Dale Van Every, for critical readings of the text at various stages and for generous and unflagging efforts to encourage my writing. Professor Engel Sluiter, University of California at Berkeley, for generous sharing of his extensive knowledge of Dutch history, especially in relation to Spanish and Portuguese overseas actions. Professor Hugh Kenner, University of California at Santa Barbara, for critical comment and advice on arrangement of materials. Dr. William L. Schurz, one of our best-known writers and specialists in Latin American history and inter-American affairs until his death, in 1962, who kindly read and criticized some early versions of the manuscript. The very courteously helpful staff of the Henry E. Huntington Library and Art Gallery—What a delightful environment they provide for the visiting scholar! I am especially indebted to Dr. Ray Allen Billington, not only for his kindness in facilitating my work in this magnificent repository, but for many years of encouragement and help in my research and writing. I am also grateful to Dr. Robert O. Dougan, Librarian, for permission to reproduce the De Bry engravings of the 1598 Frankfurt edition of Las Casas' *Brief Relation,* from the copy in the Huntington Library. My departmental colleagues in the University of California at Santa Barbara, Professors Donald M. Dozer and Wilbur R. Jacobs, for many helpful references to pertinent materials. Drs. Lucia and Lawrence Kinnaird, for valuable critical comment and constant encouragement. Sr. Ramón Bela Armada, Chief of the United States Section of the Instituto de Cultura Hispánica (Madrid), always generous and courteous in helping my work in Spain. The Honorable Charles M. Teague, M.C. (California's Thirteenth Congressional District) and the fine staff in his Washington office, who facilitated access to information pertaining to recent inter-American affairs. Dr. L. Brummel (Director, Koninklijke Bibliotheek, The Hague) and Professor H. de la Fontaine

Verney (Director, University of Amsterdam Library), for courteously facilitating my work in those repositories. Mynheer W.H. Avelinghe and others of the staff of the Dutch Royal Archives (The Hague), for assistance in many ways. Dr. L. Fuks (in charge of the Rosenthaliana Collection of the University of Amsterdam Library and of the archive of the Ets-Haim Synagogue in Amsterdam), always courteous and helpful in guiding me through the materials he knows so well and so affectionately. Miss Antoinette Chauvannes (now Mrs. van Balen), who helped greatly in locating pertinent pamphlet and other material in The Hague and in translations from the Dutch. Mr. Lennart Palme and Mr. J.C. van Eck, of Santa Barbara, who kindly aided my work in Europe through introductions in certain quarters. Mynheer H. J. van Meerendonk and Juffrouw Remeinse, for extending to me the courtesies and hospitality of the Stitching Th. Morren "Tehius voor Archiefambtenaren" (The Hague), where I resided so comfortably while working in The Netherlands.

For financial assistance in travel, in acquisition of materials, and in various other research aids, I am deeply indebted to the American Council of Learned Societies, the Del Amo Foundation (especially the sympathetic aid and interest of Mr. Eugenio Cabrero, Secretary), the Faculty Committee on Research of the University of California, Santa Barbara, and the William Volker Fund (especially the courtesy and friendly encouragement of Mr. Kenneth S. Templeton, former Liaison Officer of the Fund). Over and above the aid specifically granted for completion of the present work, I wish to express my great gratitude to Mr. Cabrero, the Marqués de Villalcázar, and others of the Del Amo Foundation for generous assistance and constant encouragement in many aspects of my research and travels in Spain.

My wife, María, and my daughters, Diana Linda and Lilia Patricia, have steadfastly borne the extra burdens placed upon them by the absences and idiosyncracies of a wandering professor trying to write a book; I am truly grateful for their affectionate fortitude under such trying circumstances. My wife has cheerfully typed all or much of several drafts; and she has been particularly helpful in that most difficult of tasks, listening to or reading experimental drafts or ideas and providing valuable criticism. If the language of the text is not always as restrained as it should be, it is not because of lack of effort on her part.

I am sure that I have not sufficiently profited by all the lessons my suffering students have exposed me to as I experimented with various ways of acquainting them with Black Legend themes. But, as captive audiences, their reactions, in one way and another, have helped me

Acknowledgments

realize what areas of popular opinion are most affected by the Legend and its modern echoes. Insofar as I can, in these few words, I wish my students of former days to know how much I appreciate both their suffering and their help.

PHILIP WAYNE POWELL

Index

Index

Index

Index

Index

"White Legend," 187

William the Silent (Prince of Orange), 5, 27, 61, 62, 64, 65, 66, 70, 71, 74, 95, 96, 107, 119, 120; assassination of, 66, 75

Williams, Stanley T., 119

Wilson, Woodrow, 148

witchcraft: deaths for, in German states, 26; Spanish Inquisition's views on, 28

World, New York, 123

World of the Elseviers, The (Davies), 104

World War I, 101

World War II, 50, 55, 138, 145, 155

Yale Review, 124

Yankeephobia, Latin American, 9, 22, 45, 58, 127, 148, 149, 151, 152, 154, 161

"yellow" press, 122

Yevtushenko, Yevgeny, 9

Zavala, Silvio, 171

Zurbarán, Francisco de, 92